"KNOW THYSELF"
Jnana Yoga

Part 1

*Newly translated from the French
Original title :* «CONNAIS-TOI TOI-MÊME»
JNANI YOGA

Omraam Mikhaël Aïvanhov

"KNOW THYSELF"
Jnana Yoga

Part 1

2nd edition

Complete Works – Volume 17

EDITIONS PROSVETA

Prosveta S.A. – B.P. 12 – 83601 Fréjus Cedex (France)

ISBN 2-85566-446-2

édition originale : ISBN 2-85566-353-9

Readers will better understand certain aspects of the lectures published in the present volume if they bear in mind that the Master Omraam Mikhaël Aïvanhov's Teaching was exclusively oral and that the editors have made every effort to respect the flavour and style of each lecture.

The Master's Teaching is more than a body of doctrines: it is an organic whole, and his way of presenting it was to approach it from countless different points of view. By repeating certain aspects in a wide variety of contexts he constantly reveals a new dimension of the whole and, at the same time, throws new light on the individual aspects and on their vital links with each other.

Omraam Mikhaël Aïvanhov

TABLE OF CONTENTS

1. 'Know Thyself' 1
2. The Synoptic Table 5
3. Spirit and Matter 27
4. The Soul 73
5. Sacrifice 83
6. Food for the Soul and the Spirit 95
7. Consciousness 111
8. The Higher Self 139
9. Truth 153
10. Freedom 207

Chapter One

"KNOW THYSELF"

I

'Man, know thyself'. Very few men have ever understood the true meaning of this formula that was once inscribed over the entrance to the temple of Delphi. Who or what is this 'self' that we must know? 'Why, that's easy,' you will say, 'We have to know our own character, our own strengths and weaknesses.' But that is not what this maxim is about. True, a knowledge of our own strengths and weaknesses is necessary but it is not enough. To know oneself is to know the different bodies of which one is constituted (physical, etheric, astral, mental, causal, buddhic and atmic) and the needs of each of these bodies. But human beings know nothing about all this. They all realize that they have certain virtues and vices. They say, 'I know myself only too well!' But they are deluding themselves: they know nothing of the being who lives deep within them. They know nothing of his desires, his needs or his aspirations or of what makes him suffer. They don't know who their 'self' is; they think that it is their physical body and spend their time giving that body food, clothes, jewellery, comfort and pleasures without realizing that their true self is asking for something quite different. The satisfaction of their purely physical, material needs has never made human beings any happier or more contented. It is only when they begin to know themselves as they are on a higher plane that they become capable of living in true splendour.

If the initiates of old laid so much emphasis on the necessity for man to know himself it was because this knowledge is the key that opens up great possibilities for making progress and achieving success. As long as we are ignorant of the needs of our higher self we continue to give everything to our physical body which becomes glutted and overfed whereas our soul and spirit suffocate and die of hunger and thirst.

But how can you expect people who don't even believe in the existence of their other, subtler bodies to do anything about nourishing or strengthening them? It is amazing to see the situation of so many people — even those who are highly cultivated: they take great pride in their university degrees and all their culture and erudition, and yet they are constantly in a state of inner torment and anxiety. Isn't this proof enough that something has gone very wrong with their lives? When someone is as ignorant as that he would do better not to be so pleased with himself.

'Know thyself'. All science and all wisdom lie in knowing oneself, in finding oneself, in the fusion of one's lower self with one's higher self. The symbol of the initiate who has succeeded in finding himself is the serpent with its tail in its mouth. In the ordinary way a serpent forms a straight or wavy line, and a line is finite, limited. But the serpent with its tail in its mouth forms a circle and a circle represents the infinite, the limitless, the eternal. He who succeeds in becoming a circle enters a world without limitations where 'above' and 'below' are no longer separated, because all the powers and all the riches and virtues of the true, higher self have been infused into the lower self. The higher and the lower become one and man becomes a divinity.

Sèvres, February 6, 1972

Chapter Two

THE SYNOPTIC TABLE

I

The table that you see here (Figure 1) sums up the whole of initiatic science and all the sacred scriptures of mankind. To be sure it is not the only valid way of illustrating man's psychic life; in fact I have already spoken to you of others. When you want to describe the human anatomy for instance, you don't try to include everything on a single chart. It is much easier to understand if you use different diagrams for the different systems: the skeleton, the muscles, the circulatory and nervous systems, etc. And we do the same when we study geography with the help of physical, political, economic and geological maps. Similarly there can be different ways of illustrating the psychic structure of human beings, and although this table is different from the Sephirotic Tree, for instance, it represents the same reality and every aspect of man is represented. I have already given you other diagrams before this and they have all been different, but that doesn't mean that they contradict each other.

You will not find the table that I am showing you today in any book. In fact this is the first time that it has ever been presented, and it is a summary and a synthesis of all the truths of life. When you first look at it all you see is a certain number of isolated words with no apparent connection between them, but once I have explained each word, its position in the table and its connection with all the others, you will be astonished by their meaning and the correspondences between them.

7

SYNOPTIC TABLE

PRINCIPLE	IDEAL	NOURISHMENT	PRICE	ACTIVITY
SPIRIT DIVINE CONSCIOUSNESS	TIME ETERNITY IMMORTALITY	FREEDOM	TRUTH	UNION CREATION IDENTIFICATION
SOUL SUPER-CONSCIOUSNESS	SPACE IMMENSITY INFINITY	IMPERSONALITY SELFLESSNESS	FUSION DILATATION ECSTASY	CONTEMPLATION ADORATION PRAYER
INTELLECT SELF-CONSCIOUSNESS	KNOWLEDGE LEARNING LIGHT	THOUGHT	WISDOM	MEDITATION PROFOUND STUDY
HEART CONSCIOUSNESS	JOY HAPPINESS WARMTH	FEELINGS	LOVE	MUSIC SONG POETRY HARMONY
WILL SUBCONSCIOUS	DOMINATION POWER MOVEMENT	STRENGTH	GESTURES BREATH	BREATHING GYMNASTICS DANCE PANEURYTHMY
PHYSICAL BODY UNCONSCIOUS	VIGOUR HEALTH LIFE	FOOD	MONEY	ACTIVITY DYNAMISM WORK

Figure 1

We call this table 'synoptic' because it gives an overall view of the structure of a human being and the activities that correspond to each element of that structure. As you see, it is divided into five vertical columns.

The first column shows the principles that constitute man: the physical body, the will, the heart, the intellect, the soul and the spirit.

The second column is headed 'Ideal', for each principle aspires to an ideal. The heart, the intellect and the soul, for instance; each strives to attain a different ideal.

Each principle needs food; it needs to be nourished, strengthened and fortified in order to attain its ideal, and we must give it what it needs so that it may continue to manifest itself. This is why the third column is headed 'Nourishment'.

The last two columns concern the 'Price' we have to pay for this nourishment, and the 'Activity', that is to say, the work we have to do in order to earn the currency with which to pay.

8

As you see, all these different notions are very clearly and logically related to each other.

Now it will make the whole thing easier to understand if we begin with the physical body, for everybody knows what the physical body is; everybody has some experience of it. It is a visible, tangible reality whose existence is beyond all doubt. The ideal of the physical body is health, life. Nothing is of greater value to the physical body than to be robust, vigorous and healthy and, in order to enjoy this vitality, it has to have all kinds of solid, liquid and gaseous foods. If the physical body does not receive the nourishment it needs it dies. We don't need a university education to know that we have to eat in order to survive. Even children know that. But in order to eat we need money. You are all familiar with the conversation between Antonio, who spent his life breaking stones, and the passer-by who asked him, 'Hey, Antonio, why do you spend your time breaking stones?' 'To earn money.' 'Why do you need money?' 'To buy macaroni.' 'And what do you want macaroni for?' 'To eat.' 'Why do you have to eat?' 'To keep up my strength.' 'But why do you have to be strong?' 'To break stones ...' Yes; it's a vicious circle! But I think you all agree that we need money in order to eat and that we have to work in order to earn money. It's as simple as that!

But just a moment: has it never occurred to you that this situation, which is self-evident on the physical plane, is equally valid on the other planes? The will, heart, intellect, soul and spirit all have their respective goals, and in order to attain those goals they too need to be nourished. Like Antonio they need money in order to buy their food, and like Antonio they have to accomplish a certain form of work in order to earn that money. Once you have got this synopsis firmly into your heads you will possess the key to the physical and psychic life of man.

As you know, the physical body is the vessel that contains all the other, subtler principles. The soul and the spirit, for example, are not wholly contained within the physical body but they manifest themselves through it – through the brain, the solar plexus, the eyes, etc. When you look at someone with a great deal of love,

9

light and purity, for instance, who is it that is manifesting himself through your eyes? The eyes belong to the physical body, but who is the being who uses them as a medium through which to manifest himself? Perhaps it is the soul or perhaps it is the spirit – perhaps it is God himself. And if, on the other hand, you say something so terrible or give someone such a black look that they fall ill and have to take to their bed, it is because you have been the tool of evil powers that sought to attack them. The physical body, therefore, is often no more than the instrument of forces that may be either beneficial or malignant and that may exist either within it or outside it.

The goal or ideal of the will is power and movement. You will say, 'But the will can also seek wisdom, intelligence and beauty, for instance.' No, these things are not what the will desires for itself; they are the goal of other principles. The powers of the will can be used in the pursuit of intelligence or in the creation of a work of art, but its own objectives, the only things it really wants for itself, are power and motion. It cannot bear to be immobile; it needs to be busy, to move about, to touch and displace things. But, like the physical body, the will cannot achieve its ideal without nourishment, and the nourishment of the will is strength. When it is nourished by strength the will becomes energetic, and if it is not nourished it wilts and fades away. Then there is the element that corresponds to the money, the currency with which the will can buy the food it needs, and this currency is movement, gestures. Yes, one has continually to drag oneself out of the rut of immobility and inertia in order to trigger, stimulate and activate the energies of the will. It is by cultivating habits of activity and movement that the will 'buys' strength and becomes powerful.

And do you know what the very first movement is? It is breath. The first act of a newborn baby is to breathe, and this breath triggers all the other functions. If you want to earn this 'money' therefore, you must get into the habit of doing the exercises recommended by the teaching: the breathing exercises, the gymnastics and the paneurythmy dances, all of which are designed to strengthen the will. Naturally you can add to these any number of other activities that are part of your daily lives. There are so many that I cannot take the time to enumerate them; I only mention here the methods recommended by the teaching, which concern more particularly the spiritual life.

You have probably never thought that these exercises could have much influence on the will; you probably believed that they were intended simply to increase the vitality of your physical body or make you feel light-hearted and joyful. Well, they can do that too because everything is connected. At the moment I am trying to make things clearer for you by distinguishing the different planes and identifying the elements that belong to each one, but in reality of course all these principles are inseparable. It is obvious that when you do the gymnastics or the breathing exercises your physical body also benefits, you feel more vigorous and not only your health but your general frame of mind also improves. Nothing is isolated; everything hangs together.

Human beings possess a faculty of feeling and emotion that we call the heart. But this heart is not the physical organ known to anatomy and physiology and which bears the same name. The heart known to anatomical science is a kind of hydraulic pump and constitutes the principal organ in the circulatory system, whereas the true organ of feeling is the solar plexus. When the initiates say that true understanding is the understanding of the heart, they are referring to the solar plexus. Actually the solar plexus is a kind of inverted brain. In the brain the grey matter is on the outside and the white matter on the inside, and in the solar plexus it is just the reverse: the white matter is outside and the grey matter is inside. But I have already explained all this before, so I shall say no more about it now[1]. The only thing I want to tell you today is that there are riches and treasures in the solar plexus that have been hidden in it from time immemorial and that, although human beings are not really aware of it, it is this organ that enables them to feel and understand. The brain understands things from the outside,

[1] See *Harmony*, Complete Works, vol. 6: chap. 9, 'The Solar Plexus and the Brain' and chap. 11, 'The Initiatic Heart'.

objectively and theoretically, and this is why people often form judgements about certain things without ever having felt or experienced them inwardly. And yet it is only when we experience, touch, feel and taste things for ourselves that we can truly understand them. It still remains for contemporary science to explore the world of the solar plexus, for it knows very little about it.

So now the question is: what is the ideal, the goal, of the heart? Does it yearn for knowledge, learning or powers? No. The heart's only aspiration is for happiness, joy and warmth, for warmth brings the heart to life whereas cold kills it. Wherever it goes the heart seeks only warmth from others.

The nourishment of the heart is feeling, sentiment: every kind of sentiment, good as well – I am sorry to say – as bad. But as our time is limited we shall only talk about good hearts, the hearts of good disciples which are nourished by good sentiments.

The money that serves to pay for happiness and joy is love. When you love your heart is immediately nourished. How often I have told you this: neither wealth nor psychic powers nor beauty can give you happiness; only love! Love is the only thing that can make you happy. Whatever else you offer your heart it will always be dissatisfied; it will continue to clamour for love because with love it can buy all that it needs. When you love someone your love is a currency that enables you to 'buy' all sorts of sensations, emotions and feelings; it gives birth to thousands of sensations every day. But when you have no more love you have no more money and consequently no more emotions or sensations. All that is finished. If you no longer love your wife you may still embrace her but you will get no joy or happiness from doing so. Whereas if you love her ... Ah! Then, even if you never even kiss her you will be filled with thousands of sentiments and sensations that defy analysis. Yes, simply because love is present[2].

---

[2] For a fuller discussion of love, see *Complete Works*, vols. 14 and 15, 'Love and Sexuality'.

Man also possesses an intellect and the goal of the intellect is knowledge and understanding. This is a very important goal, for when you are ignorant of the true nature of things you will always be confused, you will do yourself harm and you will lose your way in dangerous regions from which you will not know how to extricate yourself.

In order to attain its ideal the intellect also needs food, and the food of the intellect is thought. Here again, just as the heart can feed on both good and bad feelings, the thoughts on which the intellect feeds can be good or bad. But here in our teaching it is implicit that we only want to talk about the best and most luminous thoughts. Thought nourishes the intellect therefore; if you never think you will never know or understand things correctly. Some people say, 'Why rack your brains? It's better not to think too much, it can be dangerous; you can go mad that way!' True, one can go mad if one doesn't think correctly, but thought is still the best food for the mind. If you don't feed your mind it will lose all light and strength and die of starvation.

But in order to purchase thoughts of the very best quality you need money. You can always nibble on some of the many nonsensical, bizarre thoughts you will find lying about, but you will not get much benefit from them. Beggars cannot go to a good restaurant and buy a meal of fresh, nutritious ingredients; it costs too much, so they rummage in the dustbins for remnants of food that have been thrown away. Similarly one has to be very wealthy in order to buy the best kind of thoughts. And do you know what that wealth consists of? Wisdom. If you have no wisdom with which to buy good thoughts you will have to make do with peelings and left-overs – symbolically speaking. Only wisdom can nourish your mind with the best thoughts and thereby enable it to obtain the light it seeks. But wisdom is not, as people often imagine, a question of knowledge, science or erudition. It is, rather, an attitude. Some people are wise even though they have never had any formal education, whereas others have a tremendous amount of knowledge in their heads but not one ounce of wisdom. Wisdom is an attitude that consists first of all in knowing how to take one's bearings and set one's course in the best direction; only secondarily does it lead to science, culture and learning. The wise don't know all there is to know; they have not attained absolute knowledge; they continue to study and learn. In fact the learning process can go on for ever, for knowledge is infinite, but wisdom can be acquired instantaneously.

Wisdom is gold, the gold that comes from the sun. Yes, wisdom, spiritual gold, comes from the sun. As a matter of fact if the saints are always portrayed with a circlet of gold over their heads it is simply because wisdom emanates from them in the form of light. Just as material gold can be used to buy things in the visible world, the gold of wisdom can be used to buy whatever we want in the invisible world. When you go to a shop in the world above you will be asked if you have any gold and if you can say 'Yes', they will fill your basket to the brim. But if you have to say 'No', they will give you nothing.

And here in the mornings when we are up on the Rock[3] for the sunrise, we are collecting gold, quantities of tiny specks of gold-dust with which we can buy whatever we want in heaven: love, joy, dilatation, health, strength and fulfilment. A lot of people don't understand how valuable our custom of watching the sunrise is; they scoff at us and say that we are 'sun-struck'. Well, these people may have a lot of money in their cash boxes, but as long as they fail to understand the value of this spiritual gold their millions will not prevent them from ending in bankruptcy.

And finally in order to earn this gold we have to accomplish certain kinds of work: we have to read, study, reflect and meditate. And if the chart does not say that we have to earn this gold by watching the sun rise, add it to this last column yourself: as soon as spring comes you must be present every morning as the sun is getting up so as to collect its gold. So, set to work! You will object, 'But we don't do any work while the sun is rising; all we do is sit perfectly still and meditate.' Yes, to all outward appearances we are

---

[3] The Rock is a rocky platform at the top of a hill near the Bonfin where the Master and his disciples gather every morning, in spring and summer, to meditate and watch the sun rise.

motionless, but in reality our whole being is inwardly vibrating and pulsating with intensity.

And now let's look at the soul. In this area too there is so much ignorance and confusion in the minds of human beings. If you talk to them about the heart, the mind or the will you can sometimes reach an understanding, but the chances of doing so are very remote when it comes to discussing the soul. I have read a great many books about the soul but I have never been satisfied with any of their definitions or explanations. As for the opinion of orthodox science ... it hardly bears mentioning! The soul has quite simply been eliminated and reduced to a set of physiological processes. This is why I amused myself one day by giving a lecture about the soul. Oh, yes; I have my own ways of amusing myself! Do you remember that lecture? Many of you told me afterwards that they had found it extraordinarily clear. As a matter of fact I did not really say very much that day; I did little more than try to get the question into perspective so that you might begin to glimpse the truth, but I am far from imagining that I explained everything.

You will perhaps be surprised when I tell you that the ideal of the soul, the thing it asks for, is neither knowledge nor light nor happiness. The ideal of the soul is space, immensity; the one thing it needs is to be free to expand and reach out to embrace the infinite. Yes, the ideal of the soul is infinity. It is miserable when it is circumscribed and restricted. The human soul is a tiny fragment of the universal soul and to be confined to the physical body makes it feel so hemmed in, so stifled, that its one desire is to expand in space. People usually think that the whole of their soul dwells in their body but this is not so. The truth is that only a tiny proportion of a person's soul dwells within him; all the rest leads an independent life outside him, in the cosmic ocean. But as the universal soul has its own plans for us and wants to animate and vivify us and make us more beautiful, it is constantly working on us in order to penetrate and progressively permeate our whole being. Our soul, then, is not bounded by the narrowness of our own little person; it is something much vaster, just as our true self, our higher self, is not the puny little self that we know: it is a much more powerful entity. The soul too is infinitely more than we could ever imagine. It exists above and beyond our physical body; it can leave our body and travel to far-away regions and visit distant entities.

That portion of the universal soul that dwells in us, therefore, has a constant yearning for immensity and infinite space. But to attain its ideal the soul too needs the strength that only the appropriate nourishment can give it. The soul is nourished by all the qualities of a higher consciousness, by impersonality[4] and selflessness, by all that leads a human being to transcend himself and conquer his self-centredness. You can see for yourselves that a selfish, personal attitude always raises barriers and establishes boundaries. Every time someone says, 'That's mine!' he is erecting a fence, whereas an impersonal attitude breaks down fences and dissolves all barriers.

The soul must also have money with which to buy the food it needs, and the only money, the only means that can buy the infinite expansion that the soul seeks is fusion, dilatation and ecstasy. But ecstasy must be earned by an activity, a certain kind of work, and this work is prayer, adoration and contemplation. This is the activity that really belongs to the soul: contemplation, the contemplation of the Lord, of the angels and archangels, of the beauty of heaven. Prayer is a quest for divine splendour, and when that splendour is attained it brings with it such an intense experience of dilatation that it is as though one were torn out of one's body. This is ecstasy. All those who have experienced ecstasy tell us that they were no longer on earth, no longer bound to their limited physical body; they felt themselves to be immersed in the universal soul with which they had become one. Afterwards of course they came down to earth again, but for at least a

---

[4] This use of the term 'impersonality' may be misunderstood if it is not placed in the context of Omraam Mikhaël Aïvanhov's teaching concerning the two natures in man, the human and the divine, the lower self and the higher self or, as he calls them, the personality and the individuality. For a fuller treatment of the subject, See *Complete Works*, vol. 11, 'The Key to the Problems of Existence' and *Collection Izvor*, No. 213, 'Man's Two Natures, Human and Divine'.

few minutes or a few hours they had lived in perfect fusion with the infinite.

The truth that I am revealing to you today corresponds in every respect to the confessions or accounts left by so many saints, mystics and initiates. Ecstasy does not happen just like that, out of the blue; it is the result of an activity, the activity of prayer, adoration and contemplation, of a striving towards heaven and the Creator in order to obtain the gold with which to purchase all the joys of heaven and attain infinite expansion.

There you are my dear brothers and sisters, it is all quite clear to you now. To be sure, those who have never had even an inkling of such an experience will think that what I have said is exaggerated and bizarre. Well, let them think what they like but, for my part I put this table before you in utter simplicity and sincerity and all the initiates would agree with what I say.

And now we come to the spirit. The spirit also yearns for an ideal, but the ideal of the spirit is not that of the soul. It does not yearn to melt into space, into the infinite, because its nature is different. The soul is the feminine principle *par excellence*, the feminine principle in its most perfect, most divine expression. The spirit, on the other hand, is the divine expression of the masculine principle. The intellect and the heart also represent the masculine and feminine principles but on a lower plane and, therefore, less perfectly. The alternation of these two principles – positive and negative, emissive and receptive –is repeated on every plane and in every region of the universe, but in different forms. Wherever you look you will find only the masculine and feminine principles. But I have already said enough on this subject[5], so I shall say no more today.

What does the spirit ask for? Not space nor knowledge, not happiness nor power nor health. The spirit does not need any of these things because it has them all; it is never ill, never weak nor unhappy, never cold nor in darkness. The spirit asks for only one thing: eternity. The spirit is an immortal essence, and as such has

[5] See *Complete Works*, vols. 14 and 15.

no liking for that which is bound by the constraints of time; it seeks eternity. Just as the domain of the soul is space, so the domain of the spirit is time. Physicists and philosophers will never understand the nature of time and space until they understand the nature of the soul and the spirit. Yes, because time and space are notions of a fourth dimension which pertains to the soul and the spirit. Here too there is so much I could say, but I am waiting for the right time to say it. Today I shall simply say that even the greatest physicists, mathematicians and philosophers who study time and space will never pierce these mysteries if they have never consciously worked with their soul and spirit to reach some understanding of infinity and eternity.

In order to attain its goal of eternity the spirit too needs nourishment. It may surprise you to learn that the spirit needs to be nourished – but you will perhaps remember that I told you one day that even the Lord nourishes himself – and the nourishment of the spirit is freedom. The soul needs to expand and dilate but the spirit needs to cut the ties that bind it.

Truth is the currency with which the spirit buys freedom. Neither wisdom nor love but only truth can set the spirit free. Every truthful element that you manage to acquire about anything at all makes you freer. Jesus said, 'You shall know the truth, and the truth shall make you free'. Yes, it is truth that sets us free. You will say, 'What about love?' Love? Oh no; love is far more likely to bind you, to make you a prisoner. Do you want to bind yourself to something or someone? Call on love; nothing has more power to bind you than love! Do you want to be free? Call on truth! If you want proof of what I say look at what happens with old people: they begin to know truth, and as truth is freedom they are ready to free themselves from this world and move on into the next, whereas those who are in love don't want to free themselves; on the contrary they want to stay on earth together, billing and cooing for ever. Think about this a little and you will have to agree with me.

But you cannot buy truth just anywhere in the first shop you come to. Before you can possess truth there is something you must do, some work that you must accomplish: the work of identification with the Creator. To identify with God is to draw closer to him, to fuse into one with him, to possess the truth and become free. In a few words Jesus expressed and summed up this process of identification when he said, 'I and my Father are one'. Meditation will give you some light, but it will not set you free. Contemplation will plunge you into ecstasy, but it will not set you free either. Only this work of identification will give you the gold called truth. And what is this truth? The truth is that man is nothing but an illusion, a *maya*; that he comes from God and will return to God. As soon as you know and understand this truth, as soon as you see and feel it, you feel free – free from all passions and ambitions, free from suffering – and free to enter into eternity.

Jesus also said, 'This is eternal life, that they may know You, the only true God, and the Christ whom You have sent'. What kind of knowledge is implied here? Jesus was certainly not thinking of a purely intellectual knowledge – the knowledge of those who say that they know all about something because they have read books about it – but of true knowledge. 'To know the only true God' means to identify with God; to know God is to be fused into one with him. And it is this union, this fusion, that is eternal life. To fuse into and become one with the Creator is the only way to enter into eternal life; without this union no man can be eternal for he will still be living in time.

Actually we live both in time and in eternity: our spirit lives in eternity whilst our physical body and all that pertains to it lives in time, withers and dies. Years ago I gave a lecture about time and eternity in which I showed that eternity was not a question of duration, however unlimited, but of intensity. Eternity is an intensity of life and to possess eternal life, therefore, is not to live indefinitely but to live with intensity. We are creatures bound by the limits of time; we have all had a beginning and we must all have an end but within the boundaries of this temporal existence we can already find eternity in an intense spiritual life. Yes, because only the spirit belongs to the eternal order.

Now just to make it easier for you to see how initiates understand the meaning of the word 'know', let me give you a very simple example. Have you never noticed that a baby's way of getting to know something is to put it in its mouth? It is adults who have forgotten how to get to know things. They observe, study and read books, whereas children use the direct way of true knowledge: they put things into their mouths, that is to say they taste them. But we can take this one step further: the Bible says that Adam 'knew' Eve, and Abel was born, and that Abraham 'knew' Sarah and Isaac was born. And this shows that knowledge is a joining, a fusion. To know someone is not a question of meeting them and exchanging a few words so as to be able to say, 'Yes, I know so-and-so'. You may make his acquaintance in this way but you will not know him: only when you are one with him will you know him. The verb 'to know', therefore has two meanings: one for ordinary men and women and the other for initiates. And everything becomes perfectly clear if you realize that Jesus was speaking for initiates when he said, 'This is eternal life, that they may know you, the only true God, and the Christ whom you have sent'.

Thanks to his efforts to practise identification, contemplation, meditation, singing, breathing exercises, gymnastics and even physical labours, a disciple ceases to feel constantly hungry, thirsty and dissatisfied and begins to nourish and reinforce each of his inner principles. Of course the few indications I have given you today can be expanded and developed *ad infinitum*; you can add all kinds of details or variations, and discover all kinds of connections between the different elements. As a matter of fact isn't that what I have been doing in the lectures I have given you over the last thirty-four years? Although I have never shown you this table or referred to it explicitly before, it has always been there in the background; it has always been the basis on which all my lectures are built. In it I have attempted to include all the different notions concerning man's physical and psychic life that can be found in various traditions and bring them together in a co-ordinated whole. Yes, it is the result of my own twisted mentality which always has to unify and synthesize things.

Science has concentrated too exclusively and for too long on analysis; today's world is in dire need of a synthetic vision of reality. Well, we have this synthetic vision; all my work is achieved through synthesis. From time to time of course it is necessary to analyse some point or other, but if my method is always one of synthesis it is because only synthesis is life-giving. Thanks to synthesis you can know greatness and be rich and alive by becoming one with the Creator and with the entire universe. With analysis, on the contrary, you will gradually kill yourself, you will shrink and wither away until there is nothing left of you. Analysis is death. Synthesis is life. Doesn't a mother's work of gestation prove this? She forms the child in her womb by synthesizing billions of separate elements. A child is a living synthesis that talks and eats and walks about. Later when the time of analysis comes, each particle of the body returns to the region to which it corresponds – earth, water, air or fire – just as each little piece of type used in printing goes back into its compartment in the type-setter's box. If you persist in analysing and dismembering everything and everybody therefore, you will be heading straight towards death, spiritual death.

A personal, selfish, individualistic way of life leads to spiritual death; it cuts one off and isolates one from others; it separates one from others and that is death. A collective, brotherly way of life, on the other hand, is a synthesis which leads to life, to resurrection. If you have no desire to establish the Universal White Brotherhood on earth it means that you are working for your own spiritual death. In order to live we need a high ideal of synthesis, the ideal of the kingdom of God.

As I have already said, this table cannot contain everything. There are necessarily a certain number of notions that you will not find in it. But we can at least find the place of consciousness in it. Consciousness or, to be more accurate, self-consciousness belongs to the intellect. Superconsciousness belongs to the soul and spirit; in fact where the spirit is concerned we can speak of divine superconsciousness. Consciousness belongs to the will and the heart, whereas self-consciousness begins to appear only on the level of the mind. The subconscious corresponds to the instinctive manifestations of life (breathing, digestion, circulation of the

21

blood, elimination, growth, etc.). And finally the level of the unconscious corresponds to the physical body and the skeleton.

You are wondering where purity fits in to this synopsis, but I ask you, 'How can purity be separated from all the rest?' In the Sephirotic Tree (Figure 2) it is different; purity resides in the sephirah Yesod[6], but in this synopsis purity has no special place because it must be everywhere. On the level of the physical body purity must exist as a quality of the food you eat: your food must be pure. If it is polluted, tainted or decayed it will poison you. The same can be said on the level of the will: the forces that nourish the will must be pure. There are many different kinds of forces, and some of them produce a lot of ash and cinders. We see the same phenomenon with the different materials that we use as fuel: coal and oil both contain energy, but in order to produce as much energy as possible and at the same time as little ash as possible, you either have to use the very best clean-burning fuel or to purify and filter what you have. Otherwise you will be left with piles of cinders but very little heat, very little energy.

The heart too can only be properly nourished if you give it the purest feelings. If you feed your heart on a horrible mixture of impure feelings – anger, jealousy, greed and sensuality, etc. – you will be giving it polluted food that will poison it. And the same is true of the intellect, the soul and the spirit. There can be no wisdom, ecstasy or truth in the presence of impurity. As you see, it is all quite clear and simple.

I have not made any mention of beauty or perfection in this table either, for the same reason: they are implicit on all levels.

Nor has suffering been given a special place, and it is easy to understand why: you only have to disrupt the order that reigns amongst the different elements by giving impure food to the physical body, the heart or the mind for instance, or by giving to one principle that which belongs to another for suffering to make its appearance. If only you could hear all the complaints that go on inside you! 'Why do you give me such food? It's not what I need.'

[6] See *Complete Works*, vol. 7, 'The Mysteries of Yesod'.

'I need open space; why have you shut me up like a prisoner?' 'I need warmth; why do you leave me to shiver in the cold?'

Do you sense the truth of what I have been telling you? Of course, if your attitude in listening to me is purely intellectual and objective you may feel nothing at all. In fact you will probably find that what I say does not coincide with your opinions. Well, it is not my fault if contemporary culture has filled your head with notions that prevent you from understanding me. Hurry up and learn to look at things from my point of view and you will be full of wonder. You will say, 'Ah, I understand; I'm going to keep this table with me and wherever I go, in the bus or train, at the dentist's or even in the beauty parlour, I'll take it out and study it'. Yes, this synopsis can help you enormously. Never underestimate its importance.

Sèvres, February 6, 1972 (morning)

II

Question: *'Freedom is usually thought of in connection with the notion of space: one is free to move about, to go somewhere else. Will you explain why the synoptic table indicates that it is the spirit rather than the soul that seeks freedom?'*

Yes, everybody confuses freedom with the notion of space, but true freedom is not related to space. Picture a man who is so infuriated by his mother-in-law that, one day, he packs his bags and goes off to the top of a mountain to get away from her. The trouble is that even when he gets there he is not free. Why? Because the same old discussions and arguments with his mother-in-law continue to occupy his mind. Physically she is a long way away, but he has not escaped from her mentally because he cannot stop thinking about her. Yes, and you can imagine the good, kind thoughts he sends her! The notion of freedom is not linked to space because it is not space that gives us true freedom. It does give a certain degree of freedom: it gives us freedom of movement, it allows us to go from one place to another, but true freedom, the freedom of the spirit, is something quite different.

Take the example of a circle: the circumference can be immense but the centre will never be more than a mere dot, a point that has no dimension. The circumference represents the soul which can be infinitely vast, whereas the point at the centre represents the spirit. The spirit has no dimension but it has the particular property of vibrating with such intensity that it can displace itself instantaneously and be everywhere at once. This is why it is said that the spirit is everywhere and nowhere. The circumference of a circle is fixed but its centre is mobile. And this is so because it is alive.

The Synoptic Table

Unlike the soul which expands in space, the spirit does not occupy space. To be free in the spirit, therefore, has nothing to do with space; to be free is a state of consciousness. The spirit is not bound by space because it is not material, whereas the soul is. Of course the matter of the soul is not the dense, opaque substance that we can see and feel; it is the primeval matter which is pure light. The soul provides the marvellously subtle matter with which the spirit creates – and without which the spirit can do nothing. The spirit is enclosed in matter, and when physicists split the atom they are simply freeing the spirit, the forces imprisoned in matter. It is not matter that produces an explosion but the energy contained in it.

When we speak of 'spirit and matter' we are touching the two opposite poles of the universe, and we can move progressively down the scale and enumerate the different levels of this polarization: the heavenly Father and the divine Mother, the cosmic spirit and the universal soul, the spirit and the soul, the mind and the heart, and lower still on the physical plane, man and woman. Men represent the spirit. Even though there may be nothing spiritual about a particular man he still symbolically belongs to the category of the spirit. And women represent matter even though, of course, they are not purely material. In fact women are often more spiritual than men but they still belong symbolically to the category of matter. And when a man and a woman are united their union symbolizes that union of spirit and matter that created the universe.

Sèvres, February 6, 1972 (afternoon)

Chapter Three

SPIRIT AND MATTER

I

I have often talked to you about the difference between the conventional knowledge that is distributed in our colleges and universities, and initiatic knowledge. The main emphasis in conventional studies is on disciplines which are designed to help human beings to attain material success but which prevent them from becoming spirits and children of God. The result is that people are becoming more and more alienated from the spirit, and this is the cause of every kind of imbalance, ailment or disorder. People always look for the source of their problems elsewhere; in overwork, grief or unhealthy eating habits, for instance. No, the cause of all men's problems is the imbalance between spirit and matter; it is this that leads to all other forms of imbalance. If human beings are exclusively concerned with giving their physical body the comfort and pleasure it demands, their soul and spirit grow weak from lack of nourishment and everything in their lives is upside down.

Spirit and matter are two poles, two principles with which human beings must learn to work intelligently, reasonably and prudently; above all they must never emphasize one to the detriment of the other. It is not recommended to follow the example of the west and attach importance almost exclusively to material possessions, but nor is the example of India one to imitate either, for on the pretext of a high regard for mysticism and spirituality India has remained sunk in poverty and disease. If you want to restore the balance you must give to both spirit and matter the place that is theirs by right. Matter must not be rejected: it must be made subject and obedient to the spirit. This is the only way human beings can regain their health, beauty, strength and happiness: by restoring this balance. Use your reason! How is it that in spite of all the marvels available to them in the way of technical progress, mechanical appliances and material prosperity, human beings are more subject to illness, more discontented and more rebellious against the established order than ever before? It obviously means that something is wrong. Yes, and that something is that they have concentrated on only one way and forgotten about the other. To be sure specialization can give you very good results in a limited area. If you train to be a boxer you will be able to knock people out in the ring, but you won't be able to beat them in the area of science or philosophy. And someone who spends his life in thought may claim the advantage over every other thinker, but a child could knock him over. Just because you are a champion in one area does not mean that you will triumph in every other area.

I have already explained to you that the true philosophy of spirit and matter is perfectly summed up in the phrase in Genesis in which Moses says, 'In the beginning God created the heavens and the earth'. 'The heavens' are the soul and spirit, the splendour of virtues and qualities, whereas 'the earth' is the physical body, the material domain, worldly affairs. The fact that the world was created means that it is necessary, but Moses, who was a high initiate, put the heavens before the earth. Most human beings do just the opposite: the earth is more important to them than heaven. In fact for many only the earth exists; heaven does not come into it. And this is why nothing goes right, because the earth has been given priority. I can see that even the brothers and sisters of the Brotherhood devote nine tenths of their activity to the earth; only rarely, from time to time, do they think about heaven and the spirit. Instead of giving first place to heaven and then going about their business in the world they give the best of themselves to their worldly affairs, and then when they are bored and don't know what else to do, they take a few minutes to think about heaven.

As I have already explained to you[1], you must give three quarters to heaven and one quarter to the earth. Those who are

---

[1] See *Complete Works*, vol. 11, chap. 14, 'Render to Caesar the things that are Caesar's'.

capable of practising this will sense that there is a marvellous balance to their lives. Believe me, it is useless to look for the cause of the balance or imbalance of your lives in the nervous, circulatory, digestive or muscular system of your physical body. The origin of all balance and of all lack of balance is in the way in which each person relates inwardly to spirit and matter.

Sometimes, to be sure, I agree with those who are afraid to venture into the spiritual domain. The physical world is solid and visible and they feel safe in it because they can see where they are going and what they are doing. The spiritual world is quite another matter: it is nebulous and dangerous and unknown to them. It is full of snares and deep chasms. And then too it is obvious that there are not many people who could be an example to others, who could show them how marvellous the spiritual path is. So it is true that the spiritual world can seem very hazy and formless, and this is because the organs which would enable human beings to make contact with it are not as highly perfected as their hands and eyes and ears, etc., which they use in working with the visible world. If you examine the question more closely however, you will see that the spiritual world is not only the most real, the safest and the most clear-cut, but that it is eternally unchanging and beautiful, whereas the physical world is neither stable nor eternal: it crumbles and disintegrates. If most people are afraid to venture into the spiritual world it is because they have not developed certain senses and have no one to guide them. But the material, tangible world that is accessible to our five senses is not true reality.

True reality is that of the soul and spirit, and in order to have access to this reality human beings need to develop other senses, and above all they need a master[2]. Otherwise of course it is dangerous, and one can make a great many mistakes and do oneself a lot of harm by arousing hostile forces. If one has the proper guidance and is ready to work hard, however, there is nothing more marvellous than the spiritual world. The physical world is

---

[2] See *Complete Works*, vol. 6, chap. 4, 'A Disciple Must Develop his Spiritual Senses'.

beautiful: flowers, crystals, trees, birds, mountains, human beings and stars are all extraordinarily beautiful. But in comparison with the world of the spirit they pale into insignificance. It is no good blaming the spiritual world if you don't know how to find your way in it, the fault is yours. You started out with unbounded confidence in yourself, you would have nothing to do with a master, you refused the help of a guide, so who is to blame when you fall over the edge of a cliff?

Sèvres, February 19, 1970

II

The Master reads the Meditation for the day:

"The human spirit is omniscient and all-powerful and participates in all that happens in the universe, but as men's organs are not yet sufficiently developed to transmit the experiences of the spirit to their consciousness, they themselves neither know nor feel any of this. You will ask, 'What should we do, then? Should we try to strengthen, enlighten and educate our spirit?' No, it is the physical body that has to be strengthened, purified, spiritualized and rendered divine.

Alchemists were right to concentrate all their efforts on the attempt to transform matter. And we must work in the same direction; we must take care to give our physical body only pure food and drink, pure air, the pure rays of the sun and all that is purest and best in the way of forms, colours, sounds, music and perfume. The spirit does not need any of those things; like God the spirit is everywhere; it is omniscient and omnipresent. It is our matter that has to be cared for and transformed, and in doing this we shall be giving our spirit a better chance of manifesting itself in all its splendour."

This is another question that is still not properly understood, even by spiritualists[3]. They often think that it is the spirit that must be purified and ennobled and that they may neglect and even despise the physical body. They think that if the spirit manifests itself imperfectly on the physical plane it is because it is imperfect

---

[3] The word 'spiritualist' in the language of Omraam Mikhaël Aïvanhov denotes one who looks at things from a spiritual point of view, whose philosophy of life is based on belief in a spiritual reality.

and needs to be developed, strengthened and purified. No, the spirit is made of subtle, luminous, indestructible material; it is eternal, a spark from God; it does not need to be instructed or improved. This is very clear in the phenomenon of clairvoyance, for instance. Take the example of the American clairvoyant Edgar Cayce. He was an ordinary man with very little formal education and yet, when he was in a hypnotic trance, he showed that he had immense knowledge in all kinds of subjects such as medicine and history. He could even see people's previous incarnations, the crimes they had committed and the source of their difficulties and ailments in this life. Once he came out of his trance, however, he could remember nothing about what he had seen, and this shows that when the spirit of even the most ordinary man is given the opportunity to escape from the constraints of the physical body in which it is imprisoned, it becomes omniscient.

The capacities of the spirit are infinite but you have to give it the conditions it needs in order to manifest itself. There are certain cases, also, in which people, artists and thinkers especially, reach extraordinary heights of inspiration and enthusiasm that bring them into contact with sublime realities, and then when they revert to their normal state they understand practically nothing of what happened to them. All of this proves that if men became both more receptive and more perceptive, and if they were given conditions that would enable the spirit to manifest itself more fully, they would realize that it has the most extraordinary possibilities.

Take the example of someone who is mentally retarded or ill: it is not his spirit that is ill or retarded, the defect is in the organ, the instrument through which the spirit has to manifest itself, the person's brain. To expect the spirit to manifest itself through this inadequate instrument is exactly as though you asked a virtuoso to play on a broken piano: however willing he may be and however hard he tries he will only get horrible, discordant noises from it. It is not the pianist who is to blame, it is the piano. A human brain through which the spirit has to manifest itself is exactly like the piano on which a virtuoso plays. As you can see, therefore, it is the physical body that must be perfected and purified and made more flexible, for it is the physical body that is encumbered with so many impurities and extraneous elements that however highly evolved a spirit may be it cannot use it as a channel for its strength and light. The spirit is a divine spark; all the powers and all the knowledge of God himself are contained in its quintessence, but we have to give it a fitting instrument and the physical body is precisely one of the most perfect instruments that God has given to man; an instrument built with inexpressible wisdom and endowed with an extraordinary wealth of possibilities. And yet there are those who despise and reject the physical body because it is material, whereas the spirit, you see, is noble, divine.

Of course you will tell me that today human beings understand the importance of the physical body. Yes, but not in the right way: they take care to give it plenty of food, comfort and sexual pleasure, they do all they can to make it attractive and seductive, but they do nothing to make it an instrument of the spirit or a channel for the transmission of divine wisdom. The Bible tells us, 'For you are the temple of the living God'. Is it the spirit or the body that is God's temple? The spirit cannot be the temple because it is immaterial: the spirit is the celebrant, the one who presides at the ceremony. It is the physical body that is the temple; this is clear – except to Christians, who have never understood it. But then there are many things in the New Testament that still need to be explained.

The spirit is the son of God, an immortal principle. What more could we possibly add to it? But the physical body is quite another matter: that is where our work lies. All our difficulties, problems and suffering belong to the physical body. Our task is to make it so pure and invulnerable, so impervious to evil and disease, so subtle and so vital, that it truly becomes a mouthpiece for the spirit, a medium through which the whole of heaven can express itself and all the wonders of the universe be made manifest. At the moment of course, the physical body is not a temple; it is more like a tavern in which hell and all its inhabitants come and make merry. People use it to do abominable things; they think that that is what it is for. Nobody knows what it is really capable of, that it is capable of healing, of projecting light and perfume, that it is capable of

35

travelling through space. One day you will see all this; you will see the wonderful things that the physical body can do. It is easy for the spirit: once it frees itself from the weight of the body it can go wherever it likes. There is nothing to hold the spirit back: it can fly up to the stars or plunge into the depths of the ocean, but the physical body is not yet ready for such ventures.

Believe me, all this is extremely important. The history of mankind shows that human beings have rarely known exactly how to evaluate the relative importance of the spirit and the body. For some the spirit is everything and the body is so neglected that it wastes away. But if the body were so utterly despicable, if only the spirit mattered, we should never have come down to earth, we should have stayed above, in the realm of the spirit. But we have come down to earth, and this means that there is work to be done here. The mission of the spirit is to descend, to put on a physical body in order to work on earth and transform it into a magnificent garden for the Lord to stroll in. If we were supposed to reject matter what would be the point of our being here? Why immerse ourselves in matter if not in order to sublimate it, to make it as luminous and transparent as the spirit? When Jesus said, 'Thy will be done on earth as it is in heaven', he too was praying that the splendour of the spirit should descend and impregnate matter. Unfortunately when human beings incarnate and find themselves on earth they forget what they are here for, and they go back to the world above having despoiled and defiled this world.

A new era is opening before us, an era in which human beings have a gigantic amount of work to do in order to adapt to the new currents from heaven. Today it is the earth that is important; our task is to sublimate the earth, the physical body, matter, by bringing down the spirit into it, for only the spirit can animate and illuminate matter. We must project the spirit on to matter so that matter becomes spiritual. With your thoughts, which belong to the realm of the spirit, penetrate the cells of your body and you will see what transformations follow.

The question of spirit and matter is infinite for, in other forms, spirit and matter are to be found everywhere: as man and woman, positive and negative, emissive and receptive, heaven and earth. Nothing is more important than these two principles, and if we are to avoid attaching undue importance to one of them to the detriment of the other we have to understand the proper place and role of each. Human beings always have a tendency to go to extremes: either they consider that only the spirit is important and this leads them to neglect matter, or they are only interested in matter and they neglect the spirit. And this is what is happening today. People are only concerned with matter, and as they do nothing to imbue it with spirit it remains inert and inanimate, whereas if they put some life, some spirit into it, it could be highly expressive. What is it that makes some men and women so extraordinarily attractive and expressive? It is the spirit within them, the spirit that animates their matter. This is so true, in fact, that when a person dies not only does the matter of his body cease to be alive but it immediately begins to putrefy. It is the spirit that acts through matter. Matter without the spirit is dead.

Even I, such as I am here on earth ... I know very little; I see very little; I am nothing at all. But sometimes I realize that, far from my brain, far from my physical body, my spirit – or if you prefer, the entities that dwell in me – are seeing and feeling things. How often I have felt this! I cannot read people's minds, I am not clairvoyant, but the being that is always there behind me or inside me knows everything that happens to you or in you: he knows exactly what you are thinking and all about your worries and problems, and sometimes, by chance or just for fun, he whispers a few words in my ear. Then someone will come to me after a lecture and say, 'How did you know what was worrying me? What you said in your lecture gave me exactly the answer I needed!' The truth is that I knew nothing about it, but there is someone within each one of us who sees everything knows everything and can do everything.

We are here within the four walls of this room, but our spirits are everywhere; this is why we must give them more and more opportunity to manifest themselves through us.

The Bonfin, July 19 1975

37

III

Most human beings tend to believe that if something is refined, delicate and subtle it will not stand up to much wear and tear, but they are mistaken. Look at the different kingdoms of nature: at first sight it would seem that rocks were stronger and more durable than plants, but in point of fact, plants are less vulnerable than rocks; animals are less vulnerable than plants and so on. The cruder and more rigid the matter the more vulnerable it is because it is at the mercy of its environment. It cannot defend itself by moving away or resisting attack.

It is stone that is most helpless and vulnerable for its only defence is its matter; it cannot move. Plants on the other hand can move to a certain extent; the life that is in them is capable of defending itself. The roots and branches of trees for instance can grow round obstacles; the stems of certain flowers can bend towards the sun so as to get the light they need. As for animals, it goes without saying: they can run and jump and swim or fly from danger. And human beings have even more ways of changing their conditions, defending themselves, standing up to wear and tear. The only trouble is that as they have never worked to refine the matter of their physical bodies and make it subtler and more flexible, they are continually at the mercy of negative circumstances and evil forces and entities.

Take another example: it is easy to grasp a handful of earth, isn't it? It is much more difficult to grasp a handful of water. Air cannot be grasped at all. And as for ether ... . In order to be truly invulnerable and impregnable, therefore, man must refine himself more and more. Not in the sense of becoming weaker or more fragile, but in the sense of becoming purer and more permeated by light, of vibrating with greater and greater intensity. The higher you go in the scale of beings the more creatures you will find who have reached such a degree of physical purity and intensity of life that they have become virtually impregnable; they can be neither captured nor restricted in any way. And if you manage to rise even beyond these beings you will reach the Lord himself who is so immaterial that he is absolutely impregnable; nothing in heaven or on earth can lay hold of him, no creature can have any knowledge or conception of him.

Life oscillates between two poles: that of matter, which is animated by no more than an infinitesimal vibration, and that of pure spirit, the spirit of God, a vibration that is so intense, so vital and luminous that it cannot be grasped.

This is why those who have studied life, the initiates, make every effort to stay in contact with the pole of subtlety, intensity and light, whereas most human beings make so little effort that they drift towards the pole of inertia and become completely fossilized and amorphous; when you deal with them it is as though you were dealing with a pile of stones. Stone is useful, indispensable in fact, I agree it has its contribution to make; but disciples must understand that they must also know and draw closer to that other pole, the pole of the spirit, of God. Between the stones of the earth on the one hand, and God, who is totally unknowable, totally inaccessible, infinite and unique on the other, lies the whole range of created beings from plants to the Seraphim.

And now as you study a page of this ancient and noble philosophy that is so profound and true, it is up to each one of you to find your own place in this hierarchy. If you have the enthusiasm you need to carry you to ever greater heights in order to reach all those beings who are so much more advanced, you will get to know their life and begin to feel and taste it for yourselves. In this way you will enjoy conditions that will make it much easier for you to manifest yourselves and attain your aspirations, your ideal. The conditions we need cannot be found down here; we are subject to too many limitations, and that is why we suffer. But it is up to each human being to choose: either to sink lower and lower to the level of animals, plants and stones, or to take the upward path and rise through the ranks of the angelic hierarchies to the Creator himself. In order to achieve this he must replace the crude, dull particles of his physical, astral and mental bodies with the purest and most noble, most luminous particles, until his body becomes that of a divinity.

The whole of esoteric philosophy is summed up in these few words. In fact you will certainly have noticed that each lecture is a whole in itself while, at the same time, it always ties in with all the others. In each lecture I always tend to reach a synthesis; in fact you can base your whole life on any one of my lectures and, provided of course that you go into it in sufficient depth, it will take you a very long way even if you never read any of the others. If you take the image that I have given you today of the scale, the ladder that rises from the stones of the earth to the Godhead, you will need nothing more: it gives you all the criteria, all the yardsticks you need to make everything clear to you. When you feel that your life is slowing down, that it is stagnating, it means that you are sinking towards the level of the stones; you have ceased to evolve. Whereas if you notice that the quality of your thoughts, feelings and actions is beginning to improve it means that you are moving in the right direction, and in conformity with the eternal laws are entering another region, another domain, another dimension. And as each region has its own particular qualities you will find yourself benefiting from the new possibilities you encounter. You will begin to understand things more clearly, you will become more loving and more patient; even your health will begin to improve. If you go on in this way things will become better and better until you achieve true bliss.

Take only these few words to heart and you will need nothing more; you will have material enough to work on for the rest of your life. What more can you ask for? But I know what you will do: you will file this image away and tomorrow you will ask for another. Very well, tomorrow you shall have another, but it will point in the same direction. And after that you will want another and yet another. I have already given you hundreds of images but you keep asking for more.

Let me repeat it, my dear brothers and sisters: don't let yourselves look to matter in the hope of becoming stronger and less vulnerable. A tall tree can be split and uprooted by a storm because it is stiff and unbending, whereas a blade of grass survives by bowing before the wind. And why are women more resilient than men? They live longer, they are less easily discouraged and yet they are more fragile, more delicate than men. A man may appear to be very sturdy but he will be much more easily defeated. Yes, simply because he is less flexible than a woman. So you see, suppleness and flexibility are all-important. You must not be rigid in life; you must be flexible and adaptable. There are people who, whatever the circumstances, always apply the same methods, but as no one method can solve all problems they end by being broken and uprooted.

Flexibility is essential, and to be flexible means to use more psychological and educational dexterity, to be more diplomatic. Not diplomatic in the pejorative sense of the word; no, for me diplomacy implies wisdom. A sage is a diplomat; depending on the conditions of the moment or on the individual with whom he is dealing, he knows what method to apply in order to achieve success and do good. Whereas someone who is rigid is like the old doctor in the Bulgarian army who knew only one remedy: whenever a soldier came to the infirmary, whether he was suffering from a cold, a headache or a bilious attack, the doctor would daub him with tincture of iodine. There are people like that: whatever the problem out comes the bottle of iodine! But that won't do: iodine may be a good remedy but it cannot cure everything. Those who are too rigid, too unyielding, therefore, collide with obstacles much more powerful than themselves and are broken by them. Whereas a sage, a truly wise man, reflects, searches for and finds ways of manoeuvring, just as a navigator who knows where the dangerous currents and reefs are, knows how to steer his boat safely through them. Flexibility therefore implies wisdom. In this sense flexibility is a form of wisdom; to be flexible is to be wise, to be a good psychologist.

Of course you will tell me that in real life weeds are hardier and more tenacious than other plants, and so are the wicked. Yes, coarse, primitive, materialistic people are much more at home on earth and often survive longer and live to triumph over others, whereas those who are subtler, purer and more virtuous disappear sooner. Do you want my explanation? Present conditions on earth are not such as to make things easy for the children of God. Look at a jungle inhabited by snakes and wild beasts, or a swamp infested with mosquitoes and other insects: the creatures that live in those conditions are perfectly at home. They have been there a long time and are adapted to the environment; they have all they need for their survival. The territory belongs to them and if anyone tries to take it away from them they defend themselves: 'What right have you to hunt us and drive us out? This is our land!' And they sting and bite and claw the intruders.

Well, this is exactly what happens on earth: the earth belongs to those who have got a firm foothold and are bent on continuing their shady dealings, to those who are ready to fight to get everything for themselves. But this state of affairs will not last for ever. The earth is predestined to become the dwelling place of spirits, of the children of God, and one day great upheavals will occur to destroy the conditions that favour those who are wicked, cruel and violent and deprive them of their means of survival. Then the children of God will establish themselves on earth and it will become their homeland. At the moment to be sure they are not at home here; they are in the same situation as missionaries who try to explain to a tribe of cannibals that they should not eat each other: not only will the cannibals continue the habit, but the missionaries themselves will be eaten!

For the time being, therefore, the earth belongs to those who are violent, greedy and materialistic, and this is the cause of war. The children of God are coming to take over the earth but the others, those who feel at home here, are quick to defend themselves and it is still they who are stronger, for they have barricaded themselves in and are physically and materially well armed. You will ask, 'How long is the battle going to last?' Well, look at how many areas of the world used to be infested by man-eating beasts and other dangerous animals: they are far fewer nowadays. The same thing will happen with those who dominate the world today: the survivors will be kept in zoos for the entertainment of children – and also to ensure that their image is not completely lost. Yes, the population of wild beasts, of wild human beings, will gradually decrease because fewer and fewer of them will reincarnate and their place will be taken by children of God. But so far it is spiritualists who are always vanquished and massacred, whereas the weeds survive much longer.

Besides, why do misers and egoists live to the age of ninety-nine whereas angelic beings die in their twenties? The purest beings cannot survive in present conditions; they are too fragile, too sensitive. This does not mean that you have to be wicked and grow fangs and claws in order to survive in the world. No, because the present state of affairs will not last much longer. The wicked are destined to disappear and those who had to leave because they could struggle no longer will return as conquerors and then the earth will belong to them. Didn't Jesus say, 'Blessed are the meek, for they shall inherit the earth'? So you see: what I am saying corresponds exactly with the philosophy of Jesus: he did not say that the earth belonged already to the meek but that it would belong to them, that they would inherit it. We must always continue to live according to the philosophy of the sages and great masters of mankind, therefore, because they know that in the long run it is they who will be victorious. All the others are committed to a course that is destined to fail.

When I began by saying that you must improve things by refining them and making them subtler and more spiritual, you thought it was a strange idea, but now you are beginning to understand. Why is gold so durable? Because its matter is very spiritual, very exalted and pure. So much so in fact that we call it a noble metal. This is why we have to replace our inferior particles with particles of a higher quality. If this is not understood, of course, it is pointless to pray or meditate or contemplate the sunrise. But now that you understand this, you will understand how important it is for you to receive these particles of sunlight that vibrate with such intensity, so that your etheric body may become strong and radiant and safe from attack by disorder, illness or discouragement of any kind.

When I try to discover why human beings are so limited and unhappy, I always find that it is because their minds are focused on models and examples that are too earthbound. Yes, this is the problem: they have taken stones, plants or animals as their models. Of course this is not wholly a mistake; we live on earth and we need certain elements from the mineral, vegetable and animal kingdoms, but we must not rely exclusively on them. Believe me, human beings do not have the right philosophy; they have adopted the philosophy of their fathers, grandfathers and great-grandfathers before them: it is not the philosophy of the initiates. It is normal for certain notions or traditions that have stood the test of the centuries to be preserved, but that stale, earthbound, materialistic philosophy must now be discarded and replaced with the eternal philosophy that the initiates have held since the beginning of time. If you put all your faith in this obsolete philosophy – that will inevitably have to make way for another before long – you will always be in trouble, for it has never solved any of man's major problems. To be sure you will rub along with it somehow, but it will never enable you to do more than grope your way and nibble at the edges of life; it will never relieve you of any of the burdens that weigh you down. It will never allow you to feel free and weightless because there is nothing weightless, light or happy about it; it is only capable of burying you, of suffocating and oppressing you. If your only ambition is to be firmly established on earth you will never feel light and free because you will be obliged to bury yourself in matter, in relationships and associations, in responsibilities and commitments; you will never have a spare moment in which to breathe freely, reflect or meditate.

Those whose only concern is to expand their business interests and to earn as much money as possible by opening branch offices and subsidiaries throughout the world end by being crushed and buried under their own weight. You can go and look for them under the rubble but you will not find them; they will have disappeared without a trace. Millions of miles down under the earth they may be reaching out to you, hoping to be saved, but there is nothing you can do for them. People like that are simply too stupid; they adopt a materialistic philosophy and, of course, as they are very successful they are constantly being congratulated. Yes, idiots congratulate people like that, and not only do they congratulate them but they even want to be like them, so deeply buried in their financial calculations, their fatigue and their insomnia that they are no longer capable of breathing freely or seeing that there are stars in the sky. This is how most people understand life.

Let me take another example, the example of the strings of a violin. It is the thickest string, the G-string, that is the least resilient. You only have to pull it a little too hard and it will snap. It is the E-string, the thinnest one, that is the strongest. In the same way the physical body, which is thick and material, is weaker and less durable than the soul and the spirit, which are immortal. Now of course you must understand me correctly: you must not destroy your physical body on the pretext that it is too crude. In any case we all have the body we deserve. Before incarnating on earth a human soul looks for somewhere to live. If a soul is poor – that is to say poor in light and virtue – it will be in the same situation as someone on earth who wants to buy a house but has very little money: it will have to be content with a hovel, a tumbledown shack. In other words it will incarnate in a family from which it will receive a flawed heredity. But for a soul that is rich in qualities and virtues it will be exactly the reverse. This is why it is so important that in this incarnation you at least begin to work.

Make the most of the opportunity while you are here at the Bonfin to reflect and meditate and tidy up your inner life. Everything you see around you can be used in your spiritual life: the sky, the sun, the trees, the rocks, the air and the food. For years I have been giving you methods and exercises: use them, and by the time you leave you will be so full of treasures and riches that you will even be able to distribute some to others. Your stay here should make it possible for you to achieve something that you have never yet achieved. To begin with you will of course come up against a certain number of obstacles and an inner resistance, but at least you will have tried, and this means that you will be able to try again and keep on trying until you succeed in living continuously according to the laws of harmony, peace and light. One day you will do it effortlessly; it will become second nature to you.

The Bonfin, July 12, 1965

IV

Archimedes said that he could move the earth if someone would only show him what to lean his lever on. Well, I find myself in a better position than Archimedes, for I have found the fulcrum I need. It is the feminine principle, firm, solid matter, and my lever is the masculine principle. When the two forces combine they are capable of lifting the world. Of course you will ask me how a man can lean on a woman, and the question may seem more than a little indecent and, as far as I can see, ever since men began leaning on women they have not raised the world one inch. Not knowing how to go about it they have only managed to raise a lot of dust and a lot of devils. They all 'lean' in the old, prehistoric way. The question now, therefore, is to try to reach a true understanding of the two principles, to understand another aspect of both man and woman.

The masculine principle is the outgoing principle that emits, inseminates and gives life. The feminine principle is that which amasses and organizes what it receives so as to produce a concrete result, something complete and perfect. The work of creation therefore is shared between the two principles, and we must neither over-estimate nor under-estimate the importance of each one. Which is first? Which is the more important? The question simply does not apply. They are equally important, equally indispensable, but in different areas. The masculine principle emits waves and forces but it can accomplish nothing if the other principle is not there to respond, to receive and organize – if it is not there, in other words, to serve as a fulcrum. It is thanks to these two principles that life is possible. The whole universe is simply the result of the combined efforts of the two principles; even in areas hidden to us, even within our physical bodies, they work continuously together. In fact it is precisely when one predominates to the detriment of the other that every kind of anomaly and imbalance arises.

The science of the two principles is the science of cosmic balance. This is why all those throughout history – whether religious believers, mystics, ascetics or the many who were neither religious nor mystical nor ascetic – who considered women to be inferior beings have been in error. And not only were they in error but they were unbalanced. They had not understood God's designs. This is why I say that woman must be the fulcrum to raise the world. Of course I am not talking about this or that woman in particular. You must see woman as a collective entity, the principle that man must use as his fulcrum. I can see that if I do not make this clear, some will be scandalized and others will misinterpret what I say and take advantage of it to do something stupid.

Let's say that the masculine principle is energy. Yes, but energy can do nothing unless it is clothed in matter, unless some form of matter serves as a container. Thus we have the contents and the container, the idea and the form, the spirit and the physical body that contains it. What must you do if you want to store a highly volatile liquid? Left to itself it will evaporate. If you don't want it to disappear you have to put it in a closed vessel, and that is what the physical body is: a vessel for the spirit. Wherever we look we see only the two principles: spirit and matter, the spirit and the physical body, idea and form, etc. Everywhere, in every area, these two principles work together; we can never separate them from each other or even consider one to be more important than the other.

The masculine principle takes precedence over the feminine principle. That is true if you see things from above because it was the spirit that created the world. But if you look at things from below it is just the opposite: it is the feminine principle that embraces and holds on to the masculine principle, so it is the feminine principle that is more important. It all depends on your point of view. This is why so many people have been in a quandary when they tried to decide which came first, the chicken or the egg. How could the egg be first without the chicken? And how could the chicken be first without the egg? But what I am saying is that if you look at things from above you will see that it is the centre, the apex, that created the universe, and therefore that it is the egg that came first; it was the egg that created the chicken. But seen from below, from the level of the world, the chicken came before the egg. There is your answer. Certain problems can be solved only if you look at them from a different level; there is no other way.

The chicken represents matter and the egg represents spirit. Seen from the earth of course it is matter, material conditions, that have priority and that appear to create thoughts and feelings, the activities of the spirit. And as human beings have eyes only for the earth, they see everything from the physical point of view; for them, just as the liver secretes bile, it is the brain that secretes thoughts. From one point of view, the point of view of the earth and of human beings on this earth, that is true. But from the point of view of the cosmic spirit that created all things, matter is emanated, formed by the spirit. The universe is a thought in the mind of the eternal One, a condensation, a garment, if you like.

There is a tradition in India according to which a great bird, Kalahamsa, laid an egg, and that egg was the universe. You will object that I have been saying exactly the opposite, that it was the egg that created the chicken (the spirit that created the universe). Yes, but that is simply one way of presenting things: it all depends on the meaning you give to these two images. You can also say that the bird Kalahamsa is a symbol of the conscious, active being, the universal spirit that laid the egg – the universe – and that there are active forces working within the universe to produce another living being, another bird ... the chicken.

When you see things from the earth it seems as though the sun rises and sets, but if you were on the sun you would see things differently. Everything depends, therefore, on your point of view. If you have an earthly point of view all that is spiritual and divine will seem secondary or of no importance at all – you may even think that it does not exist. But if your point of view is that of the spirit all earthly, physical, material phenomena will be seen as peripheral, whereas the spirit will be central. This is better. For my part I have adopted the point of view of the sun, the point of view of the spirit, of cosmic intelligence, of the Creator. And it is this point of view that enables me to see the solution to a great many problems.

When Moses says in Genesis that God formed Eve out of one of Adam's ribs, it simply means that matter came from the spirit. On the higher level woman is born of man, but on earth it is woman that gives birth to man. Also it is interesting to notice that spirit and matter have opposite tendencies. The spirit tends to scatter and be dispersed in order to nourish matter, whereas matter tends to coalesce. Take the example of our organs: they have to cohere, to form a unit in order to stay alive. If our body ceases to be an integral whole it falls apart; when life leaves the body all its physical particles are dispersed and return to the four elements from which they came. Yes, but if we remain on the physical plane we cannot discover these truths. If we want to see the links, the correspondences between things, we have to rise to a higher plane, to the world of laws in which correspondences become apparent, and higher still to the world of principles, that is to say, the world of meaning.

By building the pyramids the Egyptian initiates were trying to get human beings to understand that they would never attain truth unless they focused on the peak, the highest point. But instead of understanding the lesson of the pyramids, men continually dissipate and scatter their energies. And yet there are so many examples in life that go to prove the importance of the lesson of the pyramids. What do a man (who, from the symbolic point of view, represents the spirit) and a woman (who symbolizes matter) do when they want to create a child? The man scatters his forces whereas the woman collects and gathers them together to form a child.

The tendency of the spirit is to disseminate its energies whereas that of matter is to collect, amass and unify, and this pattern can be seen in any number of areas. Let's take just one example: to the extent to which a human being is material he also tends to focus on a particular point, and for those who are not highly developed, who are too imperfect, this point is their personality, their own lower self. Those who are more highly evolved, on the other hand, focus on their individuality, their higher self. An ordinary man is only interested in himself; in eating, absorbing, monopolizing things; he sees everything as a means of satisfying his centre: his lower self. A more highly evolved man behaves in exactly the same way. He cannot change his nature; he always has to be focused on a central point. The great difference is that in his case his centre of interest is his higher self.

Where the spirit is concerned, however, there are not two different manifestations, only one. The spirit of man is in the image of the spirit of God that created the universe by disseminating, diffusing itself. Man's spirit also emanates and radiates and its emanations and radiations are what we call the aura. The more the spirit in man becomes paramount the more beautiful and expressive he becomes in his aura. The spirit is One and matter is Two. This is why woman symbolizes the Two and man the One and their union produces the Three, a child. Woman is always the Two, the two pages of an open book, whereas man is the One, the pencil or pen that writes in that book. Even the anatomical structure of their organs reflects this reality.

And then you might think about this: as with matter, it is a woman's nature to retain, to amass and absorb. She makes everything converge towards herself. Even when lit by the spirit she does not lose this tendency, but her focal point moves on to a higher level; it is her higher self. When you meditate on your higher self therefore you are manifesting the higher woman, and when you let yourself go and indulge your lower self you are manifesting the lower woman.

Why do we eat and drink and breathe? In order to sustain matter. If man doesn't collect and store up materials and energies everything disintegrates and he takes leave of this world. Every phenomenon in nature follows these two processes: *solve* and *coagula*. To create, to give form to something, is *coagula*: the process of accumulation culminates in the appearance of an object or an entity. And to make them disappear is *solve*, the law of the spirit. This is what I have found in the great book of living nature. I have not yet managed to read all that is in that book, but I can spell out some of it from time to time. Do you think that I found these truths in an ordinary book? I don't even know that such a book has ever been written. In any case you cannot say that what I am telling you is not true. The differences between the masculine and feminine principles, spirit and matter, are very subtle and they have always existed, but people have never seen them. They live, they embrace, they procreate children, but they have no inkling of these subtle things.

Let me give you another example. The second card of the Tarot represents the High Priestess, a female figure with an expression of extraordinary power and authority who is sitting with an open book clearly visible on her knees. Many scholars have spoken or written about the High Priestess or Female Pope, as she is also called, but none has ever discussed the book in her lap which is, in fact, a symbol of the female sexual organs. Yes, and man writes – or scribbles – all kinds of things in this book! The book itself is entirely passive; what is written does not depend on it and yet it is this that endures. He who does the writing therefore should have some intelligence; he should at least know what he is writing. If he is stupid, feeble or a drunkard, how can you expect his writings to be aesthetic, meaningful, profound or intelligent? The child – for the writing of course is the child – will be sickly, handicapped or unbalanced. Men have never understood how important it is to know how to write.

In the past, especially in rural areas, children did not get much schooling. They had to tend the livestock and help in the fields. In fact when governments wanted to make school obligatory there were endless arguments and disputes. Parents thought that their children would be wasting their time at school; they were much more useful at home or in the fields. But the centuries have passed and today, even in primitive societies, everybody goes to school if only to learn to read and write.

When I tell people that they don't know how to read and write they look at me indignantly. 'Why do you say that? I have been to school!' 'Ah yes, but I'm not talking about that kind of reading and writing. Have you learned to read the book of living nature? Have you learned to read the writing of birds, plants, crystals, mountains, lakes, the stars or human faces?' 'Is that what we have to read?' 'Exactly; that is the book that you must learn to read.' And that is why I say that human beings have not yet learned to read. And to write? To write on human souls, to trace sublime lines that can never be erased? No, human beings have never learned to write like that either. You write every day and you cannot even see that your writings are freaks, monstrosities. When you spend so much time every day arguing, back-biting and exchanging slanderous gossip, do you think that you are writing good things in the minds and souls of others or in nature? Human beings are constantly busy desecrating, defiling, despoiling, destroying and tearing things apart ... and this is their writing.

Writing is an act of the will and an act of detachment. To write is to kindle and take hold of something within oneself in order to bring it out and give it to others. To write is to leave a trace and there are artists who have left traces that men are still studying thousands of years later. But on a higher level than artists and philosophers are the great initiates: only they are true creators for only they work divine magic. To work divine magic is to be capable of tracing only a few words in space with letters of fire that etch themselves into minds and hearts throughout the world.

So far you have been taught to work only outside yourselves: to carve, model, draw and write, but always outside yourselves. This is why you have still not learned to write your own book, the book that is yourself, because you are always busy with external things. The great masters and initiates work at sculpturing and modelling themselves so that the whole of mankind may learn from them. They have no need of speech: we only have to be near them to learn from them.

The second card of the Tarot, therefore, is an invitation to human beings to learn to read and write. But just as it was difficult in the past to get people to go to school to learn to read and write, it is going to be equally difficult today to get them to enrol in an initiatic school in order to learn another kind of reading and writing.

If you only knew what I have learned to read in the book of woman! 'Aha!' you will say; 'I suppose you have read every woman's book!' No, not at all; it is not necessary to do so. In fact it is because I have never done so that I can understand what no one else has ever understood. Women, those who possess this book, don't even know what they possess; their book is at the disposal of every idiot, every criminal or unprincipled rogue that comes along. It lies open for anybody to write in or to tear the pages.

And men, those who have a pencil, do they know how to use it? No, they have no notion of its value or power, no notion of the immensity, the essence of what they possess. This is why it is perfectly true to say that you do not know how to read or write. And it is not in bars, night-clubs or on the beach that men and women will learn to read and write.

Sèvres, January 9, 1977

V

The Master reads the Meditation for the day:

'You think that I talk too often about the same subjects, and as you are not used to this method you are always eager to hear something new. The fact is though that it is necessary to deal constantly with the same things but from different angles: in the morning, in the evening, before and after meals, at night, etc. If you do this you will discover that every subject has many different aspects, that it breathes and changes. Look at a garden in spring or summer and then in the autumn or winter. It is the same garden, but how different it looks! And this is true of spiritual realities too: we have to keep coming back to the same subjects but we have to turn them all ways and look at every possible aspect. The truths I give you are essential, and if you understand them and study them in depth they will open up extraordinary possibilities in your lives.'

To be sure we need to throw a little more light on this passage, for you could object with perfect truth that, although I tell you that you must keep coming back to the same thing, life obliges you to concern yourself with all kinds of different things. Actually there is no incompatibility here. Once you have a central, guiding idea firmly entrenched within you, it is possible to take care of all the other things you have to do without dissipating your energies. For all those other things are only details, forms, different approaches, whereas the spirit, that is to say the idea, remains central. In the centre, therefore, is your spiritual life and everything else fits into place around this centre. This is the only way to unify your life. Anything else means disorder and dislocation. I remember a brother saying to me one day, 'The thing that astonishes me most in your lectures is that

55

although you have been talking to us for years, there is never one idea in all that you say that contradicts another. Everything ties into everything else!' Yes, that is because there is a centre, a summit, in my head around which everything else revolves harmoniously. And this is not something that you will find in many writers – whose latest books often contradict those that have gone before! With me everything hangs together. In spite of the novelty and diversity of my lectures they never contradict each other because they all have the same orientation, they are all guided by this one point. Without this point there would be no unity. Man needs a lodestar to guide him. If you try to find your way through a forest or across the ocean without a landmark or a star to steer by, you will get lost. This is why we have compasses: to prevent us from losing our way. And I have a compass in my mind which points directly to my lodestar, that is to say, to the Prime Cause, the Creator, the Spirit.

True spirituality consists in never losing sight of the spirit, whatever you may be doing. Whether you are eating, sleeping, working or just walking about, the spirit must always be present to you. This is what people fail to understand: for them everything is dispersed and disconnected; things just drift apart. And to think that they take themselves for spiritualists! No, a true spiritualist does not disperse his activities; the spirit is always at the centre of everything he does.

The anatomy of a human being shows that everything converges towards the head. Yes, because the brain is the centre that governs all other functions. And this is the key: only the spirit has the right to be dispersed because it is thanks to the dispersion of the spirit that the whole of creation is nourished. But we have no right to be dispersed; our duty is to move towards unification. For us dispersion means death. The spirit descends into matter and matter must rise to meet the spirit. We who represent matter, therefore, must make everything converge towards the spirit, towards our own spirit and towards the spirit of God. This is why my work consists in bringing you back constantly to the central point, to the peak. The means I use vary depending on the circumstances, but my aim is always the same.

I mentioned the example of the brain which is the centre from which the nerves spread out into the body, but I could give you others. The torrent of water flowing from its source high in the mountains has the right to split up into many little streams in order to irrigate the land as it flows down to the sea. The sun, too, has the right to be dispersed throughout space in order to bring life to the whole solar system. But we who are at the periphery have to move in the opposite direction: we have to turn to the centre, for it is from the centre that we receive life and strength. One day to be sure we shall have the right to be dispersed like the sun, but not until we have reached total fulfilment. When we have reached fullness of being we shall, like the sun, be capable of pouring out our love and light on all creatures. When a woman is carrying a baby in her womb her organism works to unify and concentrate the scattered particles around an image, an idea, the structure of the child, until a magnificent, healthy, living human being is born. But once those particles are dispersed again it means that that human being is dead. You could define life and death in this way: life is the concentration of forces towards a goal, and death is the dispersion of those forces.

My dear brothers and sisters, you must understand that if you want to become radiant and full of life and power you must strive tirelessly and with your whole being towards a single point, a sublime goal, capable of giving meaning to everything you do in life. Unfortunately children have never been told this in their families or at school. This is why we see so many people who are always sad, depressed and confused. They have never understood that they needed to focus on an ideal, a sublime goal, for even if there is little likelihood of their ever achieving that ideal it can still be very beneficial for their inner life. This is why so few people have discovered the meaning of life; this is why, in spite of the great beauty and richness of life, so many people take their own lives ... all because of a lack of education, a lack of light; because they have rejected the philosophy of the initiates.

The Bonfin, September 15, 1976

VI

The Master reads the Meditation for the day:

'Man is only what he is; he cannot give what he has not got. In order to give, you must first possess. And in order to create, you must possess the elements of that creation within you and be able to express what is in your soul and spirit. If there is nothing in you you will never create anything.

Some people show you such monstrous creations that one wonders where they could possibly have found them: in themselves to be sure! A man cannot produce divine works of art if he is not inhabited by heavenly beings, nor can he produce diabolical works if he is not inhabited by creatures from hell. In order to produce something that is greater than oneself, one has to go out from oneself, rise above oneself, detach oneself and enter higher regions so as to capture elements from those regions. This is the secret of the new art.'

I'm afraid that this page will be completely incomprehensible to you if I don't explain it a little further. It says that man is only what he is and that he cannot give what he has not got, and yet in other lectures I have said that God has put every treasure, every possibility, and all forces at the disposal of man. Isn't it a contradiction then to say that he is only what he is, and can only give what he has got? No, there is no contradiction here; it is simply a different way of presenting things. Man possesses the most extraordinary riches, but they are so deeply buried in regions within him that they are virtually inaccessible; on the surface it is as though he possessed nothing. But this is only what we see on the surface. In reality all those gifts and possibilities are there within

58

him. However as he has never worked to develop them he cannot use them. In order to manifest them he will have to undergo a long apprenticeship and a discipline that is still unknown to him. This is why very few people have clear ideas on this subject; most people complain and are miserable or angry when they believe themselves to be deprived of the possibilities enjoyed by others.

You will remember what I told you in the recorded lecture that we listened to again yesterday[4]. The spirit possesses all virtues and all knowledge, but the physical body is not in perfect condition and it is this that makes it impossible for the qualities of the spirit to manifest themselves. If the physical body were perfectly tuned and adjusted the spirit would be able to manifest itself fully. But I have already explained this to you so I shall not repeat it today.

The differences between human beings exist, therefore, not because their spirits have reached different degrees of evolution but because their physical bodies are different. Every spirit is a flame; every spirit is a living spark, a quintessence, a fragment of the Lord, just as every drop of water is a fragment of the ocean. All human spirits are identical except in the mission entrusted to them and in the experiences encountered in the course of their successive reincarnations. When they first separated from God they were identical, but as each one sought to accomplish its mission it had to traverse different regions and, consequently, picked up different knowledge and experienced different impressions and emotions. This is the only difference: some passed through one region, others through another, but in their essence and quintessence, in their sublime nature, all human spirits are the same. Men's physical bodies, on the other hand, are not the same: although they are all built on the same model of ideal perfection the degree of evolution of each one is different. In each incarnation a spirit has a different body and a different face and sometimes a different sex, and this means that its destiny and experiences will also be different. But in their essence all spirits are identical; in this sense they are all one.

The unity that we are talking about, the unity that all men seek

---

[4] See Part II of this chapter.

instinctively, resides in the spirit, nowhere else. Apart from the spirit, all is diversity, multiplicity. To speak of unity, therefore, implies the presence of the divine Spirit. Hostility and all the arbitrary manifestations that stem from it – the acquisitive instinct, the tendency to think oneself different and apart from others, even patriotism – find their origin in the fact that human beings have drifted away from the state of perfection in which all spirits are united and know themselves to be one. No negative, discordant elements can manifest themselves in the presence of unity. Certain initiates have reached such heights in this experience of unity that they have the sensation of vibrating in unison with all creatures; they are so keenly aware that there is no longer any separation, that all souls and all spirits are one, that they feel all that happens to others as though it were happening to them. And this is precisely the purpose of initiatic science: to bring all creatures back to the consciousness of their fundamental oneness. On the higher plane we are all united; it is on the lower planes that we are separate. On the higher plane we all experience the same joys, the same sense of wonder, the same perception of all that is truly perfect.

It is because human beings have strayed so far from their source that their tastes and attitudes, their way of doing things have become so different. Yes, so different that there are people who delight in the filthiest, most perverted and most disgusting realities and find them magnificent. This distortion comes from their having abandoned that original unity. No wonder human beings can no longer understand each other! It is as though everybody was sick or insane. Sick people never agree about things: one cannot stand fresh air because he has a cold; another cannot stand the light because his eyes hurt him, etc., etc. In one way or another almost all human beings are in this situation: they are all deformed, and there can never be any unity in the tastes, criteria or conceptions of those who are deformed. To be sure they still have a number of things in common. If you slap or bite them or prick them with a pin they will cry out and retaliate. And they will all be pleased if you give them food or money or affection, but this is about all that is left of their original unity. If this trend towards separation continues the situation will become so terrible that men will end by exterminating each other; instead of finding any joy or pleasure in being together, they will be overcome by such a sense of hostility at the sight of other human beings that they will massacre each other ... just like that, for no reason at all.

This is why, in the Universal White Brotherhood, we are learning more and more how to love, help and understand others so as to come closer and closer to the state of unity. But the hardest thing in the world today is to try to convince human beings of this. They simply cannot get it into their heads! You can get them to understand electronics or pure mathematics, but they cannot understand this question of unity; they cannot see the point of it. Initiates on the other hand seek nothing but this: the path that leads back to that perfect unity. Inwardly we are one; in our spirit we are all one, but this oneness has not yet been achieved on the physical plane; it is this that remains to be achieved.

When the spirit leaves the physical body it moves on to the etheric plane. After a little while, just as it left its physical envelope, it leaves its etheric envelope and rises to the astral plane. It remains on the astral plane until it has accomplished certain tasks and then moves on again to the mental plane, and so on. heaven begins with the higher mental plane, the causal plane; it is on the causal plane that the spirit begins to come closer and closer to God until it becomes one with him and possesses the absolute knowledge and absolute power of the Lord himself. In the birth of a child the process is reversed: the entity that incarnates dies to the spiritual world and descends into planes that are progressively more material. If we only knew where a newborn baby comes from and how many bodies it has put on! What a journey! And what an adventure!

In the meditation I read to you earlier it says that you cannot give what you have not got. Yes, he who is not pure cannot purify others. He who is poor cannot enrich them. He who is weak cannot give them support. Human beings are so ignorant that they really believe they can give others what they have not got. Especially the young: a boy tells his sweetheart, 'Darling, I'll make you happy!'

but he has not yet found happiness himself; how can he make someone else happy? Or he says, 'I'll make you rich', when he himself is out of work. And he really believes it! Later on perhaps, when he has found work, when he has found happiness, he will be in a position to give her everything, but not before. But I find that I am the only one who does not believe that he can give what he has not got. I am the only doubter!

Before we can produce a celestial, perfect creation, we must possess and then express that perfection, that celestial quality. This means that we must transcend and rise above ourselves. Of course to say that we must rise above ourselves is a figure of speech: we don't go out of ourselves, we don't detach ourselves from our soul and spirit, for everything is within us; it is our consciousness that rises to a higher plane. You can find everything within yourself. When you feel that you have been in heaven, that you have walked amongst the stars and touched God himself, in reality you have simply gone further and deeper inwards and reached your higher self. And it is your higher self that possesses the power to create. When we talk about the realities of our inner world we have to use concrete language as though we were talking about physical space, distances and volumes, but all this goes on within us, in our higher, divine self.

The truth is that everything is within us. And this means that, although I say that a man cannot give what he has not got, if he works hard he can give it, because it is all there stored up within him. When man strayed from the Lord his spirit contained everything in potentiality. It must be understood of course that the concrete materialization and manifestation of the powers lying dormant in the spirit take time, but that does not mean that they are not there: they are. If you thought about this truth more often it would be a tremendous help for your evolution.

The initiates say that man is a microcosm because he is a reflection, a reiteration of the macrocosm: the whole universe exists within him. This is why, as I told you one day, we possess within ourselves all the chemical elements necessary to heal ourselves. Believe me this is so; the only problem is how to bring them up to the surface and activate them. At the moment we are so far from being able to do this that we still have to buy our medicines at the pharmacy. But all those medicines are within us; in fact we possess other elements as well, those of the etheric or even the astral plane, whose properties have still not been studied by chemists. Yes, chemistry also exists on the astral plane; in fact if you learn to use the elements that belong to the domain of feelings, emotions and sensations, they can be just as potent and effective as the others. And this is also true of the mental plane. There is a whole chemistry laboratory within us in which the elements are our thoughts, feelings and emotions. This means that, if you are lacking in a certain quality, you will be lacking in the corresponding element and this can cause certain anomalies. To remedy the situation you can do what you are in the habit of doing and go and buy the elements you need on the physical plane, but it is far more important to look for them on the other planes. Those that can be found only on the physical plane are not enough.

Let me show you another correspondence: organic life is only possible if four chemical substances are present: hydrogen, oxygen, nitrogen and carbon. These four substances correspond to the four elements: hydrogen corresponds to water, oxygen to fire, carbon to earth and nitrogen to air. As you see, therefore, the four alchemical elements – earth, water, air and fire – are represented by the four chemical elements that go to make up a cell.

The question should be quite clear to you now: although it is true that we cannot give what we do not possess, it is also true that we possess everything. The only thing is that in order to bring all that wealth out into the open, we have to go and look for it within ourselves. The Lord is within us, in our higher self; we are indissolubly bound to him.

And now let me explain the practical applications of the fact that you possess everything within you, for it will save you a great deal of sorrow and disillusionment. For example, you are sad or furious because your beloved is not by your side: if you remember that she is within you, you will immediately be happy and at peace. Why do you never think about this? Why do you always have to have things externally, physically? Also, you have a master: if he is not with you, talking to you on the physical plane, is that a reason to vegetate? Why not remember that he is within you, that he is constantly speaking to you, helping and protecting you? You must get used to looking at things in this new way and you will see: things will go more smoothly and you will feel less miserable, less weak and deprived.

If you always look for satisfaction on the physical plane you have to receive or to take what you want from others, and when it is not given to you, you begin to look for ways to get hold of it – and this is where things begin to go bad. Whereas if you remember that everything you need is within you, you will always feel rich; you will feel your wealth gushing up and overflowing, and then you will feel the need to get rid of some of that wealth by giving it to others. This is how we begin to resemble the Deity: by having a constant need to give. This is why an initiate has such a great need to give, whereas others think they will die if they cannot take, and while waiting for the chance to take something they feel deprived, weak, unhappy, neglected and angry. Adopt my way of thinking and you will seek out other human beings in order to share your abundance of riches with them. You have to become fraternal if you need to love, otherwise you will always be looking for someone to love you, and that is where all tribulation, fear, suspicion, anger, and jealousy begins; you become dependent on others; you are never in command of the situation.

Accept this philosophy; I know from daily experience that it is the only philosophy that really works. Yes, I prove it every day; I live by it. I consider that you are all within me. When I want to talk to you – or if I have to tweak your ears from time to time – I can always find you there, inside me. You cannot escape me.

The Bonfin, August 4, 1975

VII

Generally speaking we can have a very good idea of how something will end when we see the way it begins. It is possible, however, if we make a great effort to change the course of events so that the end does not resemble the beginning. To be sure there are certain events in life that can be accurately foreseen, because they unfold with the same implacable rigour as eclipses or the conjunctions and oppositions of the planets, which occur in obedience to mathematical laws. But on the whole life does not unfold according to such rigorous laws, and when the spirit is involved it can always intervene to add or subtract or remedy something. When the seal of the spirit is on it life is transformed, and becomes purer, more beautiful and more perfect.

Take the example of the physical body: it obeys the natural laws of birth, growth, decay and death. This is the normal sequence of events and there is nothing one can do about it; it is automatic and inevitable. Yes, but if the spirit decides to intervene it can retard or hasten certain processes. In the present state of our evolution our spirit cannot manifest itself fully or in an absolute way, for it is subject to the constraints of matter. In its essence, on its own higher level, its powers are without limit, it is almighty; but on the level of matter it is not almighty for it takes a long time to get everything organized and in order. Thanks to the efforts we continue to make every day however, the work of the spirit gradually progresses, and in the long run it will emerge victorious and begin to rule and transform everything. The spirit possesses what are called 'supernatural' powers. In reality there is nothing supernatural: miracles, prodigies and events which seem to contradict the laws of nature are neither supernatural, nor supra-natural, nor anti-natural; they simply obey other laws which are those of the spirit.

The task of a disciple can be summed up in a few words: instead of allowing his ordinary, material, animal nature to dominate him, enslave his spirit, smother the living spark and bar the road to paradise, he must work according to the laws of heaven, the laws of the spirit. He must live in harmony with the forces and powers of eternity so as to imbue his ordinary, everyday life with the elements and quintessences of another order that are hidden away on the highest planes of his being. By his thoughts and feelings, his faith and his efforts, he adds something to the ordinary course of events, something radiant, something that flows and manifests the presence of the spirit, the splendour of the divine world. For true beauty is found only in the spirit.

However extraordinary the beauty of crystals, flowers, animals, birds and men, it is never more than a reflection. The spirit is reflected in the beauty of creation but the beauty of creation is not perfect. We do not yet know the beauty of the spirit. That which we see in trees, flowers, crystals, fish, butterflies, mountains or human faces is far from expressing, manifesting or exhausting the indescribable beauty of the spirit. All that is not the spirit can be no more than an imprint, a reflection of the spirit; it can speak of the spirit and lead us to it but it can only show it very inadequately.

A disciple is someone who is conscious of possessing a higher principle that transforms everything within him. Thanks to this consciousness the life he emanates is the life of the spirit and gradually as this life continues to flow from him even his physical appearance begins to change; it becomes more and more harmonious, expressive and luminous. This is why, when a disciple looks at a photograph of his master, he cannot help but sense that that form, that physical body, speaks to him of other things: it leads him to form bonds with other regions; it awakens other memories, memories of the past. An initiate emanates, expresses and reveals the things of the spirit through the medium of his physical body. And this is precisely what you must work towards. Yes, you must work towards this because it is beautiful, because it is rich, because it is potent ... and because it gives you great possibilities and makes you feel happy and alive. Do away with this philosophy, wipe out this wisdom, and man becomes an animal.

This fact seems to me so self-evident that I am constantly amazed to see that even the most intelligent and enlightened people never seem to understand it. Their research delves into every imaginable area but it never takes them in the direction of the spirit. They believe that they have wonderful ideas and the will to achieve tremendous results but they are deluding themselves. If they were on the right path things would be very different. Of course, sooner or later they are going to understand their error, but unfortunately this realization will not come until a great deal of damage has been done and a great deal of time and energy wasted. But it will come, because heaven is going to intervene, and when it does so, they will be forced to understand. The divine world has decided to turn everything upside down so that the heads of those who imagine themselves to be so powerful and intelligent will be forced to 'ripen'. The future of those who are willing to understand and live in harmony with this light from heaven will be indescribable. It would be impossible to explain to you the marvels, the immensity, the eternity, all the splendour that awaits them. All the better for you if you believe me, but if you refuse to believe me there are others who will make it their business to convince you; it will not be my business any longer. My business is to proclaim truths that are truly truthful and that have never changed from all eternity. The form can change but the truths remain the same.

The explanation for the catastrophic state in which mankind finds itself today lies in the fact that it has drifted away from these great truths of the spirit. The intellect is the only thing that counts; all the rest is despised. But above the intellect there is the spirit. The intellect is not yet the spirit, it is a manifestation of the spirit, but it is not the spirit itself.

This means that in all his reasoning, all the decisions he makes and the work he does, a disciple must always give priority to the spirit, to the kingship of the spirit. On everything he does and wherever he goes, a disciple seeks to leave the seal of the spirit, and in this way everything ends by being transformed. If you understand what I am saying the clouds will gradually thin and disappear and your whole life will be like today. What transparency in the sky this morning at sunrise! What extraordinary light!

Keep an eye on yourselves, study and analyse yourselves at every moment of the day so as to see if you are obeying only your animal nature or if you are giving your divine nature a chance to manifest itself. I am not saying that you should do away with your animal nature. No, you cannot and must not do away with it, it has a right to its own existence, but it must not be allowed to overshadow or destroy the rest. It should be something for the spirit to lean on, not something that smothers and absorbs every other aspect. Watch yourselves, therefore, and when you see that your spiritual life, the divine life in you, is beginning to slow down and the physical body with its desires and its appetite for food and drink, etc., is taking over, be careful. Do whatever needs to be done to make sure that this state of affairs does not last long. When the course of your physical life is even and regular and you feel that alongside it there is something else, an awakening, something that shines and flows – the spirit – then you can be glad, for this means that it is the spirit that will eventually take over, it is the spirit that will rule and leave its mark, and when this happens you will truly live with intensity.

Most people have no notion of what it means to live a life of intensity because the meaning of the word 'intense' is not clear to them. In fact you could say that this lack of understanding explains the unbalanced state of their psychic and physical life. They think that intensity is the equivalent of agitation and nervous tension; in reality an intense life is a life of peace and harmony. And you must do your best to live the life of intensity every day for it is a plentiful fountain whose flowing waters will wash away all the impurities that are clogging up the passages in your organism. If you succeed in living with intensity you will find that not only your health but also your intelligence and understanding will improve.

Unfortunately material prosperity and well-being are often incompatible with what initiates call the intense life. When people have everything they cease to make an effort, they let themselves go, and then without their realizing it the life of the spirit loses its intensity. This is why the invisible world often sends us privations and tribulations so that we shall be forced to face up to them and free ourselves by overcoming them. Naturally, if nobody ever crosses you, if your path is smooth and you never have to contend with an enemy, you will be content, but your inner life will be simply ticking over and the result will be very bad: all kinds of waste matter will accumulate and start to rot within you. Without the cleansing stream of an intense spiritual life there will be no force capable of eliminating them.

Nowadays, in every country in the world, people's one ambition is not to have to work any more. If they were intelligent though, even on holiday or when they are of an age to retire, they would work more than ever. Believe me, work is the only thing that can save us. Those who want to spend their lives doing nothing have no idea of the dangers involved. To be sure there are jobs that are so debilitating and bad for one's health that they can do nothing but harm. But when I talk about work I am referring above all to the inner activity by which man gives the spirit priority over matter.

Let me give you an example: human beings are in the habit of expecting everything to come from outside them. In one way this is normal, for we could not survive if we did not receive a certain number of things from outside ourselves: water, air, sunshine and food, for instance. We are created beings and all created beings – and creation as a whole – are obliged to receive something from outside, if only their nourishment. Only the Creator is above this law; only he has no need to be nourished. True, but the Creator has planted within every creature a fragment of himself, a spark, a spirit of the same nature as himself and, thanks to this spirit, every creature can become a creator. And this means that instead of always waiting for their needs to be satisfied by some external source, human beings can work inwardly by means of their thought, their will and their spirit to obtain the nourishing, healing elements they need. This is why the teaching I bring you is of the spirit, of the Creator, and not of matter, of creation. If you reject this teaching you will always be weak and dependent, at the mercy of circumstances.

The mistake that human beings make is to identify so completely with the outside world, with matter, that they no longer have the strength to react. But the teaching of the Universal White Brotherhood urges us to work towards something different, towards the kingdom of the spirit, the spirit which has no need of external elements in order to create, the spirit which draws all the elements it needs from its own being, just as the Lord drew on his own quintessence to create the world.

My dear brothers and sisters, it is time to extract yourselves from the false reality of matter and enter into the inner reality of the spirit, the reality of all the great masters. Think deeply about the Creator and creatures. It is up to you to determine whether you will remain a creature or become a creator. Do you believe me? Perhaps there is not one among you who believes me? No, I think you do believe me, but you say, 'Yes, but life is so difficult; you don't know the conditions, the circumstances we have to contend with!' Oh but I do know! Believe me, I know better than you. Where do you think I live myself? In exactly the same conditions as you, in the same circumstances, in the same world. The only difference between us is in our attitude, in the way we think. So stop expecting to get the help you need from outside yourselves. And stop believing that all your problems come from outside yourselves also. Most people think that they themselves are blameless; they blame all their problems on their husband, the neighbours, the government, something they have eaten or the weather. Never will they admit that it is their own hateful philosophy that is preparing a catastrophic future for them, and yet it is this philosophy that is dragging them little by little into an inextricable situation. It is time you replaced your old philosophy with the one we are offering you; only in this way will you become strong, powerful, independent and free.

Think about all this therefore. What is true for a creature is not true for the Creator. A creature is too dependent on the outside world, on his circumstances: he can be pushed hither and thither and there is nothing he can do about it. Become creators; enter the realm of the spirit which is free to create, fashion and mould events and you will see that everything changes: you will no longer be so dependent on the outside world; you will be the master of your own destiny.

The Bonfin, August 19, 1967

Chapter Four

THE SOUL

I

There are three worlds: the physical world, the spiritual world and the divine world. Or if you prefer: the world of facts, the world of laws, and the world of principles. Or again: form, content and meaning. However you express it, it is always the same trinity of body, soul and spirit. The spirit is the expression of the divine world; the soul corresponds to the spiritual world, and the body corresponds to the physical world. The soul, therefore, lies between matter and the spirit; it is an intermediary, a vehicle which conveys elements from heaven to earth and from earth to heaven. All that descends from above and all that rises from below passes through the soul. The spirit only knows how to descend and the body only knows how to rise, but the soul rises and descends between the two. This is why the spirit can have power over matter only by using the soul as its intermediary. The soul's potential for action is tremendous; it is the soul not the spirit that acts directly on matter.

Look at what happens in nature. The sun cannot have much direct influence on the earth except to warm it; for anything else it needs air and water to act as intermediaries. In the same way our spirit cannot touch our physical body directly, it needs our thoughts and feelings to act as its intermediaries. Intermediaries are always extremely important.

If a disciple improves the way he lives by learning how to eat, breathe, love, think and meditate, he will be in a position to draw down from heaven the subtlest materials, currents, energies, forces and lights and the most exalted entities. At the same time he will be capable of rendering certain material elements more subtle by projecting them on to a higher plane. This is how sexual energy can be sublimated. Yes, and it is particularly in this domain that there are such great energies, some of which need to be brought down while others need to be projected to a higher level.

The Bonfin, September 19, 1973

II

Many people believe that when a child comes into this world his soul and all his moral and intellectual faculties have to grow with his physical body, and that as his body gradually gets older and loses its strength and vitality, the soul does the same. Not at all. Before incarnating the soul is already fully in possession of all its faculties; it has reached a very advanced stage of evolution, but it cannot manifest itself as it is through a physical human body. This is why it remains largely outside the child's body while it works to prepare it and make it fit to house it completely. In reality it will never quite achieve that goal, but that is what it works towards throughout the child's life. As the years go by and the child grows up, he gradually manifests new talents and new faculties as his soul enters more deeply into his body, dwells in him more fully, and succeeds in manifesting itself through him. And then there are days when the soul leaves the body and travels far from it. At these times the body can only lie there, paralysed and motionless, and it takes a great deal of time and effort to reanimate it and bring the person back to his senses.

When a person becomes old and weak it is only his body that is affected; the soul never gets old and weak. No. It is simply that the body can no longer be animated as well as before because it has become crystallized and clogged up by too many heavy elements. It is like an old engine that is beyond repair or a battered old piano whose notes are no longer true: it is not the pianist who is decrepit, it is his instrument. The soul and spirit are still present, but as the body, the muscular and nervous systems, etc., are less and less responsive, they can no longer manifest themselves very well.

Soul and body are two completely distinct realities. If a man's soul succeeded in manifesting itself completely through the

77

medium of his body he would be a divinity. And this is precisely the goal of all the methods of the teaching: to allow the soul to be wholly contained within the physical body so that it may express itself perfectly.

Look at what happens when you drink wine or spirits: the alcohol has the effect of driving your soul from your body. Certain substances, therefore, have the power to make the soul leave the physical body. Doctors, magicians and sorcerers all know that small doses of certain mushrooms or herbs can trigger an out-of-body experience. The soul leaves the physical body and goes to other regions, and when it returns it brings back revelations of what it has seen. It is possible to develop divination and clairvoyance with the aid of these substances but only to the detriment of the physical organs; in the long run experiments of this kind end by ruining one's health. External means like these can be used to develop one's psychic faculties therefore, but they are always dangerous and our teaching is absolutely opposed to them.

You are all aware that drugs have become a scourge in society and that young people are particularly threatened. The young feel a growing need to escape, to get away from all the ugliness of life that makes them unhappy. I cannot approve of all the things they do, but we have to admit that adolescents have become so sensitive that they are less and less capable of putting up with certain conditions. There is nothing wrong with wanting to escape, on the contrary; but the teaching of the Universal White Brotherhood can offer them means of escape that are far, far better than drugs. The synoptic table that I showed you[1] can help young people to understand what kinds of nourishment will give them joy, rapture and the expanded consciousness they seek. The external solutions are always very costly: drugs and physical pleasure can never bring fulfilment, and one day human beings will be obliged to recognize that cosmic intelligence intends us to find happiness only in the elements that can satisfy the needs of the soul, spirit, heart and mind; that is to say in very subtle elements, subtler even than

[1] See chapter 2.

those of the etheric plane; in thoughts, feelings, forces, prayer, contemplation and ecstasy; in other words, in spiritual work.

The human soul is completely distinct from the body. When the body declines and grows old the soul flourishes and blossoms. When the poor old body has to go down into the grave the soul, which is rich and powerful, abandons it, for it can no longer manifest itself through the medium of a shrivelled old body. Soul and body work together but they are totally different in essence and in nature. A moment ago you were astonished when I told you that the soul was only partially within the body. The soul of a child, for example, dwells largely outside his body, but it is present and it understands everything, better even than we do. It can see and think and reason but it has no means of expressing itself. A baby can hear what you say to it, though it cannot understand; but the baby's soul hears and understands everything you say, for it is already fully formed and in possession of the intelligence and sensitivity and all the other qualities that will gradually be manifested as the child grows and becomes adult. Yes, the soul is already in full possession of all its faculties, but it is going to take years to manifest them.

It sometimes happens that the soul makes a special effort and the baby speaks by its gestures or its facial expression; the look in a baby's eyes can sometimes be so eloquent that you are bowled over. This means that its soul is trying to respond to you and show you that it understands. Although most educators have never seen instances of this kind, they do exist; I am not inventing it. There have even been cases in which a baby that was much too little to talk has actually spoken. In one instance the child's mother was on the point of going to bed with a man who was not her husband when she heard her baby say, 'Mummy, don't do it!' Tiny baby though it was, it managed to say those few words. A similar phenomenon sometimes occurs with animals.

In the very distant past man's soul floated in space and was so loosely connected to him that he had no sensation of pain at all; he could be killed and cut up in bits without feeling anything. He had neither sensitivity nor intelligence. It took millions and millions of years for the soul to descend and gradually take possession of the body. And now this has been achieved, but not completely. In the present era the soul is taking possession more fully of the intellect; that is why the human intellect has developed to such an extraordinary degree. Animals and plants have a collective soul which is wholly outside their body. Each species of plant has its own group soul. Each forest also has its collective soul. The same is true of animals: lions, for instance, and all the different animal species have a group soul which endeavours to manifest itself through the species as a whole.

It is only in men that the soul begins to be individual. But what a long and tortuous road had to be travelled before a human being first took possession of that 'ego' and began to say 'I, me'! It was on the level of human beings, therefore, that this new phenomenon of individualization first appeared and men became free, independent entities. And it was this phenomenon that was to be the source of all their misfortunes. For it is precisely man's independence that poses a problem: human beings have the ambition to be free, separate individuals; they want to be ruled by none but themselves, to be masters of their own destiny, and it is this that causes them to oppose the divine laws and abuse their freedom. Yes, this is the cause of every misfortune. Man must be free and independent, to be sure, but without disobeying the laws of heavenly harmony, of cosmic order. This is why he must now reverse the situation and submit once again to divine laws and decrees. Without being coerced, by a decision of his own free will – for he must always retain his individual independence – man must turn back to an attitude of obedience to the divine order. Only when he does this will he regain his eternity, his happiness and beauty, his former lustre and true freedom.

When human beings remain in ignorance of the grandeur of their destiny, their one idea is take advantage of their freedom to commit every kind of folly. Doesn't every young man and girl long to leave home and live their lives in their own way? They are bound to make the most disastrous mistakes but that doesn't matter as long as they can be independent! This desire for independence is perfectly normal and good but it so often goes astray and causes a great deal of damage. Personally I am in favour of freedom, but not when it is used for experiences that lead straight to the caverns and cesspools of the underworld, and ultimately to hell. The young who clamour for freedom must be given proper guidance. They are a long way from understanding that if they give a free rein to all their tendencies without discrimination it is bound to end in disaster. They have to learn to be free, yes, but they also have to learn to choose the upward path, for freedom belongs to the highest spiritual plane. Only the spirit is free. The more deeply one is immersed in matter the more one is dependent. When you descend to the level of passion, greed and the pursuit of pleasure, when you hasten to gratify every wish or whim that enters your head, you are limiting your freedom and allowing yourself to be shackled. But the realization of this only comes later. Believe me, freedom can be found only on the highest spiritual plane.

A disciple becomes free when he decides to do God's will and obey his laws so as to achieve the harmony that heaven asks of him. Others, all those young men and girls who are bent on following only their own inclinations will end as slaves – as slaves to some hooligan, to their own passions, to money, etc. Wherever you look you see nothing but slaves; the world is peopled by slaves. Why? Because men have always refused to learn the great laws of divine harmony, and sooner or later they have to pay dearly for this refusal.

Human beings must be free; yes, but with the freedom that is divine. When that kind of freedom is yours everything is yours and whatever you do you will always manifest yourself divinely. Of course adults have never given young people this light because they don't possess it themselves, and so today they see themselves mirrored in their children: like father like son. 'My son is nothing but a hooligan, a gangster!' 'Yes, but it was you who made him what he is; you and none other. You have only yourself to blame. If you had learned certain laws you would have known that it was in your power to give him what he needed to become a divinity.' Children are what they are, but it is often their parents' fault. It is the parents rather than the children who need to be educated therefore. You will see that one day the whole world will be enlightened, guided and helped by the sublime philosophy of this teaching. Of course, anyone who chooses to seek personal independence, profit and pleasure rather than a sound philosophy is free to do so but, sooner or later, it will only lead to disaster.

We must seek freedom, joy, happiness and wealth. Yes, but we must look for them above, not below.

Sèvres, February 12, 1972

Chapter Five

SACRIFICE

I

For most human beings the word 'sacrifice' is associated with the idea of difficulty, privation and suffering[1]. For an initiate, on the contrary, it is associated with the idea of love and joy, for an initiate knows what sacrifice really is and how it should be used. This is why he is interested above all in making sacrifices.

Sacrifice is the transformation of one form of matter into another, of one form of energy into another. To sacrifice something is simply to deprive oneself of it in order to replace it with something better. Take a piece of coal: look how black and dirty and ugly it is until it is sacrificed. Then it becomes heat, fire, light and beauty. If you refuse to make any sacrifices you will always be ugly, weak and impure. Obviously, as long as you are convinced that sacrifice implies suffering and deprivation it will never have any attraction for you. You have to adopt the initiatic point of view which teaches that if we renounce something it must only be in order to replace it with something better. Suppose you want to rid yourself of a bad habit: gambling, women, or drink, for instance; if you don't put something else in the place of that habit the temptation will continue to torment you and you will end by giving in to it. Yes, simply because you have not cultivated another need strong enough to overcome the first one. As long as human beings fail to understand this they will continue to feel sacrifice as something painful and then, of course, they will say that it is not worth trying to make a sacrifice because not only do they always fail, but they only succeed in making themselves even more miserable.

[1] For further discussion of this subject, see *Complete Works*, vol. 5, chap. 9; vol. 11, chap. 12, and vol. 14, chap. 25.

You will never succeed in overcoming something pernicious if you don't try to replace it with another force, another quality or another entity. You could certainly find many examples of this in your own life. Suppose you associate constantly with someone who has a bad influence on you: unconsciously you will imitate the remarks he makes, his attitude and reactions, and after a time you will notice that your other friends are beginning to avoid you: you have lost their affection. At this point even if you decide to break off your association with that person and free yourself from his influence you will not succeed: the only answer is to associate with someone else. Actually human beings often discover this solution for themselves. When a man wants to free himself from a wife who causes him nothing but problems, he starts to look for another one!

Instinctively therefore human beings behave according to the precepts of eternal wisdom. The only trouble is that they don't always apply them correctly. When a man changes wives in the hope of being happier there is no guarantee that he will find what he is looking for. He may well free himself from the clutches of one shrew only to find himself tied to one who is even worse. And it is the same with political regimes: if you overthrow one government there is no guarantee that the next one will be any better. Man's instinctive desire for change is very strong, but there is just one problem: if a man is tired of his wife and thinks that a new one would be more exciting, more stimulating, what is he supposed to do with the first one? The laws of karma are always there and have to be reckoned with, but human beings forget this. They are eager for change and in itself this is all right, but to make a change for the better requires a great deal of knowledge which they simply haven't got. All they have is a vague impression that something needs to be changed: they don't realize that it is not on the outside but within themselves that they must work for change.

Would you like to know, for instance, how to replace your vanity? Vanity is a desire to dazzle human beings, to be noticed, respected, appreciated, lionized, invited everywhere – and much photographed! And however hard you may try to stifle that desire you will never succeed: it will always be there. So what should you do? First of all you have to understand that it is absolutely normal to want to shine, but instead of trying to shine in the sight of men, you must ask to shine in the sight of the angels and archangels. In other words, you exchange earthly glory for heavenly glory and you are saved. In this way, if you understand that it is heaven that you must try to dazzle, not human beings, your vanity can actually lead you to heaven. This kind of vanity is not only permissible, it is highly recommended.

You cannot make sacrifices if you see no useful purpose in doing so. In any case if a sacrifice is not useful it is better not to make it. As you see, I am just as utilitarian as anyone: I have no desire to do something that is not useful. And now, you may ask, why should you make sacrifices for the Brotherhood? Why should you dedicate your life and all your time and energy to it? Because it is very much in your own interest to do so. The sacrifices you make for the sake of an ideal are transformed into gold, light and love. This is the key to the power of sacrifice: the idea that motivates you, the ideal for which you are working. If you are working for yourself, for the satisfaction of your own desires, needs, instincts, passions and lusts, the sacrifices you make in the hope of winning the respect and trust of others will not be transformed into light or divine energy. Many people sacrifice their health and a great deal of money for an ideal, but as that ideal is too worldly their sacrifices are not very beneficial. Yes, this is what people fail to understand: the importance of the idea behind their actions. The idea is the magical aspect, the philosophers' stone that transforms everything into gold. This is why I urge you to work for this divine idea: the triumph of light, the establishment of the Great Universal White Brotherhood on earth, the coming of the kingdom of God. Whatever you do for this idea will turn to gold, that is to say: to health, beauty, light and strength.

So be sure that the sacrifices you decide to make are sensible. There are women who are so eager to sacrifice themselves that they are ready to marry a drunkard – or men who are ready to marry a woman who is neurasthenic – in the belief that in this way they can save them. But only the Lord knows if they really will save them.

It is not kindness or generosity that is lacking. No, what is lacking is light. People are blind; they don't foresee what will happen and it is such a pity that all their qualities and virtues should be just thrown away. It would be so much better if they were dedicated to a divine work that would help not one but thousands of human beings. Besides you cannot be sure that that person will be helped. What you can be sure of is that the one who wants to help them will become a victim.

A lot of people behave like the little acorn whose heart was bursting with so much love that it decided to go out into the world to do good. The old oak told it, 'Listen little one, you're still very young; you would do better to learn to be patient. You must start by burying yourself in the ground and later, when your roots, trunk, branches and leaves have grown, you can begin to be useful. Then you will help to purify the air; birds will come and take shelter in your branches; you will be an inspiration for painters; your acorns will feed the livestock; you will provide a shady swing for lovers, and the poor will collect your dead branches for their fires.' 'Oh, you're too old!' said the little acorn. 'That's all nonsense; you don't understand what I'm talking about. I'm overflowing with love and the desire to sacrifice myself,' and it went and sat down in the middle of the path. But a hog that happened to be passing that way spied it and gobbled it up and that was the end of all the acorn's noble intentions. Well, for my part I have followed the advice of the old oak. For years I buried myself in the ground so that my roots, trunk and branches should grow, and now perhaps I can give a little shade to those who need it, and the birds can come and shelter in my branches. But I see many who have been disciples for only a year and they know nothing, nothing at all, and yet they believe that they are capable of doing good to the whole world! This is why they will be snapped up and devoured by the first swine that comes along. Even before trying to sacrifice yourself, therefore, you have to prepare yourself; you have to study and become strong, otherwise you will be incapable of helping others.

So I repeat: sacrifice is always a question of knowing how to replace one thing by something better. And it is something that needs to be done every day in order to set up a movement, a circulation of energies. If you don't do this, if you don't keep a stream of fresh water flowing constantly within you in this way, you will stagnate and dry up and your system will end by being clogged with rotting, mouldy matter. This is why we have to meditate and pray every day: in order to wash away the old worn-out particles and replace them with new particles that are purer and more luminous.

Sèvres, December 30, 1974

II

Fire is one of the greatest of all mysteries. How many of you, I wonder, can ever hope to understand it? A little while ago we collected piles of dead wood, bundles of twisted, blackened twigs and branches that had nothing beautiful about them, and now look at them. What a bright and glorious sight they are now that they are burning.

When initiates or priests are preparing to conduct a magic rite or to say Mass, why do they always light a candle or a vigil light? Why do they make sure that light shall be present at the ceremony? You all know about these things but you have never examined them or tried to understand them better. What I am about to reveal to you is extremely important, and when you know it you will be obliged to put it into practice in your lives. A candle feeds the flame by supplying it with materials drawn from its own substance and in doing so it diminishes. Combustion therefore is a sacrifice. If there were no sacrifice there would be no light. Some form of nourishment is necessary for light and fire to exist and the candle represents this nourishment. And we are like candles; we are made up of combustible materials which of themselves are drab and lifeless; only fire can make them alive and luminous. But before this can happen there must be a spark to set fire to us, to our matter.

As long as a human being lives an ordinary, prosaic kind of life, his matter is as lifeless and inert as a dead branch. Only when he has been visited by the fire of the spirit can he begin to shine and become warm, beautiful and alive. But in order for this to happen he has to sacrifice his personal life and it is this that is difficult: the one thing that prevents human beings from making this sacrifice is the fear that it will lead to disintegration and disappearance. Of course, something will have to disappear – that is true; but it disappears only in order to make way for something else, something better, to appear. The matter of the candle disappears so that light and warmth may appear. You will say that before long there is nothing left of the candle. Yes, but a man can burn indefinitely without disappearing. Once lit he can no longer be extinguished; there will always be some material in him that can be burned.

The one thing that you should desire most is to burn with the sacred fire of divine love, for it is in this fire that you will find the secret of life. Most human beings are not yet alight, their personality is intact. They are not ready to be consumed; they are like candles that have not yet been lit. But they are going to have to make up their minds: sooner or later if they want to possess that light and warmth they are going to have to burn everything. We all enjoyed collecting these twigs and branches for the fire, didn't we? They might have lain where they were for years and been no good to anyone, and now look at them. Just to see them burning so brightly gives us a feeling of happiness and joy. And all the energies locked up in them are flying back to the sun from which they came. The cheerful, crackling sounds you hear are an expression of joy and jubilation, the sounds of these energies being set free: the prisoners' chains are snapping and they are being released and set free.

If the ancient custom exists, therefore, of lighting a candle or burning incense when one prays, it is because the candle and incense symbolize the sacrifice of something that is consumed in order to obtain a certain result. Nothing can be obtained without sacrifice. Sacrifice is the only thing that can heal and illuminate man for it is the only thing that can transform energies by changing them from one state to another. You see: the simple gesture of lighting a candle is significant. In fact none of the gestures we make in life are without meaning; even those that seem most insignificant have a profound meaning. Every time I light a fire or a candle the extraordinary depth of the phenomenon of sacrifice strikes me anew; it always brings me back to the thought that in order to obtain light, even inner light, the light of the mind, the light of the spirit, there has to be some form of sacrifice; we always have to burn some of our inner matter.

If human beings only realized it there is so much within them that could be burned. Why can't they burn all their impurities and selfishness, all the tendencies of their passions that are driving them into darkness? If they did this they would have a fire so strong and bright that they would be completely transformed. Unfortunately, instead of throwing these things on to the fire they cling to them with all their might. They obstinately refuse to burn them until the cold is too great to bear – that is to say, until they are deprived of all love, friendship, tenderness and sweetness – just as, in periods of intense cold when people have no fuel left, they are forced to burn their old tables and chairs and cupboards so as not to freeze to death. Yes, men have to endure great tribulations, misfortunes and disappointments before they are willing to burn some of the rubbish that has been accumulating within them for centuries. But one day they will come round to it; one day everyone will do it. And those of you who understand what I am saying today will delight in collecting everything within them that is rotten, mouldy and worm-eaten and throwing it all into the fire. What a blaze it will make! You can be sure that if you yourself are no more than a feeble little flame you will soon be blown out; the first puff of wind and you will be no more. But if you are a blazing furnace no one will be able to put you out: on the contrary the stronger the wind, the brighter the blaze.

As long as someone is little, weak and puny, as long as his flame is not burning strongly, the slightest affliction will extinguish it. But once his flame is bright and strong all the difficulties, misfortunes and hostility he encounters will only serve to reinforce his inner fire, his inner dynamism and power. Yes, if you are strong everything that happens fans your inner flame. This is why the wind can be so dangerous in the event of a forest fire: it is very difficult to put it out if there is a wind to fan the flames. But if the fire is very small you only need to blow on it and it goes out! Haven't you seen this time and time again? At the first sign of contradiction or opposition the weak are discouraged and give up the struggle. But those who are like a furnace are exalted by difficulties; they become even more determined to persevere and face up to every contradiction. Now there is no need to ask me whether you are a furnace or a candle flame: you can find that out for yourselves. If every little obstacle in life discourages you then you are not a furnace.

Those who feel that their flame has gone out can come to me for a match. I have all kinds of matches. In fact that is all I have. I have spent my whole life collecting matches and now I have tons of them. So if there are any customers for my matches they only have to come and ask and I'll give them some. The only danger is that instead of setting fire to themselves they might set fire to other people's haystacks and barns, and that would never do. No, absolutely not ... but you don't understand what I am saying.

Did you notice how quickly and vigorously the fire took hold today as though it were full of joy? Sometimes it hesitates, but this evening the blaze was tremendous. And look at it now: it is pleased that I am talking about it! The question now is how to preserve the sacred flame. Well, you can preserve it by feeding it every day with bits of your personality. That is what the personality is predestined to be: food for the spirit. You have still not understood how useful the personality is; you are always wondering how you can get rid of it. But you must not get rid of it; without it you could not survive on earth, whereas with it you will always have plenty of elements with which to feed the spirit. It is important that you understand the law of magic which says that if you want to obtain results on a higher level, you have to sacrifice something of your personality.

If you go to an initiate, a magus or a great master and ask him to heal you or a member of your family, or to ensure the success of an undertaking, he will tell you that in order to obtain the grace you are asking for you must give up a vice or a bad habit. If for instance you have a weakness for scandalous gossip, stealing or lying, you will have to give it up, and it is this renunciation that releases the energy needed for the success you are seeking. All the sacrifices prescribed by all the religions of the world from time immemorial are based on this principle, but the sad thing is that religious men and women will be the last to understand this magical secret

93

of success. You all know that in ancient times a petition was frequently accompanied by the sacrifice of an animal. The energies contained in the animal's blood were communicated to the surrounding atmosphere thereby nourishing entities that could contribute to granting the petition. But then Jesus came and he taught human beings not to sacrifice their external belongings any more – such things as livestock, fruit, flour or oil – for even though these things represented a sacrifice for the one who offered them, they were less essential than the sacrifice of certain weaknesses, appetites or lusts. It is the sacrifice of these inner belongings that constitutes true sacrifice.

As I say, when Jesus came he asked men not to sacrifice their poor, suffering livestock any longer but their inner animals, and as it is the personality that harbours these inner animals, it is the personality that must be burned on the altar of sacrifice. In this way all the forces stored up in the personality are released and the spirit, in the form of light, warmth and life, is present in abundance. Of course there is always a form of combustion going on in man and it is thanks to this combustion that life exists. But it is a purely biological, animal form of life; the life I am talking about is the spiritual life and the combustion that makes it possible is quite different. It is no longer the physical body, the cells, that burn, but the personality. And although the personality is invisible it is immense: it can provide fuel enough to warm and illuminate you for centuries.

Unfortunately today it is not the personality that men burn but their physical body. Look at how people shrink and shrivel up as they get older! But it is not this physical combustion that we should be concerned about, for that is natural and normal for everyone; it is the combustion of the personality that is important.

The Bonfin, August 12, 1964

Chapter Six

FOOD FOR THE SOUL AND THE SPIRIT

I

How good that so many of you are able to be here today! When human beings go somewhere it is never without a reason; it is always in order to get something. When you go to the library, to the baker's or the grocer's, or even when you go to your sweetheart's, it is always because you want something. So let's see what you are looking for when you come here. We have never talked about this before.

Oh yes, I know that you are all living in the world, and that in this world there are all kinds of things that you have to understand and all kinds of problems that have to be solved, and none of it is easy. From the day you are born you are obliged to struggle and face up to difficulties in order to survive, in order to eat, earn your living, marry, build a house, etc. You never have a moment's peace, I can see that. From time to time you feel happy and quite satisfied; you think that you have found what you are looking for and you say, 'At last I'm happy!' But that happiness never lasts long, and this fact brings us to something that you must understand: all of you, all human beings, have only one basic need and that is to find something stable that they can rely on.

Consciously or unconsciously human beings are all looking for something lasting, and they know to their cost that the pleasures, joys and satisfactions that come their way, all the things they enjoy and all the things they do in life, never last long. Over and over again, the very next day or next week, everything has to be done again as though for the first time; it never ends. Even those who are truly happy, those who are always lucky, those who succeed in everything they put their hand to ... even they can never be sure that their happiness will endure. They too are worried and plagued by doubts, they too try to create something durable: guaranteed financial security, lasting success, unfailing health. What they are looking for is the one thing that is most elusive. There are many reasons why this one thing is so difficult to obtain and the principal reason is that people don't know how to set about it. They hunt in all the wrong places; they read books, travel round the world and consult other people, always hoping to grasp something that is virtually unattainable. This is what is so tragic. Everybody thinks that tragedy consists in being deprived of money, health, a house, a wife or children. No, all that is of very little importance; that is not the tragedy.

The real tragedy lies in being incapable even of analysing the reality of what goes on inside oneself or of understanding one's real needs. Everybody thinks that what he wants is money or a wife for instance, but that is not really so. And you are in the same position: you have come here today in the hope of finding something, but you don't really know what. Consciously or unconsciously what you are looking for is something stable, something indestructible and eternal.

The Bible says that God created the heavens and the earth and this means that the earth has a role to play. But it is not the earth that can give man true satisfaction or fulfilment. All the realities of heaven are matched by a corresponding reality on earth, because the earth is the mirror image of heaven, but it is not the quintessence, the truth, the heart of reality. If you really want to obtain fulfilment, which is a state of the soul and spirit, you must look for it elsewhere. Truth is to be found in the combination of the two: the world of outer, objective reality and the world of inner, subjective reality. Man comes from heaven, he is a spirit, but he is obliged to put on a physical body in order to dwell in the physical world. A person's physical body stands in the same relation to his spirit as the universe stands in relation to God. Yes, the universe, nature, is God's physical body. God has a body and he has distributed thousands of things throughout his body, the cosmos, as well as in our own bodies. But he has not entrusted everything to the physical body; he has placed his most precious treasures – life, strength, consciousness – in the spirit, and when the spirit leaves the body it takes all these treasures with it. The dead body is left with nothing but the physical elements which end by disintegrating.

God has given us a physical body so that we may be in touch with the world. A body is necessary, indispensable even, for work and manifestation, but it is not more than that. Human beings are deluding themselves when they believe that the objective dimension, the physical body and the universe, are everything. The universe is not everything; God is everything, and if God were to withdraw from the universe it would disintegrate and crumble into dust. The universe exists only because the spirit of God dwells in it to animate and vivify it. If God were no longer there the universe would revert to nothingness. And the same is true of man, who is a reflection of his Creator. Henceforth try to understand that you must look to the soul and spirit for what cannot be found on the physical plane, while at the same time continuing to use, to perfect and harmonize and work with the elements that God has placed on the physical plane. Even if you possessed the whole universe, even if you were capable of controlling the course of the planets, you would still not know fulfilment. Go ahead; try it! You will explore and work and make sensational discoveries, you will acquire great possessions, conquer all comers and have more than you want of everything, but you will still not find what you are looking for because you are not looking in the right place. You can possess the whole world and still be dissatisfied because you are neglecting the needs of your soul and spirit.

Human beings think that it is their physical body that is always clamouring for things and that they will be happy if they stuff it with food, pet it and spoil it and give it everything. But the physical body is very soon replete and glutted; it complains that you are smothering it. It tells you, 'It's no good expecting me to give you what you're looking for. I can't do it.' But people persist; they think, 'Well, that didn't do the trick, but perhaps if I tried this or that I'd find what I'm looking for ...'. And once again they encounter only emptiness. So they try again ... and again. The fact is that the physical body is content with very little. The dissatisfaction men experience comes not from their physical body but from their soul and spirit which cry out ceaselessly: 'We need to contemplate the sun and the stars. We yearn for Brotherhood, for the kingdom of God on earth, for peace among all nations. We long to be united with God. We need purity and light and space ... .' But human beings are deaf to these things, totally insensitive to the needs of their soul and spirit. When a man wants to please his wife he gives her a present, but always a material present: jewellery, a car, etc. It never occurs to him that his wife has a soul and a spirit which also have needs.

Contemporary civilization is based essentially on the needs of the physical body. I am not against this, it is not intrinsically bad: but human beings should not devote all their energies to satisfying their physical needs and forget about the soul and spirit so completely that, deprived of the nourishment they need, they wilt and fade away. So many of the people one meets today give one no sense of the soul and spirit; they seem to be no more than a crudely formed body mechanically gesticulating and moving about. What people fail to understand is that a philosophy founded on something as fragile and vulnerable as the physical body rather than on a stable, immutable, eternal principle is bound to have catastrophic consequences. As the premise on which it is based is not divine, the conclusions it leads to will always be false and even dangerous for they will necessarily resemble that premise, the physical body.

In order to satisfy the needs of the physical body we have to have money, and although people sometimes come by their money honestly they very often obtain it by dishonest means: by theft and lies. In order to gratify their physical needs human beings are capable of every sort of crime – even of devouring each other in times of famine – and it is this that is the cause of almost every war. There have been many great human beings in the past whose only concern was to satisfy the needs of their soul and spirit and who feared neither hunger nor fire nor death itself. These were the great masters, the great initiates, the martyrs, saints, prophets and heroes, who were afraid of nothing. Their behaviour proved that they had an immortal soul and spirit and that they preferred to die rather than betray their soul's need for magnanimity, nobility, fidelity and purity. The physical body cannot create these needs in man; on the contrary, it is entirely without moral principles and always urges man to steal, destroy and kill.

If you build a philosophy on the needs of the physical body you will always be weak, mean, small-minded, ignoble and incapable of great deeds. Don't expect much from someone who is only interested in his physical body: to satisfy the demands of his body he is capable of selling his wife, his country and the Lord himself. I am not saying that you must neglect your physical body, but it must be subject to your soul and spirit so that the higher, nobler, more glorious needs of the soul and spirit – light, the eternity of the spirit and the immensity of the soul – may be reflected in all your words and deeds. In this way all that you do and say will bear the mark of the Deity for, as soon as you accept a philosophy of the soul and spirit, that philosophy begins to work within you and transform you and then you will no longer be fearful, selfish beings who tremble and are ready to abandon everything noble for the sake of a few pennies. Accept this philosophy of the spirit and begin this inner work, the noblest, most glorious, most divine work that exists. You will see the transformations that begin to take place within you first of all, and then in your family and friends, and eventually in the entire world, and as far away as the stars. Yes, for everything is connected.

Suppose that you have met with so much injustice or are so worn out by worry and anxiety that your peace of mind has abandoned you. Then one night you look at the starlit sky and meditate on the tiny earth lost in the midst of that infinite space, and you say to yourself, 'He who created so many worlds must certainly have peopled them with creatures more intelligent, more beautiful and more powerful than man. How is it possible to believe that the Creator has given intelligence only to the inhabitants of the earth – this earth which is no more than a speck of dust in the vastness of the universe? It is inconceivable that these pygmies whom we call men and who spend their days arguing, weaving their ridiculous philosophical theories or quarrelling and destroying each other, should be the only intelligent beings in the universe.' Gazing at the starry sky overhead you begin to sense that the problems and anxieties that have reached gigantic proportions in your mind are almost nothing. And if you remember that the stars you are looking at have existed for billions of years, that the intelligence that created all these worlds is eternal and that you were created in his image, you will begin to feel that your spirit too is eternal. Or again suppose that you are hungry for all kinds of things, that you are impatient and tense because you are unable to do all the things you want to do as quickly as you would like; if you meditate on immensity and eternity you will begin to understand that it is really very stupid to try to impose your own will on things and to get into such a state about it.

I am not saying that in order to conquer your lower appetites and tendencies you have to do away with them completely. No, not at all. But instead of allowing all your divine energies to be absorbed by your physical body, you must channel your physical appetites and make them flow in another direction. You must muster all the forces and energies stored up in your body and give them some spiritual work to do. Even your stomach should participate in your spiritual work. This is possible, for the physical body possesses all the qualities of heaven.

The philosophy of materialism has clipped the wings of man's soul by attempting to prove that he is nothing but dust, that there is no such thing as God or heaven, that he has no hope of raising himself up and becoming something sublime. Materialistic philosophy has killed and eliminated all that is beautiful in man.

Of course I know that materialists have some very good qualities; for one thing they are tireless in their activity. How magnificent it would be if they could put these qualities in the service of the soul and spirit, and work inwardly to expand their consciousness and obtain light and peace! They are intent on achieving physical well-being; yes, but physical well-being is nothing compared to the sensations we experience when we are in harmony with the cosmos, with all the creatures of the universe. Even if you are famished and in rags this harmony can fill you with indescribable joy, with the infinitely subtle sensations which are manifestations of the soul and spirit.

In reality the soul and spirit exist not only in the physical body but also outside the body, in their own spiritual dimension. As they are linked to the physical body they communicate their experiences to it from time to time, but the frequency and intensity of this communication depends on whether the body has antennae capable of receiving impressions transmitted by the subtle world, and whether the brain is capable of recording these impressions. The soul and spirit do not need to open their eyes to see the treasures of the spiritual world; – they can always see and feel them, – but they are not always able to transmit those treasures to the physical body because in order to do so they have to use a brain which is not always sufficiently developed.

Never forget that your soul and spirit have needs of their own. A man's physical body needs to eat and sleep. His astral body wants pleasure, it needs love and emotions. His mental body wants to learn, to know. That is all well and good, but you would be justified in saying to the majority of people in this world: 'You always give your physical body everything it asks for. You obviously give your astral and mental bodies what they ask for too, since you have had several mistresses and have earned degrees from several universities. Why are you still not satisfied? Because you have neglected your other bodies; they are still hungry and thirsty.' It is not enough to see to the needs of the physical body, the heart and the mind. The increasing popularity of drugs, particularly amongst the young, is a warning sign. It warns us that the soul is stifled because it cannot make itself heard or understood; it longs to escape to heavenly regions and, as human beings don't know how to satisfy the soul's need to escape, they take drugs. But drugs are not the answer; they are still something that we give to the physical body. It is the soul that feels the need to escape, not the physical body. The craze for drugs is simply an indication that the soul yearns to escape into the vastness of space, but drugs can never satisfy the soul or answer that need. And not only can they never satisfy the soul, they destroy the body.

The only thing that can save mankind is the teaching of the Universal White Brotherhood. At the moment nobody cares two hoots about this teaching, but when there are so many anomalies in the world that life has become impossible, then people will try the teaching. Today however, they turn up their noses at it! They prefer drugs because it is so much easier to take drugs than to make an effort to nourish one's soul and spirit.

Why, after an exercise in meditation, contemplation or identification, do you feel so fulfilled? Nothing has happened to you outwardly; you are no different from what you were before, and yet you feel fulfilled, as though all the hunger within you had been satisfied and all your thirst quenched. Why? Of course those who are ignorant will say that it is an illusion. But would they admit that when they suffer and feel miserable that too is an illusion? No, never; their suffering is real enough! It is joy and ecstasy that are illusions. Well, that is not a very scientific attitude.

Make up your minds to come regularly to this restaurant that caters to the soul and spirit; eat and drink heartily and you will find the solution to this insoluble problem of fulfilment. Spiritual nourishment is not like the food we eat and drink on the physical plane. On the physical plane you have to eat every day otherwise you will be hungry and feel weak, whereas the nourishment you find in the sublime regions of the soul and spirit will satisfy your hunger for days and days. In the divine world there are elements that are so rich that you only need to taste them once for the sensation of fulfilment they give you stay with you for ever. Once you have experienced the sensation of eternity nothing can ever take it away. Obviously, before you can hope to reach this level you are going to have to practise and go back to eat the same meals over and over again, just as we do for the sake of our physical stomach. But once you succeed in reaching the highest and most sublime regions all that is over, nothing can ever rob you of that state of fulfilment. You will be in a position to say, with the Egyptian initiate, 'I am stable, son of one who is stable, conceived and engendered in the realm of stability.'

If you want to find joy and happiness you must turn your mind away from the world of matter and raise it to heaven. And when you reach heaven you will instantly find yourself flooded with joy, for heaven is a region of joy. Every creature in heaven is brimming over with joy and happiness. Hurry up and find this out for yourselves; try to rise to a higher level. Sometimes the experience can be so intense that one is almost afraid. Yes, and an experience of this kind is recorded within you and can never be erased. It is as though you had a magnetic tape recorder inside you; at any time you can put on a tape that was recorded while you were in a state of light and love and live that state all over again. Once again you will experience the same love and the same light; the experience may not be as intense of course, but even so it is important to be able to relive these sublime moments. There is not a creature on earth to whom heaven has never given a few moments of hope and joy. All men, even the poorest and most destitute, have known such moments in their lives and it is good to live those moments over again in one's thoughts.

Do you see how simple it is? How clear it all is? You will say, 'Yes, we know all that already. You have explained it before.' But it needs to be explained again, over and over again, if you are to understand it properly. I have so often seen this: I may have explained something to you ninety-nine times but it is when I explain it for the hundredth time that you understand. I know that I make myself ridiculous by constantly talking about the needs of the soul and spirit, but it is only because I am so anxious for you to understand how useful this can be in practice. Besides you should be glad when I repeat something, because there is always a difference, I always use different words, a different tone of voice, and above all the psychic conditions are always different. One can sometimes put life into words in a way that one has never done before. The subjects and even the phrases may be the same but the life, the force, the love and the light that I put into those phrases are never the same. I have already used the example of a river: the Seine, the Thames and the Mississippi have been the same rivers for centuries, but the water that flows in them is never the same.

So don't hold it against me if I often repeat the same things, because this question of the soul and spirit is absolutely essential. The soul and the spirit – spirit and matter – the heavens and the earth ... As long as these two concepts are not clear to you, you can never boast of being able to solve life's problems. Only when the spirit, light, God, have priority in your life can you be truly strong, lucid, alive and free. I insist on this because it is this that is the most important: light must have first place; the sun, the Creator, the spirit, must be given first place in your life. All the rest comes second. The head must come before the tail. Unfortunately human beings do just the opposite: they put the tail first and the head has to follow as best it may. This is why they are sick and unbalanced.

There is nothing that makes me happier than to be useful to you and I cannot see any use in distributing millions – of dollars, or of anything else. The only thing that can be useful to you for all eternity is this truth.

Sèvres, March 15 1969

II

You ate your meals as usual yesterday and yet you are hungry again today. And you expect me to tell you something again today, too. The nourishment I gave you yesterday was for yesterday, and today you are hungry again. Good; that's very good! The Gospels tell us, 'Blessed are those who hunger and thirst ...'. So you see, you are blessed! The only trouble is that you don't know it. Why do you always need me to tell you that you are very privileged, very blessed? Why can't you feel it for yourselves? As a matter of fact I can see from your expressions that you don't really believe me when I say this. I assure you, it is true. Do you want me to prove it to you? All right; I will do so with pleasure! I always get great pleasure from proving something to you and it seems to me that I shall never be deprived of this pleasure.

When you get up in the morning why are you not immediately conscious that you are blessed? You have your arms and legs, hands, a mouth, ears and eyes. Suppose you woke up one morning and found that you could neither see nor hear nor move a limb. It could happen you know; it could even happen that you did not wake up at all! So you see my dear brothers and sisters, you are very blessed but you don't know it. You wake up every morning in possession of all your faculties and you are not even aware of it; you are not even grateful. This is why initiates think that human beings are really stupid: because they are not conscious of all that they possess and are forever grumbling and demanding more. They possess treasures; they have been given extraordinary possibilities, and yet they get into a terrible state simply because they haven't got all the clothes or all the money they would like. Think about this for a moment and try to see how deep this ingratitude and lack of intelligence goes: you will never reach the bottom of it; it is unfathomable.

To you I say: learn to be grateful and to give thanks every single day. Give thanks in the morning when you wake up and find yourself intact and in possession of all your faculties, and in doing so you will feel blessed. Continue to be hungry and thirsty, but not with physical hunger and thirst, of course. When Jesus said 'Blessed are those who hunger and thirst', he was not talking about physical hunger and thirst, he was talking about a hunger and thirst for truth, light, wisdom, righteousness and liberty. He was saying that we should hunger and thirst for nothing but light. The soul hungers and the spirit thirsts. The soul eats fire and the spirit drinks light. Fire is a masculine principle and the soul is a feminine principle and each one is nourished by the complementary principle. The soul eats fire because it hungers for a positive, active, dynamic principle. The spirit, which is masculine, drinks light because it thirsts for a feminine principle. Just as the masculine principle engenders the feminine principle, it is fire that engenders light. Light is a manifestation, an emanation of fire. When you set fire to something it produces light, and the purer the fuel, the purer and subtler the light it produces. There is no smoke, no soot. The pure soul feeds on pure spirit and the pure spirit feeds on pure light.

Light is the garment in which fire is clothed and for this reason light is always related to matter. In the sublime regions of the world above light is related to matter and fire to the spirit. This is why light was created first by God, the Primordial Fire, and it was light that created the world; nothing was created without light. This evening, God willing, we shall have the ceremony of fire and you will see the re-enactment of the creation of the world unfolding before your eyes.

In the cosmogony that has been handed down to us by the initiates it is said that fire existed before anything else. Light appeared only later. You will wonder whether it is possible for fire to exist without light: yes, primeval fire, non-manifested fire, is not luminous. For fire to be accompanied by light it has to manifest itself. Actually there is fire in everything: in stones, water and air, but this fire is not manifested. In the beginning was fire and the fire produced light, the light with which it is said that God created the

108

world. Light, which is itself a condensation, created matter, and this is why light is always related to matter, but not to physical matter. It is sound that relates directly to physical matter, and this means that light must be transformed into sound before it can touch physical matter. Light can only touch spiritual matter, and this means that if you want to create by means of light you can only do so with an extremely subtle form of matter.

The soul which is feminine, feeds on fire which is masculine; and the spirit which is masculine, feeds on light which is feminine. In the same way the intellect, which is the son of the spirit on a lower plane and therefore masculine, prefers a feminine nourishment; and the heart, which is feminine, prefers the masculine nourishment that it finds in feelings. Yes, feelings, sentiments, are dynamic forces; they are another kind of fire manifesting itself on a lower plane. Sentiments are inverted fire, that is to say, water. If you look at the forms in running water, in streams, torrents and waterfalls, you will see that they are the same as those you see in fire, but reversed. Water is simply a down-turned fire. The intellect, on the other hand, feeds on thoughts because thoughts are feminine. Thought is not so active and dynamic as feeling; this is why it is not generally recognized as a reality. What is the impact of a thought compared to that of a feeling? A thought is not powerful; it accomplishes nothing, produces nothing, whereas a feeling has formidable, shattering power. In reality thought and feeling both have the same power but in different forms. At first sight water seems to be docile and obedient; you can do what you like with it. If you scoop up a handful it will flow through your fingers without hurting you. But if you try to take a handful of fire .... And yet water is just as powerful as fire but in different conditions.

The heart feeds on feelings and the intellect feeds on thoughts. But there is no purity in the regions of the heart and the intellect; the good must constantly be sorted out and separated from the dirt, waste and ashes. Purity is to be found only above in the realm of the soul and spirit.

The soul feeds on fire. It yearns for and feeds on the fire of the spirit. And the spirit, which is fire, feeds on the light of the soul.

And this idea must be constantly present within you: the cosmic spirit that is fire, and the universal soul that is light. When you meditate, concentrate exclusively on the highest aspects of the two principles, masculine and feminine, for it is here that the most extraordinary illumination awaits you. Raise yourself every day to this region and stay there; nothing is more beautiful. Some of you may want to say, 'Yes, but I don't like the idea of fire. Nor of light either for that matter!' Very well, you can use other words instead: you can speak of love and wisdom, for instance. Wisdom is light and love is fire. If you hate the idea of fire because it burns and of light because it dazzles you, treat yourself to a feast of love and wisdom!

The Bonfin, August 12, 1964

Chapter Seven

CONSCIOUSNESS

I

Our consciousness is the common meeting ground for all the physical and psychic forces of our organism. It is a kind of Geneva. The city of Geneva offers a neutral environment in which the representatives of different powers – whether friends or rivals – can meet for discussions, and while these discussions, negotiations and decisions are taking place Geneva becomes the temporary consciousness of the world. In the same way the human consciousness is a neutral setting to which forces of all kinds send delegations to represent them and express their point of view. It is like a blank screen on which is written all that goes on in the world of a human being, and the legibility of what is written depends, of course, on the breadth or narrowness, light or darkness, of a person's consciousness.

Picture an old-time village in which the village crier comes into the market square with his trumpet or bell and announces the news of the day: what is being bought and sold, the decisions of the mayor, etc. Neighbouring villages are too far away to hear any of this, but if his announcements were written in gigantic letters of fire in the sky, then everybody in the world would be able to read them. Our consciousness can be so narrow that it can take in no more than the announcements of the village crier, but it can also reach to the outer limits of the universe. Your consciousness varies therefore according to circumstances: it can be broad or narrow, but it is never an absolute, because without your realizing it other people can project their own will on to it and make you obey them. You may believe that you are acting of your own volition but in reality someone else is controlling you from a distance.

As you see, there is a great deal that is still unknown to you. Human beings need to be instructed in initiatic science so as to gain control of their own consciousness and not allow themselves to be swayed by all the forces that come at them from every corner of the world. The voice of your own consciousness must make itself heard more clearly than all the other voices bickering and quarrelling within you. Even an initiate cannot prevent certain images, certain impressions, from reaching his consciousness and doing their best to hinder him in his work, but he knows how to get rid of them; whereas the consciousness of the man in the street is a screen on which anybody can project anything, and this makes it impossible for him to live his life independently. He is continually harassed and exploited, continually the theatre of dispute and conflict. His belly and stomach, his genitals and his liver, his brain and his heart, all have their representatives clamouring to make their conflicting claims heard.

An initiate is someone who has learned to impose his own will on all these different representatives and to make the interests of each of his organs converge and contribute to the welfare of his being as a whole; in this way his consciousness becomes superconsciousness. The consciousness of most people is often no more than the manifestation of their subconscious: all the memories and instincts inherited from the past, all their animal tendencies, rise to the surface and project their image on the screen of their consciousness. This is why, when a disciple sets out on the path of initiation, he must expect a certain number of surprises. He wants to pray, he wants to be virtuous and pure, but other desires set up a tumult within him, clamouring for this or that and often enough the poor wretch gives in. But if he remains firm and continues to struggle against his baser appetites he will gradually free himself from them, gain his independence and begin to live on the level of his superconsciousness. Yes, because his perseverance wins him the friendship and support of heavenly entities; upheld by their help and the light they pour into him, he begins to feel his consciousness expanding and becoming more enlightened. This does not mean that he will suddenly be completely free of all ties to the subterranean world. No, that world will continue to try and drag him back into its own cacophonous, chaotic sphere, but if a disciple perseveres in his efforts and continues to look for help from heaven it is as though a barrier gradually grew up and cut him off from that lower world. And when this happens nothing can intervene to destroy the images of indescribable beauty that heaven projects on to the screen of his consciousness. At this point the disciple triumphs at last; he enters into a new life; he is in communion with all the most highly evolved creatures of the universe; he has become a child of God.

Sèvres, April 18, 1968

II

Consciousness, as we have seen, is an inner screen and all that goes on in man is projected on to it. Actually it would be more accurate to say that not everything that goes on in man is projected on to this screen, only a small proportion of it; all the rest, all that fails to reach his consciousness, remains in what we call the unconscious. But there are two quite distinct zones of unconsciousness: that of the lower consciousness, which we call the subconscious, and that of the higher consciousness or superconsciousness. In fact very little of what goes on inside us ever reaches our consciousness; it is a screen with a very limited scope. The vital processes – digestion, circulation, respiration, elimination and growth, for example – are completely outside the range of our consciousness, and yet if we managed to develop the possibility even these processes would become conscious.

Years ago I gave you a diagram that represented all the different bodies that go to make up a human being (See Figure 3). Beginning at the bottom we see the physical body (which includes the etheric body); the astral body (seat of feelings and emotions), and the mental body (which is the conductor of thought). Above these three bodies you see a dividing line, and above this line the causal body, which is the body of wisdom and omniscience; the buddhic body, which is the seat of selfless love; and finally the atmic body, the body of divine omnipotence. In most human beings it is only the three lower bodies that have reached some degree of development; the three higher bodies are no more than the germ of what they will become, they hardly manifest themselves at all. The three lower bodies correspond to the personality and the three higher bodies to the individuality. Man possesses two natures, therefore, both of which have the power to act, to feel and to think, but on two

116

different levels: the personality on a lower level and the individuality on a higher level.

INDIVIDUALITY

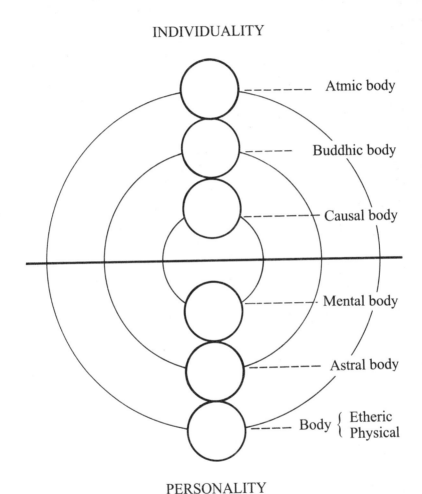

PERSONALITY

Figure 3

In reality these two natures are not separated from each other. As you can see from the diagram, each of the lower bodies is linked to the corresponding body on the higher level: the physical body is linked to the atmic body, the astral body to the buddhic body and the mental body to the causal body. And this is precisely the goal of human evolution: the incarnation of each of the higher bodies in the corresponding lower body so that man is illumined by the divine nature within him.

The line between the lower and the higher bodies represents consciousness; it is like a screen between the personality and the individuality on which both natures are reflected and if it is too limited it means that we ourselves will be limited in our activity. All human beings possess the germ of their higher bodies and one day they will be fully matured. In fact I am sure that you have all felt their presence at one time or another. You hear a snatch of music or glimpse a face that causes something to stir within you and gives you the desire to accomplish deeds of extraordinary generosity for the good of the whole world: this is a manifestation of your buddhic body which is beginning to vibrate within you. Or perhaps you feel an inner force rising within you that is capable of moving the whole earth: your atmic body is beginning to stir. Or again, you experience such illumination that you begin to perceive the structure of the universe and to understand how it functions: this is your causal body which is beginning to filter into your brain. If these manifestations occur frequently it means that your three higher bodies – causal, buddhic and atmic – are already beginning to take possession of your whole being.

Generally speaking, one could say that a person's consciousness is a reflection of his interests and of his way of life. If you reinforce your personality – that is to say, the coarse, primitive, animal side of your nature – your consciousness will shrink and be darkened and the images it reflects will be distorted. Whereas if you give much greater scope to your higher nature the thoughts, sentiments and sensations it projects on to your consciousness will be of a divine quintessence. If you want to expand your consciousness, therefore, you must encourage the manifestation of your higher nature, for it is clairvoyant, omniscient, all-loving and all-powerful. Men and women speak of their consciousness without realizing that because of the way they live they project images of hell on to it. They abandon themselves to all the impulses of their lower nature with the result, of course, that they are obsessed by monsters. All their mental anguish, neuroses and nightmares come from the lower half of their being which is nourished and strengthened by their disordered way of life. No one, neither doctors nor psychoanalysts, can heal or help them, for the rot is within, their torment comes from within; nothing external can save them.

Consciousness exists as a consequence of all that goes on within a human being. Just as a cameraman can project nothing on to a screen if he has no film, we cannot project something on to our consciousness without an intermediary of some kind. This means that it is the quality of the film, the quality of our life, that we must take care of, for it is our life that is projected on to the screen of consciousness. Consciousness manifests itself on the level of the brain but it is the result of what goes on in all our cells. It is on our cells that must we act, therefore, if we want to change our consciousness, not on the screen, for the screen is purely passive. Our will and vitality are not part of our consciousness; they are outside it but they are reflected by it.

Through nutrition, respiration, spiritual exercises and certain kinds of thoughts and feelings, a person can influence the cells of his body, and the state of his cells will be reflected in his consciousness. And vice versa: the images reflected by the screen of a person's consciousness can influence him so that he will be at one and the same time the screen and the film projected on to the screen.

As a human being is made up of several bodies he also possesses several levels of consciousness. On the physical level each cell of his body has its own consciousness; it is not something that concerns only the brain. Every cell of every organ possesses its own very limited, but very real, consciousness. On the lowest rung of the evolutionary ladder, stones, rocks and metals also have a form of consciousness but it does not dwell within them: it dwells very far away on the outer edge of the universe. The consciousness of plants on the other hand dwells in the centre of the earth; this is where we have to go to reach it if we want them to understand us and do things for us. The consciousness of animals is not individual either; they have a collective consciousness that exists outside them. Each species is ruled by its own group-soul. Man is the only creature that possesses an individual, indwelling consciousness; in all creatures of all the other kingdoms of nature consciousness is external. This is why animals mate, spawn and moult, for example, at set times: because they obey their group-soul. Only human beings, although they too belong to the universe, have a self, an individual consciousness, individual volition.

As I was saying, every cell of every organ has its own consciousness. The cells of the liver, the spleen, the lungs, and so on, all have different activities and responsibilities and consequently a different consciousness; but as they are all closely bound to each other, they are like the animals in that they have a representative, a group-soul, in the brain. All the cells of the body therefore have their representatives in the brain to look after their interests, transmit their demands and express their pleasure or their displeasure. The system is exactly like that used by a group of citizens to elect a member of parliament or by the workers in a factory to choose a trade-union delegate. Yes, it is exactly the same process, for human beings cannot discover anything that does not already exist somewhere in their own organism or in the universe. Through intuition, vague memories of the past or their own persistent groping, they are led to discover realities that have already been created by cosmic intelligence.

In the front of the human brain are cells that are the conscious representatives of the whole body. The other cells of the brain are representatives also, but unconsciously or subconsciously. Our self-consciousness resides in a few cells here in the front of the brain: all the rest corresponds to the subconscious. In the rear of the brain for instance is the cerebellum which is the seat of sexuality, and the cells of the cerebellum also have representatives who come to the front of the brain to clamour for what they want:

'We need this, we want that ...'. As a matter of fact we often experience certain needs without really being aware of them consciously and this is why people are astonished at the dreams they have at night. Their desires had not reached their waking consciousness, but they were there all the same. As I have said then, consciousness is a screen on which all kinds of demands are written and obviously our divine nature also sends its representatives to write on that screen.

This screen that lies between the two natures therefore is a kind of no man's land, a buffer zone in which two countries meet and attempt to negotiate before resorting to war. A human being is both of his natures at the same time. In fact he is not only his higher and his lower nature, he is also the screen on which they project themselves. This explains how he can indirectly cause certain changes on that screen by acting on one or other of his natures, for he is in both of them. And this explains also why his actions are capable of affecting heaven and hell and the whole universe. A human being is an immensity, his roots reach into every corner of the universe and this means that it is very difficult – impossible, in fact – for him to know himself: he manifests himself sometimes in one world and sometimes in the other, and it is the screen of his consciousness that allows him to have some idea of what he is doing. This screen is like a mirror: it enables him to study and get to know himself. He cannot act in any direct way on that mirror but because he has a will, an imagination and the capacity to think, he can act on every level of the universe and the mirror will simply send back to him the reflected image of his acts.

Yes, a human being is an immensity that has worked for thousands of years to acquire the qualities and elements that have enabled him to construct his physical, etheric, astral and mental bodies and the germ of his causal, buddhic and atmic bodies, and this is why his roots reach into every corner of the universe. His being is spread throughout all these different bodies, these different regions, and is in touch with a great variety of forces and powers which are reflected in his consciousness. If he is intelligent and lucid he can look at that screen and understand and learn from what is reflected there. He can see whether his thoughts and desires and the movements of his will have succeeded only in dredging up slime from the depths or whether they have reached the heavens and produced images of heavenly splendour. In this way, as he gradually becomes aware of the true nature of things and of the reality of certain laws, he is in a position to opt for a more intelligent way of life, to become wiser, more prudent, and more reasonable and to stop projecting images of ugliness and disorder on to his screen. But there is a great deal more to a human being than that which is reflected on his consciousness; he can act in many other ways without even knowing where or how. His consciousness reflects only a tiny proportion of his life; it is a stage on which a few representatives appear, sent either by his egotistical personality or by his vast, disinterested individuality, and it is brightly lit or in darkness depending on which elements are on stage at the time.

As we have seen, therefore, we cannot act directly on our consciousness; we have to act on our cells and organs or on the different regions of creation, on the angelic hierarchies. You go for a walk or sing or pray, and within a few minutes you begin to feel better about things because you have acted on certain positive factors which are then reflected on the screen of your consciousness. A human being dwells in every region of space and is composed of particles from all those regions. Consciousness is only a result, a reflection; it is not a constituent component. This is why you must always try to see the meaning and the source of what goes on within you. You must discern whether your desires, thoughts and feelings stem from your lower or your higher nature; you must even discern their colour and their scent and know which entities they correspond to, for everything belongs to a specific category or order. You must get into the habit of working in this way with the mirror of consciousness.

Everything that reaches our consciousness is related either to heaven or to earth. But when I speak of consciousness it can equally refer to the unconscious, the subconscious, self-consciousness or superconsciousness; it all depends on who or what is acting and manifesting itself on that screen. While we are asleep for instance it is the lower regions, the regions of the subconscious, that manifest themselves in dreams. But if the manifestations are luminous and sublime it means that the superconsciousness is manifesting itself. As I have told you consciousness is a neutral zone in which both good and bad can express themselves. Naturally not everything that goes on within us is manifested in our consciousness: if we had to be aware for instance of all that goes on in our stomach and liver, we would go mad.

There is a whole world within us that we know nothing about and we sometimes see evidence of this for the first time when, one fine day, an enemy that had been in hiding for ages suddenly shows its face. As it had never manifested itself on the screen of our consciousness before we had no idea that it was there, and then when it comes out into the open it manifests itself in physical or psychic illness. But there can also be angels dwelling in us unknown to ourselves and they too can suddenly appear within our consciousness; then we are amazed to discover that these friends have been helping and supporting us for a long time.

As I have said a human being is immense but he doesn't know himself. He may know himself on a higher level, in the divine world, but he needs to know himself here, through his brain, through matter, and it is this that is so difficult. You have all seen a kitten playing with its tail: as it doesn't know what its tail is it bites it and then it is surprised by the pain it feels. And you are like kittens: one day you find the tip of a tail which seems to be moving about all on its own so you bite it, and then of course you squeal with pain when you discover that that tail is part of you.

At the moment man's being is scattered throughout space, but one day he is going to have to find himself: our tail is our physical body and it is through that tail, through the matter of our physical body, that we have to find ourselves. This is what makes life so difficult and so complicated, for we often come into conflict with people and things without realizing that they are ourselves. This truth is the foundation of all moral law. If it is written that we must not wrong our neighbour it is because in wronging our neighbour we are wronging ourselves. Our true being is everywhere and it is we ourselves therefore who are the first to be affected by the injuries we do to others. In the same way we are the first to benefit from the joy we give to others. All moral law is based on the knowledge that man's being fills the whole of creation. This is why we must always try to do good because it is to ourselves that we are doing it, to the self that is there in our neighbour.

As I have already told you everything that exists possesses consciousness but, depending on the level of evolution it has reached, its consciousness can be close to it or very far away. The consciousness of minerals is the most remote; that is why minerals are inert. The consciousness of plants is closer and that of animals closer still, whereas man possesses his consciousness within himself and this is why he is capable of thought. One day I will explain to you in detail just how animals, plants and minerals appeared. In reality they came from man, for man possessed all the kingdoms of nature within himself. In the beginning man contained everything – minerals, plants and animals – and they only appeared externally when he gradually detached them from himself.

A few minutes ago, when we were talking about man's different bodies, I showed you how his higher bodies were linked to the lower bodies. This means that if you work to cultivate wisdom and light you develop your causal body and the causal body becomes one with your mental body. If you work to cultivate absolutely disinterested love you develop your buddhic body, which blends into your astral body. And if you work to cultivate power and to do God's will you develop your atmic body, which becomes one with your physical body. In this way therefore man's personality and individuality become one: on the physical plane he becomes all-powerful, his heart becomes all-loving and his intellect becomes omniscient. It is important to remember that that which is below is like that which is above, but reversed; otherwise nothing makes sense. The body that is at the top of man's higher nature is linked not to the highest region of his lower nature but to the lowest. For the time being the two natures are separated by the screen that lies between them and on which each projects the image of itself, but one day when they have become one that screen will no longer exist, or rather everything will serve as a screen, for it is not possible for us to know everything and be everywhere with nothing but this one little screen. If you yourself are very limited you will have only a very narrow screen, but if you are unlimited the whole universe becomes your screen and you can be everywhere and know everything.

Of course human beings are not yet capable of reaching this level of comprehension; sooner or later however they are going to be obliged to obey the currents from heaven that are sweeping them on towards perfection. Even if at the moment they are going in the opposite direction, it is only temporary: cosmic intelligence will eventually lead them to their true goal.

Sèvres, March 21, 1970

III

People sometimes come and tell me that they have been tormented for years by mental images, nightmares and obsessions and don't know how to get rid of them. I tell them, 'It is you who created all these images that haunt you today. Over the course of many incarnations you have been storing them up inside you and now the film has been handed to an operator and is being projected on to the screen of your consciousness.' Yes, all the images that torment human beings come from a long way back; it is not their present consciousness that is creating them. All their consciousness does is serve as a screen. The film has been in the making for a long time, and now that it is running you have no choice but to watch it. You will see that some sequences are very bright and beautiful and others are very dark, but as there is practically nothing you can do to change the film that already exists the best solution is to work at creating a new one. We must not put the blame on our wretched consciousness; it is not responsible either for the good things or the bad things it reflects. The most we can expect is that if a person is intelligent his consciousness will let him see that he needs to ask for another kind of film. heaven is always willing to give us other films but it will not change your screen for you. The one you already have is quite big enough and perfectly suitable for its purpose. It is the pictures that are projected on to it that are not good; the screen itself is what it is meant to be.

Take the case of a thief or a murderer: his consciousness is perpetually haunted by the spectre of the police and prison. Yes, simply because he has set certain processes in motion which are now reflected in his consciousness and are destroying his peace of mind. The consciousness of someone who has done nothing wrong on the other hand has no reason to be disturbed by such fears. This is clear: as soon as someone does something dishonest his consciousness can no longer be at peace for it receives worrying images from all sides. He may try to calm its fears but he will not succeed because it does not depend on his consciousness; his consciousness cannot know peace as long as the other aspects of his life are not in order. You can see now how ignorant human beings are: they never know what to do to improve their situation. Try to appease your conscience and sleep peacefully in your bed after committing a crime! You cannot do it. You will always have to worry that perhaps someone saw you ... somebody suspects ... they are going to come and get you! This is how people make themselves ill.

Sooner or later, although there is no way of convincing human beings of this, every fault we commit leads to illness. People think that they have power over themselves, that they can do whatever they like with impunity. But this conviction is soon brought low. If they do wrong they will never succeed in healing the psychological damage their wrongdoing causes. It is no good their thinking they will because no one has ever succeeded ... no one! Even the power of a great magus who has reached the point of commanding and being obeyed by the spirits of nature will not save him if he does something wrong. No, because there is no power capable of appeasing a tormented conscience. Believe me; I am telling you the absolute truth. You must count neither on your power nor on your own will, but only on your clean, honest, upright behaviour. This is the only way to set yourself free. As soon as you do wrong and transgress a law all your powers are reduced to nothing; they can only be restored to you if you make reparation. And it is precisely this that sets a true magus apart from ordinary men, the fact that he makes swift reparation for his mistakes. His true power lies in this: in the fact that he puts things right at once. For all his power, if he failed to put things right he would be incapable of setting his conscience at rest. As soon as he makes reparation it acts directly on his consciousness and he is at peace again.

There is a great deal that needs to be said about this question, for the truth is unknown to most thinkers. So many false ideas about human consciousness have been spread abroad that it is impossible to get things straightened out in people's minds. They believe that they should have the power to persuade their consciousness to be at peace. No, never: neither thought nor auto-suggestion nor faith has this power. I repeat, there is only one way and that is to make reparation: when you do so, your strength, health and harmony is immediately restored. Jesus who knew this law told us: 'Before the sun sets, go and forgive your brother.'

You see, without seeming to I am giving you a commentary on the Gospels. Yes, I say 'without seeming to', because it is no good trying to preach about the Gospels or quote from them today; people just won't listen. This is why I try not to refer too often to the Bible; it is no longer acceptable. In point of fact though I draw all the truths I reveal to you from the Bible – particularly the Gospels – or directly from nature, but without always saying so, because people are so bored by all that that they are leaving the Church. So I bring you back to the Bible by other ways, by roundabout routes. Oh, the beauty of roundabout routes!

The Bonfin, July 30, 1971

IV

Since our physical body – and even our astral and mental bodies – represent only a very small part of ourselves, we must try to get to know the other, far greater, part which is so far away, so far above us. This higher part of ourselves has its own life, which is quite different and often in direct contradiction to the life we live on earth. Suppose you do something really wrong: why does that other pole of your being let you do it? It may be far away but it is still attached to you; it knew that you would regret your actions and have to suffer for them, and yet it did nothing to intervene or prevent you from making a fool of yourself. Why not? Sometimes in fact it seems that it is that other pole of your being that drives you to do wrong. What a mystery this is! It has allowed you to stray and make mistakes – for nothing ever happens without its knowledge and consent – and now that you are suffering the consequences and up to your neck in boiling oil it is away somewhere, on a cloud of beatitude without a thought for your distress!

It would take too long to explain the reason for this. Let's just say that there are ways for a disciple to reach and get to know his higher self and become one with it. And once he has achieved this all weakness, darkness and suffering disappear from his life and other forces are set in motion. The phenomenon is very similar to the phenomenon of metamorphosis of a caterpillar. A caterpillar wraps itself up in a cocoon and shortly after a different being appears: a beautiful, dainty, brilliantly coloured butterfly.

Nature has placed many such signs throughout creation so that disciples may learn from them and understand the transformations that they too must undergo. Human beings have a very high opinion of themselves, but in reality they are like ugly, lumpy little caterpillars that spend their time doing all kinds of damage by devouring the leaves of plants and trees. But once a caterpillar decides to withdraw into itself to reflect, meditate and renounce some of its baser tendencies, it triggers new forces within itself and the butterfly that soon emerges no longer destroys the leaves but feeds instead on the nectar of flowers. A butterfly is a symbol of a soul that has escaped from all that bound and limited it, and this is resurrection, true resurrection. You must not think that the resurrection that the Bible talks about applies to the physical body. There is no resurrection of the physical body; there is only the quickening of a spiritual element that lay dormant within that body and that is now ready to awaken and blossom.

All this means of course that a disciple must not concentrate on what he is here below, for it is not very glorious; he must concentrate on becoming what he is on high. And in order to achieve this, in order to get all those energies, all that power and strength and beauty, to descend to his level, there is something specific he must do: he must raise himself to a great height to the level of his higher self, and implore it to change him. This is something that only our higher self can do, but it will not do it unless it is asked. Don't delude yourselves: if you don't ask your higher self to help you it will do nothing; it will leave you to suffer and be miserable.

Since our whole being is reflected on the screen of our consciousness, the reflection of our higher self is also there, however faint, and it is this reflection that makes it possible for us to be united to our self, our true self. Man is a fragile, puny little being, but if he is enlightened, if he has someone to instruct him, he is capable of making his cry for help heard on a very high level. I have never fully explained this to you before, but you can now understand how the screen of your consciousness makes it possible for you to know yourself. It is only a reflection and yet it contains the quintessence of your being; even though it is only your reflection, it is part of you.

Even a person's reflection in a looking glass contains some of his fluids, some of his forces. Even your shadow is a reality. In fact there are magical practices in Africa in which a sorcerer needs nothing but the fluidic traces left by a person's shadow in order to cast a spell on him. People think that their shadow is not a reality, but it is: it is the trace of one's fluidic emanations. Why do you suppose that dogs can track down people simply by following the scent of their fluids? And if we can learn to follow the 'scent' of our higher self on the screen of our consciousness, one day we shall be able to 'track down' that self that is above us. This screen is not there without reason. Even though what a disciple sees on it is no more than a reflection of his true self, if he works to make contact and get to know that self, his consciousness begins to expand until one day he feels that his being is as vast as the universe itself, that he is the cosmic being, that he dwells in eternity.

The sages of India have a mystical formula that is very profound. It is 'I am That', and it means 'I have no separate, independent existence. I exist simply as his reflection. In discovering myself I shall be discovering him, That which created me. I myself am an illusion, a non-being. Only That is a reality.' Yes, God amused himself by scattering himself amongst his creatures. In reality though we should say that there are no creatures, nothing exists but God, for that is the truth. All creatures and the whole of creation are simply thoughts in the mind of God. We are going to have to pass through many different stages of course before we discover this for ourselves. To find oneself is a tremendous task. There are times when you suddenly feel flooded with light as though you had been catapulted on to the level of superconsciousness and you are overawed and dazzled by the immensity and the beauty of what you perceive. Unfortunately though this perception does not last and you find yourself back again in the daily routine with all your old worries and weaknesses. Once again you feel cut off from the Godhead and from your higher self; like a piece of flotsam drifting in the void. And then again a new light, a new illumination, comes to you, but this too does not last long. And these ups and downs go on until one day at last light fills your being and never leaves you again. You have crossed to the other side; you are safe once and for all.

My dear brothers and sisters, even if you have not fully

understood what I have been telling you, try to accept it, for I have verified so many things for myself and I am impatient to share them with you. Trust me and persevere even if you cannot see any results. Imitate the caterpillar which enters into itself and becomes a chrysalis. The example of the caterpillar which turns into a butterfly shows that even the most inferior beings possess amazing possibilities and can become butterflies – that is to say, angels. You must die to your life as a caterpillar and live the life of a butterfly. This is why Jesus said, 'Except you die you shall not live'. Yes, you have to die to your lower life so as to live the divine life.

Sèvres, January 16, 1968

V

A disciple has to bring into the present all that existed in the past and all that will exist in the future in order to make use of it. You must understand of course that when I speak of the past I imply only that which belongs to the veritable, divine tradition which has been handed down to us in its entirety from time immemorial. Similarly, the future implies all that is divine and universal that is still to come. Yes, for the future, the real future, necessarily tends in the direction of greatness, infinity, immortality, the expansion of the soul and the power of the spirit. That is what the future is. And this is why I say that a disciple must live in the present with all that he has acquired in the past (all the riches he has amassed in the course of his evolution) and with all that will be his in the future. Only by living in this way can he possess the fullness of life.

Some people are always living in the past, their own past: they remember the parties they enjoyed, the day they got engaged or what happened to them during the war. If their past was unhappy they spend their time regretting it; the present is unimportant, they are incapable of enjoying anything. Others live perpetually in the future, but in a future of their own fantasy that will never exist anywhere but in their imagination. It is good to recall the past, but not if one does so in order to live its tragedies all over again and make oneself miserable. No, we should only recall the past in order to learn from it and understand where we were wrong and where we were right. We must use all that accumulated wealth of experience in order to learn to act with greater intelligence. But at the same time we must project ourselves into the distant future and try to understand what God has in store for mankind, try to perceive something of the splendour and light in which human beings are destined to live. You can even picture yourself in that distant future and see that you will no longer be puny, mediocre and pitiful: you will be a divinity; you will emanate the most exquisite music, perfume and colour; you will be one of the elect in the assembly of God's children. And you will be so entranced by what you see that you will not want to come back into the present; you will live in the eternal future.

I know that people think a lot about the future – but what kind of future do they think about? They think, 'In a few years I'll be married and have lots of children. We'll live in a little house and keep chickens. In the evenings we'll sit in front of the house and I'll smoke my pipe and enjoy the peace, watching the cows – or the trains – go by and smelling the dust. Then we'll go in and have supper, have a little drink ... and so to bed!' What a beautiful future! You will say, 'But people don't really look forward to that kind of life'. No, I know; they look forward to earning a lot of money and making a name for themselves in business, or to being a brilliant general at the head of an army. Some will plan to be a university professor, a Cabinet minister or president. Others will dream of having a pretty girl to make love to night and day. But all that is less than nothing – it's pitiful!

Unfortunately there are very few who are ready to look any further than their own dubious future and try to perceive the future that God has in mind for humanity. It is time for human beings to begin looking to new horizons, to open a window on to infinity and begin to see the future of the whole of creation. But above all you must never be put off by the time factor. You must never say, 'Yes, but by the time all that happens I shall not be here any more,' because in saying that you will be cutting yourself off from true beauty. It is amazing to see how ingenious human beings are at finding ways to limit themselves! Yes, because it is they who limit themselves. They are afraid to reach out and touch the magnificent, limitless treasures of their soul and spirit. They are so narrow, so small-minded. Where are those who are brave enough to break through their self-imposed barriers and venture out into the vast world? They are not very numerous. But initiates and spiritual masters constantly break through barriers; in fact they go much further back into the past than historians.

Historians study no more than a few thousand years of the past – Babylon, China, India, Egypt or Assyria, etc. – whereas initiates go back much further than that. You will probably wonder if they can still find any vestiges of such an ancient past, and the answer is yes, for nothing has disappeared; the descendants of the distant past are still all around us. If you knew how to decipher the messages of insects – ants or bees for instance – you would be astonished at what they could reveal. They are the descendants of some of the extraordinary beings that existed in the past and which, in fact, still exist. Nature has eliminated some of these creatures but others still exist. In fact even those that have disappeared from the face of the earth still exist: there are regions underground in which every animal and vegetable species that has ever existed is kept under the care of highly evolved beings so that science, true science, shall always be intact and one day these beings will reveal this science to human beings.

But we will talk about all that some other time. As I was saying, a disciple must not limit himself. He has to live in the present to be sure, but his present must reflect the wisdom learned from the past and the promises of the future. The present must be a time of conscious, enlightened action which draws on the lessons of wisdom stored up in the past and is stimulated by the boundless hope of all that the future holds. This is the perfect balance: the lessons of the past (and the Lord knows what great lessons mankind's past holds for us!) and the infinite promises of the future. A disciple who is capable of living in the present and expressing both the experience of the past and the splendours of the future begins to resemble the Deity. What is it that the Seraphim sing as they stand before the throne of God? 'Holy, holy, holy, Lord God Almighty, Who was and is and is to come.' Yes, this is how the consciousness of a disciple expands to the dimensions of divine consciousness. But it is very difficult for you to understand this for you have no notion of what past, present and future really are.

Man's true past is not his historical past but the period in which, in his primeval splendour, he dwelt in the bosom of the eternal One. He lived in God, he was with God, he was God himself. Man's true past is not the few thousand years that have led up to today; it is the period that preceded his descent into matter, that preceded original sin. When I was very young, nearly fifty years ago, I spent whole days trying to rediscover that past; sometimes I would go so far back that I felt my head spinning. It was as though I were plunging straight into a bottomless pit. It was a frightening experience! I was very young at the time and I was fascinated by such bold experiments but it was a dangerous thing to do and I certainly don't advise you to try it, for it can lead to serious trouble.

Today there are therapists who experiment on their patients with hypnosis: they put them to sleep and then begin to take them back into the past. They will ask them for instance what they were doing ten years ago and the patient will tell them exactly where they were and what they were doing. Then gradually the hypnotist will take them back to their childhood and birth and further still, and they will begin to remember being born into another family in another period and another country. Experiments of this kind have already been done and they correspond to the reality. One day conventional science will decide to do some research in this area and it will make some tremendous discoveries. It will be obliged at last to admit that men are not on earth for the first time and that all the misfortunes, illnesses and failures they experience in this life, as well as all their qualities, wealth or success, can be explained by their previous incarnations. Once this is understood the laws of destiny, divine justice, and so on, all become clear.

As long as people refuse to believe in reincarnation they will never learn to resolve their problems correctly; they will never reach the truth. Even the Church keeps mankind in a state of error and ignorance and bars the road to progress. But the day will come when the Church is startled by the reproaches of her own children: 'Mother Church, you have deceived us for too long with your lies; the truth is not what you say'. Then the Church will be obliged to catch up with her children who are far in advance of her. May the

Church forgive me, but that is what will happen if she doesn't change. Children forge ahead while their parents stay behind.

A disciple who knows how to use both past and future expands his consciousness. The matter of the past is congealed and frozen stiff; it cannot be changed: whereas the matter of the future is so subtle that it cannot be seen; it seems unreal. But it exists at a distance and it is gradually getting closer and becoming real. As for the present, it partakes both of the past and of the future. In reality the present does not exist; there is no such thing. Or rather neither the past nor the future exists: there is only the eternal present. But for us it is the present that does not exist, because as soon as we become aware of it, it is already the past. Whatever you say and whatever you think is already in the past. As soon as a thought finds form in your mind, as soon as you express it, it is already in the past. We cannot grasp and hold on to the present. For us, limited as we are, there is no present; there is only the past and the future. But for God there is neither past nor future, there is only the present. You will say, 'But I am living in the present!' No, you are wrong; it is already the past. You can live to a very small extent in the future, but the future is always something that is not yet there; the future is always beyond the scope of our consciousness. 'But you said a moment ago that we could have a foretaste of the future, that we could live in the anticipation, the expectation, of the future.' That is true, but it is only a foretaste; if it were already present it would no longer be the future. The future is always still to come.

But enough of that! The one thing to remember is that there is neither past nor future for God, only the eternal present, and that God's present is our future. Some years ago I told you that the present of animals was man's past, for man has evolved; that the present of men was the future for animals, and that the present of angels was man's future, etc. Past, present and future, therefore, can also be seen as different degrees of evolution. Would you like to have an idea of the beauty of our past? Look at the muzzles and snouts of animals! Would you like to see what we are at present? Well, I won't tell you to look at the 'snouts' of human beings ... but look at their behaviour. And if you want to know what your future will be, go and ask the angels. Yes, you can go in thought to where the angels are and feel, see and understand what your future will be.

The Bonfin, August 4, 1964

Chapter Eight

THE HIGHER SELF

I

The sun is always new. The water in a river is always new. Human beings renew themselves also; the cells of their bodies are constantly renewed. This being so we might well ask: 'Why is man always the same? Why does he always have the same attitude, the same reflexes, the same weaknesses?'

Let me give you a comparison: when an employee in an office or factory retires or dies, the person who replaces him is obliged to learn his job and do exactly the same work as he did. In the same way, when our cells die their work is carried on by the new ones that replace them. But there is something we don't realize, and that is that offices, archives and memory banks are not confined to governments or business; they exist in man too, and the new particles and cells are trained to vibrate and behave exactly as their predecessors behaved. It is because of this memory in man that, in spite of the constant renewal of the matter of his physical body, an individual is always the same. If you knew the secret of how to change the memory of your cells, therefore, you could change everything: both your matter and your mentality could be renewed.

At the moment human beings are content to renew themselves physically in the way of children. Look at a young child, and then look at him twenty or thirty years later: he will have grown and his face will have changed, but his self, his ego, will still be the same. It takes a great deal of spiritual work to change that. This is why a disciple must learn to identify with a heavenly entity: Christ, the heavenly Father or the divine Mother. You will say, 'But that's madness!' Yes, in some cases it can be madness. There is not much distance between madness and initiation. Let that be an encouragement to you! Everybody knows that a genius is only a step away from madness. Someone who thinks that he is Christ can be quite mad: he wanted to be initiated but went about it the wrong way and lost his mind. If he had known the right methods he would have really and truly become Christ. Other very highly evolved beings before him have succeeded in identifying with Christ. The important thing therefore is to know certain rules and methods.

To make the transition from the ordinary level of consciousness to the level of the superconscious involves such a fundamental renewal, such a dramatic change of personality that, if you don't know the method to use to ensure that this change takes place harmoniously, things can go very wrong and you can go out of your mind. So as I say there is not much difference between a madman and an initiate: with the madman the attempt to change his level of consciousness is undertaken in such a disorderly, chaotic way that he has to be shut up, whereas with an initiate the change is effected so perfectly that he becomes a divinity. Yes, it is important to know that if you don't proceed according to certain rules all kinds of bizarre things can happen. There have been a great many mystics and spiritualists who have played havoc with their nervous system or have attracted and been possessed by malignant entities, simply because they did not know how to set about things and had no notion of moderation or respect for the laws involved. And this is why nowadays everybody thinks that spiritualists are all a little mad.

You must know that by the way you live and work you put yourself on the same wavelength as certain entities; this is why they are attracted to you. An Egyptian initiate, for instance, would concentrate and repeat certain formulas and sometimes wear masks or special robes in order to identify with the god Osiris or Horus. For a brief moment, because he managed to vibrate on exactly the right wavelength, he truly became the incarnation of this sublime entity who could then speak and manifest himself through him. In order to create this bond one has to vibrate on the same wavelength. This is a law of physics, the law that makes radio possible. Long before the physicists however, initiates were familiar with this law and knew that it applied not only on the physical but also on the psychic and spiritual planes, so they instructed their disciples in the rules and methods they should use in order to vibrate in unison with a specific entity and be a channel for its messages. Later, after being brought back to their normal state, some of the disciples could not even remember what they had said. Another being had spoken through their mouths. In a way you could say that this is what happens with people who are mad and who, without knowing it, have formed a bond with noxious currents or creatures of darkness.

As a matter of fact one might wonder why sickly people often have gifts of clairvoyance and mediumship that normal people don't have. Or why it is that such gifts sometimes appear after a severe shock or illness. Yes, this is often what happens: a shock, a fall, an accident or a great grief of some kind will trigger certain inner processes and not long afterwards the person begins to manifest psychic gifts. As nobody knows how to explain such things they say that they are abnormal. Well, there is some truth in that, but you must not conclude that to have psychic gifts one must necessarily be unbalanced or ill. In reality the explanation is that a person's subconscious makes contact with the superconscious. This brings us back to the question of the personality and the individuality, the lower and higher natures, that I have already talked so much about[1].

Sèvres, April 1, 1968

---

[1] See *Complete Works*, vol. 11, 'The Key to the Problems of Existence'.

II

Our higher self is perfect, omniscient and almighty, a fragment of God himself, a pure, transparent, luminous quintessence. Yes, but if this is so how is it that this self allows us to make mistakes? It is this that is so difficult to understand: how can there be a being within us who sees and knows everything and is all-powerful and yet who is totally unmoved, who never feels or expresses any pain whatever we do? Why does he accept situations that are not in his best interest? And when we speak to him of our philosophy and all our dreams, hopes and plans, why does he do nothing to put them into effect? We are not separated from him, and yet when we are suffering and trying to improve the situation he remains coldly indifferent and leaves us to our plight. Is there no way of touching him? It is very important to get to know this higher self, for he is so far above our own being that when he does decide to act nothing is impossible for him. We are composed of physical, etheric, astral and mental bodies and his nature is far superior to this. Superior even to our causal, buddhic and atmic bodies, for these are still bodies and he is not a body; he manifests himself through these bodies, but he belongs to the region known to cabbalists as Ain Soph Aur: limitless light.

So, as we have said, everything is possible to our higher self; the only problem is in getting him to act, and as we don't know how to make him want what we want, it is a problem that can reach tragic proportions in our lives. How can we spark the goodwill of this being who is so far above us and whom we represent so inadequately here on earth?

Our earthly being is made up of many different fickle, changeable 'selves', but it is we who are responsible for them and for all their silly mistakes, so it is we who suffer and have to make reparation. Our true self never makes a mistake or commits a crime; he remains in the purity and light of the higher world, and it is up to us to scale those heights and one day become one with him. In the meantime, though, there is always the 'me' on earth that combines in itself and serves as an 'identity card' for all those other bizarre 'selves': – the poet, the miser, the cook and the liar, – who are so different from each other but who all live at the same address. But we ourselves ... what are we? We don't know. There is this one fictitious self who encompasses all the others and who is rewarded or punished for their good deeds or their crimes. One of these 'selves' steals from his neighbour and is caught in the act by an honest 'self' who is scandalized and deeply distressed. He cannot understand how such a thing could happen. Remember the lecture I gave several years ago about the different 'tenants' that we carry about with us wherever we go.

When we want to know ourselves, that is to say, when we make up our minds that we really do want to be united with him, our higher self is immediately aware of it and delighted to know that at last the most important work on earth has begun. Whatever else we do leaves him absolutely cold and indifferent. It is all the same to him if we become a general, a Cabinet minister or an emperor or if we have an accident or live in destitution and despair; none of that moves him. He only begins to notice us and give us his attention when we finally decide that we want to get to know him.

There are actually two methods that a disciple can use in order to find and make contact with his true self. The first consists in focusing on his ego, his human self. This self is illusory and very limited, to be sure, but it is nonetheless a reality. Even if you say that it doesn't exist, at least it exists as non-existence. So the first method consists in making use of this feeble means; this screen on which your self, your consciousness, is reflected; this screen which is not you and yet which is you, which is part of you, a distant manifestation of your higher self. You grasp and hold on to that consciousness, doing nothing else, simply clinging to this consciousness for several minutes, keeping it alive within you. In this way, as your consciousness is already linked to the infinity of your superconsciousness on the higher plane, little by little your concentration will put you in touch with your higher self.

But if you want the qualities of your higher self to flow down into your lower self, you are going to have to bring your imagination into play. With your imagination you can do the exercise that I described before when talking about the sun[2]. You are down here on earth and you focus on your higher self in the world above and picture him looking down at you; in other words, from that higher level you look down and see yourself and the imperfect conditions in which you live. Keeping this thought before you, you set in motion a current that flows between the self that is above and the self that is below. In this way you are restoring the vital link between you, for from down here you are thinking that you are up there, and up there you are conscious that you are down here, thinking of your self up above.

It is very difficult to explain this clearly: at the same time you divide yourself and unify yourself. You divide yourself into two, one above and one below: the one above – your true self – watches the one below as he meditates on that self above, and in this way an extraordinary current is established between the two, making it possible for your superconscious to develop. You stay with your eyes closed, conscious at the same time that you are there, in your room, a living, thinking being, while your all-powerful, omniscient higher self above sees his reflection and recognizes himself in you. Seeing himself, he smiles at you – perhaps even laughs a little – and you watch him from below and begin to get to know him while he watches you from above. In this way the gulf between the higher and lower poles of your being begins to narrow until one day it disappears and they are fused into one. When this happens your lower self no longer exists. That lower self – which is not a true reality – disappears, and all that is left is your real, higher self. No more weakness, no more discouragement or darkness! You become omniscient, immortal and eternal.

So you have to imagine not only that your higher self watches

[2] See *Complete Works*, vol. 10, chap. 3.

you, but that he is conscious of seeing himself in you through your mind; that he recognizes the close bond between you. In this way, thanks to the extraordinary closeness of communication, your superconsciousness will begin to stir and awaken.

Or there is another exercise that you can use: it consists in concentrating on the occiput, the region at the back of your skull. Try it for a few minutes and you will notice that something begins to happen: your whole body begins to vibrate and you feel as though sparks were coursing through you. But this is not an exercise that should be continued for long: as soon as you feel a tension, a tingling, as though you had touched a nerve centre that made your whole body vibrate, it is time to stop. The first few times you must be very careful and be sure not to go on for too long.

Very few human beings have ever achieved identification with their higher self, for the amount of work involved is gigantic. This is why certain initiates do well to abandon everything and retire to a forest, a cave or the desert, so as to free themselves from all distractions and everything that might absorb their energies and turn them from their goal. But conditions are different here in Europe, and except in very exceptional cases this is not something I recommend. It is one thing to make a retreat for a short time in order to work better afterwards, but to decide to withdraw from the world for the rest of one's life and never be available to give others the help or comfort they need seems to me to be very selfish. This is very common in India: a person will abandon everything, his family, his possessions and his job, and devote himself exclusively to the spiritual life. Well, that may be fine, but here in Europe it is preferable to achieve a balance between the material life and the spiritual life.

Many Eastern spiritual masters have come to teach in the West – there is no point in naming them – but the exercises they teach their disciples have often destroyed their health or their psychic balance. As these exercises are excellent in themselves and have long been practised in the monasteries of Mongolia, Tibet or India, these teachers see no reason why they should not teach them also in Europe and America. But westerners need other methods.

Many of them have gone out of their minds or become the victims of grave sexual disorders because of the inner tornadoes triggered by these exercises; they were incapable of controlling them and had not learned how to use them. There are thousands of different exercises and practices in use in the East, but I have rarely met a westerner who has achieved a truly sublime result by using them.

A long time ago I was at a variety show at which an Indian yogi appeared. After the first few numbers this half-naked, skinny little man came on to the stage and began rolling all the muscles of his body in the most frightful way. You could see his aorta throbbing, his lungs inflating, his intestines moving about, etc. It was so terrifying that several women in the audience fainted. Can you imagine! It seems to me utterly pointless to spend years of one's life learning to do this! I just wonder whether all these yogis who have achieved such an extraordinary degree of control over their physical bodies take as much care of the spiritual dimension. Do they work at controlling their feelings? Sometimes they cannot even find their way about in their own inner life. The physical body is important, to be sure; without it we could achieve nothing on this earth, but in my opinion we are doing all we need to do for the physical body by being vegetarians, doing the few exercises of gymnastics that you all know and living a pure, well-balanced life. The thing that matters most is to know the spiritual laws and apply them by living as we should, to have a genuine understanding of the universe, the hierarchies and human beings, and to attain perfect mastery of oneself.

Before you go off and experiment with all kinds of dangerous knowledge, you must begin by learning to nourish yourself properly by learning to breathe and love and think and act. Science will come to you later, and when it comes it will be immense, infinite. The thing that matters most is to know how to live properly so as to become stronger. Unfortunately human beings neglect this and prefer to collect masses of useless information. They are like the man who had such a passion for books that he had a special coat made with huge pockets and he would go out and buy all the books he could and bring them home in his pockets. He piled up all these books in his one little room until one fine day the floor gave way and collapsed on to the head of the man below. You see the poor fellow had spent his life studying but there was one thing he had neglected to study and that was how many tons of books his floor would hold before it collapsed.

And this happens very often: people spend years amassing information and then the floor collapses. What do I mean by the floor? The nervous system. Yes, this is something people forget about; they think that it will take any amount of strain, but it won't. Not unless you reinforce it. If it is properly reinforced you can pile up all the books you want. So now you understand why I tell you that you must begin by learning to eat properly, to breathe properly, to sleep and behave properly: these things are the 'floor'. Once it is really strong you can pile the whole universe on it without causing it to collapse. If you want an example in nature, look at a melon or a vegetable marrow and you will understand this law of consolidation. If you see a melon hanging on the vine you will see that its stem, which begins by being very slender and fragile, becomes gradually thicker and tougher until it can bear the weight of a huge fruit without breaking. But there are people who instead of reinforcing their nervous system spend their time piling up heavy burdens until eventually everything breaks down and collapses within them.

Sèvres, January 17, 1971

III

When I have been travelling by train at night I have often opened the window while all the other passengers were asleep, and looked out at the engine up ahead and thought of the driver. I would say to myself, 'Up there in the front of the train is the fine fellow who is looking after all these sleeping people; his face black with soot and only his eyes glinting in the dark'. The idea of this poor man, who was there all alone and who did not have the right to go to sleep because he was responsible for the lives of all of us, used to make a deep impression on me.

You will probably think that I have been given a very strange mentality because I always think about things that no one else bothers about. But that is how it is. As it says in the Gospels, 'The stone which the builders rejected has become the chief corner-stone.' But the thing that you have never thought about is that there is another train whose driver must never sleep, and that train is ourselves. Our body, our cells, must be allowed to sleep, but our higher self never sleeps. It is always awake and vigilant, always there to guide us towards our destination. At least, this is so with initiates and enlightened disciples, but ordinary human beings are so out of touch with their higher self that they are like a train in which everyone is asleep, the engine driver as well as the passengers.

You must always be sure that something within you is awake. In fact before you go to sleep at night you should remember to leave someone on guard to keep watch within you while you are sleeping. Jesus said, 'Watch and pray', and many Christians, thinking that this meant that they should keep watch physically, would wake themselves up in the middle of the night to recite the office or meditate. But the poor things often exhausted themselves to such an extent that the natural rhythms of their body were completely disrupted. It is on a higher level that we must watch and pray.

Wakefulness on the physical plane is not essential; you have to transpose your vigilance on to a much higher plane; the cells of your physical body must be allowed to sleep and rest while you keep watch on a higher level. In other words you have to ally yourself with the constant watcher, with him who never sleeps; you must find him and become one with him. And where will you find this eternal watcher? Here, between your two eyebrows; this is his home. And that is why, although he remains motionless and utterly impassive, he sees and records and understands everything. So you must find and unite yourself with him. Yes, if you succeed in watching and formulating your requests from this centre you will have spiritual eyes with which to explore regions invisible to your physical eyes, and while your body is resting you will be in touch with the most marvellous realities.

The Bonfin, July 14, 1964

Chapter Nine

TRUTH

I

Simplicity

Ask for light, ask to understand things correctly, to think correctly. You still don't understand how important it is to think correctly according to the rules and criteria of the divine world. A lot of people believe that they think correctly because they refer to norms which the world approves of. But in that case everyone thinks correctly: all those who never break the rules or overstep the boundaries of social traditions and good manners can be said to think correctly. The only thing is that what ordinary human beings consider correct is still not correct for initiates. This is why you are going to have to re-examine your opinions with reference to the norms recognized by initiates.

Oh yes, I know: you are thinking that I am asking you to do something that is far too complicated for you. Not at all; quite the contrary in fact: I am leading you in the direction of simplicity. It is you who are entangled in complications; that is why you are always unhappy. Yes, you are unhappy simply because you are so complicated. Once you have recovered your simplicity you will be happy.

People don't understand what simplicity is; they think of it only in terms of external manifestations: simplicity of dress or manners, the 'simple life', etc. But it is not that at all. Simplicity is a philosophical attitude, which consists in ceasing to be concerned with the material world of phenomena and rising to the level of principles. That is simplicity: a turning back to the centre, to the summit. Whereas complication is the opposite; it is a movement away from the centre, a scattering, a downward movement. When you turn away from the light, from simplicity and unity, you find yourself faced with such variety and multiplicity that you can no longer see things clearly; you can no longer see how things relate to each other according to the laws of affinity. To be simple is to know how to direct one's steps upwards. People's heads are filled with far too many complications. I fully recognize that they have great talents and great learning, but they lack this element of unity, and this is why they never attain truth, for truth is simple; truth is pure light.

The reason why everything becomes so complicated is because our personality sees only the countless facets of physical and material life and we lose our way amongst them. The individuality on the other hand – because it is a spirit and belongs to the world of unity – is always looking for simplicity, always longing to get back to primeval simplicity. The personality complicates everything; it is the personality that is the cause of so many disasters and misunderstandings and that drives us to busy ourselves with so many useless activities. People mistakenly believe that all this agitation will bring them happiness. No, it is important to get rid of this misapprehension, and in order to do that we need the guidance of beings who come from the region of unity, who have attained unity for themselves and are capable of teaching it to us. Then, at last, there will be no more complications!

There, you see: all of a sudden you no longer feel tired, because while I have been speaking to you I have been leading you without your realizing it towards unity, the unity that is always there, vibrant and generous, overflowing with life. Whereas in the midst of multiplicity and complication our energies are scattered, our vibrations become weaker and concentration becomes impossible. When your head is filled with too many different things, when you have several different goals in view, you are torn in different directions and your strength ebbs away. Whereas when you succeed in concentrating on one idea, one desire, all your forces converge towards this one goal and you become fantastically powerful. If a country at war is obliged to defend itself on several different fronts, its fighting forces are scattered and their efforts are much less effective than if they were concentrated in one direction. This is so obvious and so easy to understand!

Take a magnifying glass and use it to focus the sun's rays on to one point and you can set fire to the whole world; but if the rays remain scattered over a wide area you can stand there with a magnifying glass in your hand for years and you will never set anything on fire. It is the concentration of fire, the concentration of light or thought or activity, that produces such incalculable power. The laser is a fantastic example of the power of concentrated light, and man himself is built like a laser: his spinal column is the ruby rod and the spiral flash lamp is kundalini, the serpent that rises the length of the spinal column. Initiates who succeed in bringing the serpent all the way to the summit develop a fantastic power with which they can work wonders when it is projected from the top of their head.

Well, my dear brothers and sisters, we can talk more about this another time. For the moment think about simplicity; try to become simple. Everybody underrates simplicity (what do we mean for instance when we say that someone is simple-minded?). This is why 'Blessed are the simple in spirit' is a very unfortunate translation of the first Beatitude; and 'poor in spirit' is no better: the kingdom of heaven will never belong to those who are poor in spirit. There is no place in heaven for them; they will be sent back to earth to learn their lesson.

Sèvres, April 20, 1965

II

Unity and Multiplicity

i

Yes, my dear brothers and sisters, I am simple, uncomplicated, without pretence, like a child. I appear before you exactly as I am. And it is because I am simple that I am beginning to resemble truth, for truth is simple, undiluted. When you begin to be synchronized with something, to vibrate on the same frequency, you begin to receive the currents and forces emanating from it. This is why I have been able to discover truth: thanks to simplicity. It is simplicity that shows us truth. Children are unsophisticated; it is only as they grow up that their families and schools deform them and put all kinds of false notions into their heads so that they are no longer natural and unfeigned.

How can we get back to that simplicity? Unfortunately people are not too fond of it; if you appear to be simple they lose their respect for you. No, you have to think things out carefully in advance and become skilled in pulling the wool over people's eyes; then they will think you are someone to be reckoned with and bestow respect and admiration on you. But if you are simple and natural people brush you aside and take no interest in you. When a girl is natural and unaffected and refuses to use all kinds of allurements, men are not attracted to her.

To be simple is to have only one idea, one desire. As long as you allow all sorts of conflicting thoughts and desires to co-exist within you, you will always be in a complete muddle. A lot of people come to me and tell me that they are completely lost and it is easy to see that this is because they are bogged down in complications: they have been trying to satisfy all kinds of contradictory desires and ambitions. Why do they think they need everything? Some people go into a bar and start mixing their drinks: a glass of port, a glass of whisky, a tot of brandy, and when it is time to go home they are dead drunk. They would do much better to be simple and drink pure spring water! And what do young men and girls do? It is not enough for them to sleep with one person; they have to complicate their lives by sleeping with two, three, ten, or more. It is all this indiscriminate mixing that is so ruinous.

I have often given you the example of a diamond. If a diamond is so pure it is because it is simple; it is pure carbon with nothing else mixed in. Add just one element to it and it will no longer be a diamond. And disciples who constantly mix all kinds of thoughts and feelings create a dense, murky swamp within themselves and not a ray of light can get in. If they became simple, that is to say if they made sure that all their food and all their thoughts and feelings were pure, if they lived in the light of the sun, they would become like diamonds, pure light. Light makes everything simple. Disciples who are eager to taste, touch, experience and know everything lose their value as diamonds; they are no more than opaque stones. A true disciple must always move in the same direction, have one ideal, one desire, one kind of nourishment. For him everything is simple, that is to say, pure.

Simplicity therefore is the equivalent of purity. But it can also be seen as the equivalent of sincerity, honesty or integrity. The word simplicity can be applied in every area.

Simplicity is a quality of the intellect as well as of the heart and will. On the intellectual level, to be simple is to be guided by only one philosophy, the philosophy of light. On the level of the heart, simplicity means to have the one overruling desire to love the Lord and be united to him. And on the level of the will, simplicity means to have one constant, unchanging activity. You see? It's clear. And this is precisely what simplicity is when it is applied to thought: it is clarity, lucidity. And for our being as a whole, simplicity manifests itself as harmony and peace. In the midst of too many disparate and contradictory elements, peace vanishes and is replaced by inner disorder, turmoil and distress. This is exactly what happens in a family in which the members all want something different: they do nothing but quarrel and the family ends by falling apart. Why have people become so complicated? It is more and more difficult to find a united family or a long-standing friendship because, instead of taking the path of simplicity that leads to a higher plane, people have chosen a downward path. And once you start on the downward path everything becomes more complicated and differences and contradictions become more and more evident.

When you rise to a higher plane, on the other hand, the multiplicity of facts and phenomena tends to be simplified until it is eventually reduced to a handful of laws; rising still further, these laws are encompassed in even fewer principles; and on a higher level still, all that remains is unity. Unity; simplicity; One. It is when we move away from our source, our Creator, and start exploring the periphery that complications begin and we find ourselves up against all kinds of problems. All misunderstandings and conflicts between human beings stem from the fact that they have left their Father's house and gone out to seek adventure and a fortune at the periphery.

Everything can be explained in terms of simplicity (unity, the return to the source) and complication (multiplicity, estrangement from the source). This is where I look for the explanation of every event. All complications, mishaps and tragedies stem from the fact that in his ignorance man has distanced himself from the source. And all happiness and prosperity come from his turning back towards the source, towards unity, the universal soul, the Lord – towards simplicity.

It is because human beings don't possess the right criteria that they search through philosophical treatises in the hope of finding an explanation for what happens to them in life; but the explanations they find are so complicated ... and the truth is so simple! When you feel an inner uneasiness, when you sense that something within you is not vibrating in unison with the first cause, it simply means that you are drifting away; that's all. There is no need to look for any other explanation. And when you sense that your inner life is progressing more smoothly, that you are becoming a child of God, it means that you are drawing closer to the spiritual sun and that you must continue on the same course. To be sure, we must always expect some variations in our inner 'weather': there will always be the seasons of spring, summer, autumn and winter. Your winters and your springs can last for a few hours or a few days – sometimes a few years – but you must learn to be patient and put up with hard times: winter will not last for ever; spring will come again. We all have to go through such periods but the important thing is to steer constantly in the direction of unity, otherwise no one can come to our rescue or really help us. The only solution lies in this philosophy; there is no other way.

I am telling you the truth and it is clear and simple; don't look elsewhere. Give up everything else if you want to, but never give up your pursuit of unity, never deviate from the path that leads to the centre of the universe, to the Lord, to that dazzling light. Don't worry about how long it is going to take you, the ups and downs you will encounter, all the sacrifices you will have to make and the tribulations you will have to endure – none of that is important; it has all been planned and foreseen. There are debts to be paid and it is all part of your karma. But throughout everything you must pursue the same course, the course that leads to simplicity, unity, truth. As long as you seek solutions in other directions you will never be free of suffering and complications.

What I have been saying today sums up for you in a few words the teaching of all the sacred books of mankind; this is the quintessence of wisdom, religion and truth. You can see how simple it is: why look for anything more? Unfortunately people have no liking for simplicity; they don't believe that something simple can be really effective. They want to be told something outlandish: 'Take the tooth of a rabid wolf, the heart of a blue swallow and the liver of a special kind of green fish. Grind them all together in a mortar, etc., etc., and all doors will open before you; you will have access to the treasure-chests of the world.' Yes, this is what people are looking for! Don't make the mistake of thinking that they want something simple. I have often spoken to doctors about the efficacy of boiling water for instance, and they say, 'Yes, of course; we know that hot water can be extremely effective, but if we prescribed that to our patients we would have to shut the shop'. Hot water is not appreciated because it is too cheap and easy. Human nature is very peculiar: people only believe in remedies if they are complicated. This is why doctors have to impress them with all kinds of instruments and machines that are often quite useless.

Simplicity and complication; nearness and distance. You come closer to the source and everything becomes simpler. You move further away from it and the complications begin in your mind to start with, and then in your feelings and your actions, until your whole life becomes so complicated that you no longer know where you are. If you don't believe me you can verify what I say: consult all the books and all initiates and they will tell you the same thing. It is not so difficult as all that to find the truth. I have always wanted to be simple and it is thanks to this simplicity that truth, which is simple, has revealed itself to me. People are always looking for something spectacular but this is a mistake: you must get back to the 1, the number One.

Simplicity is 1. Complication begins with 2, for 2 signifies division, polarization, contradiction, and consequently war. And 2 is followed by 3, 4, 5 and 6, etc., all the way to infinity, which is the nth degree of complication. There is a mathematical formula which states that one divided by infinity tends to zero ($\frac{1}{\infty} \to 0$). You can interpret this symbolically to mean that when a human being departs from the centre he is so scattered and torn apart by the complications of the periphery that there is almost nothing left of him; he is dead and buried, wiped out, zero. If you divide one indefinitely the inevitable result is death. Life resides in the 1; this is why we have to make a constant daily effort to draw nearer to the One, to God himself. When Jesus said, 'The Father and I are one', he showed that he had achieved this tremendous truth, this tremendous simplicity. He wanted to melt into the Father and be one with him. All those who are not animated by the same philosophy complicate their existence. Bear these few words in mind, and if you have understood me you will give your life a new direction and it will begin to take on a new countenance, a new light, a new colour, a new meaning: the meaning of life.

Throughout the centuries the prophets of the Old Testament continued to repeat the call to the people of Israel: '*Shema Israel, Adonai Elohenu, Adonai ehad*; Hear O Israel, the Lord our God, the Lord is One'. But the people did not understand. They sought other gods: Baal, Bel and Astarte, all the Babylonian, Syrian and Phoenician deities. What a struggle between unity and multiplicity!

Light a fire and the flames rise, reaching for unity. Water on the other hand tends towards multiplicity. This is why fire (and air) were chosen as the symbol of the spirit, whereas water (and earth) were chosen to symbolize matter. Air feeds fire; without air fire would go out. Air and fire understand each other because they always tend to rise. Fire and air are brothers, whereas water and earth are very loving sisters. Water is absorbed by earth.

Some of you will perhaps say, 'But it is life that obliges us to be complicated. It is because life is what it is that we need so many different things and have to struggle and fight for them.' Yes, but who has created that life? Human beings! And the human beings who created that life were not very enlightened. The life created by sages and initiates will take a very different direction.

The Bonfin, July 18, 1967

Today I want to add a few words to what I said yesterday about simplicity and complication. You have already understood that simplicity is the number One, the Godhead, and that to reach the Godhead we have to climb to the summit or, to use another comparison, to move from the periphery to the centre. Today I want to emphasize the philosophical significance of this phenomenon of separation, estrangement from the centre, which is the phenomenon of creation, manifestation, materialization. He who understands this twofold process of movement to and from the centre possesses the key to all knowledge.

The return to the source, the ultimate union, the fusing into one with our heavenly Father is the goal of all religions. This is what is known as the re-integration of beings. The essential concern of all religions is to help man to return to his primordial state, to the state of equilibrium, peace, joy, ecstasy and light that he enjoyed in the bosom of the eternal Lord. Religion has never been very concerned about the process of creation. Moses for instance wrote no more than one page to describe how God created the world. To be sure, many philosophers, theologians and high initiates have studied the question, but generally speaking it has never been considered very important to instruct human beings about questions of this kind. It has always seemed far more important to give them advice, methods and exercises to help them return to the centre.

The very notion of creation implies materialization, and human beings are already so deeply immersed in matter that it would only be to their detriment to tell them to continue to explore the question of materialization. This is why it has been left to one side until they have sufficient light, ethical sense and balance to deal with it. So there you have it: the departure from and the return to the centre, involution and evolution. You all know the story of the prodigal son who left his father's house to go and seek adventure in the world and who returned home to his father ill, penniless and half-starved. All the sacred scriptures of mankind have stories of the same kind that illustrate this twofold process.

The *solve* and *coagula* of the alchemists is another way of presenting the question. Nature itself speaks to us of these twin processes: at one moment you look up at a sky which is blue, transparent and cloudless and then a few minutes later it begins to cloud over, a veil is drawn across it as the water vapour in the air condenses and forms clouds. Later again the sky is swept clean and the clouds seem to dissolve. Everywhere throughout the universe these two phenomena, *solve* and *coagula*, are visible and they are an invitation to a disciple to reflect on them and understand them: appearance and disappearance, birth and death, creation and the return to nothingness.

Now if you ask why and how the Lord created the world no one can answer you; it is the greatest of all mysteries. Did space exist? Did God fill that space? What is God in reality? No one knows. The Vedas even say that the gods appeared after the world was created.

But if you want my opinion I think that the Lord created the world because he was bored. he was all alone you see, and it is very difficult to live alone. So he created human beings for his own entertainment – and they certainly give the Lord a great deal of amusement. He looks down at them from above and laughs at what he sees; yes, he laughs until his sides ache! Don't you think that this is the best explanation? Well, all right, but I have heard so many preposterous theories about the origin of creation that I thought I might as well invent my own. And perhaps this is the most plausible explanation: the Lord was bored.

Why did God create the world? Perhaps he wanted to suffer at the hands of human beings! Yes, because every other creature in the universe, even the devil himself, obeys God; only human beings do exactly as they please. In fact the Book of Genesis says that God regretted having created man, so that must mean that man is not something very remarkable. Oh dear, how complicated it all is!

In the beginning nothing existed apart from God. God was all there was. He was One. Division and polarization only made their appearance with the creation of the world, for every manifestation is a polarization involving positive and negative, light and darkness, good and evil, the subtle and the gross. To begin with there was neither good nor evil, nothing but some vague forms, the seeds of the good and evil which were to manifest themselves only gradually as matter became more and more condensed. But these manifestations were already potentially in existence. The Cabbalah explains the creation in terms of emanations. God emanated a substance, a quintessence – it would be too much to say a form of matter, but one might say a suggestion, a first notion of matter – and this substance was the Sephirah Kether, light, the light that Moses was referring to when he said that it was the first thing that God created. 'Let there be light!' and this light is the Sephirah Kether. But this emanation from God, this first subtle light, is not the physical light that is visible to us and which, by comparison, is very dense and crude, grossly material. You have only one word for light but in Bulgarian we have two different words: *svetlina*, which is physical light, and *videlina*, which is the inner, mystic, spiritual light, the light that initiates possess. The word *videlina* corresponds to the Hebrew word *Zohar*, and *Zohar* is the title of the book that contains the traditional teaching of the Cabbalah.

Genesis speaks of 'The beginning', but the notion of beginning is also incomprehensible; how can one speak of a beginning if time did not yet exist? Our time is measured by the sun, the moon and the stars, which were not created until the fourth day. Besides what was a 'day' in this context? There can be no such thing as day unless the earth is already spinning on its axis in orbit around the sun, and the sun had not yet been created. And when Genesis says, 'The evening and the morning were the first day', and 'The evening and the morning were the second day', what was this day? For from evening to morning is not day, it is night! So as you see, we are now in the midst of endless complications, whereas before everything was simple and clear: we shall have to turn back to the centre if we want to get back to unity.

Once you leave the simplicity of the centre, all kinds of possibilities are open to you, for innumerable paths radiate outwards to an infinite distance. There are 360 degrees in a circle, and this means that there are a great many different ways of getting from the centre to the circumference. There is only one path leading back from the periphery to the centre, but if you want to go from the centre to the periphery you have a wide choice of paths: to the left or to the right, in front or behind, and even above or below. There are six directions and 360 degrees, so you have innumerable rays to choose from.

As I was saying, therefore, as it emanated from the centre the primordial light formed the first Sephirah, Kether, which means 'crown', and in that light dwelt the Seraphim. The Seraphim were the first creatures to leave the bosom of the Lord. Following the example of God himself, Kether drew on its own abundance and wealth to emanate the second Sephirah, Chokmah. Chokmah is denser, more material than Kether, but it is also a world in itself with its own organization, its own creatures, forces, colours and music. Chokmah in turn emanated Binah, and starting with Binah another kind of organization begins. Binah represents a frontier, a border line which marks the beginning of the stabilization of the systems that form the framework, the skeleton, of the universe. Binah emanated Chesed; Chesed emanated Geburah; Geburah emanated Tiphareth; Tiphareth emanated Netzach; Netzach emanated Hod; Hod emanated Yesod; and finally Yesod emanated Malkuth. And Malkuth is the region of the earth which is the densest, heaviest and most opaque of worlds. This is how the universe was created. Each Sephirah is a world and each of these worlds has its own substance, organization and density, and the level at which materialization is the most dense is that of the physical world in which we live. In order to get back to the subtlety, light and splendour of the higher worlds we have to follow the path of evolution once again.

Why did we leave all that splendour and reach such a degree of materialization? Why did God have to go to such lengths? He could have created the universe differently or not created it at all. Why did God knowingly make man such that he would inevitably lose his way and then decree that he must find his own way back to his source? These questions are all mysteries. It is possible to understand them, but only on a very high level. Here on earth no one can understand them. Suppose someone asks you why evil exists. You can tell him that evil does not exist of itself, that the existence of evil depends on the source, the Creator. But at the same time you know that the Creator cannot create anything evil since he is perfect. What a conundrum! In the same way hell and the devil have no existence on their own. Since all life comes from God, even the life of the devil must necessarily come from God. It is God who sustains and nourishes the evil and if he withdrew his support the devil would disappear. And yet the devil is always represented as God's enemy: what is the explanation? I have studied these questions for a long time and I have already explained a good many things to you[1], but today there are not going to be any explanations. We are up to our necks in complication and we are going to stay there!

When man leaves the centre and moves out to the periphery he can no longer understand God's manifestations. There is no light at the periphery. The further one goes from the centre the darker it becomes and it is this darkness that makes it impossible to understand anything. This is why human beings are continually arguing and quarrelling; everyone defends his own pet theory but no one is any nearer to the truth than anyone else. Yes, simply because they are all at the periphery. In order to understand it is necessary to turn back to the centre, to God. This is why all religions teach man to seek God, to think of him and love him. In this way light is gradually restored, because when you take the ascending path that leads back to the source you receive the particular quality of each Sephirah. Yesod gives you purity; Hod gives you intelligence; Netzach, beauty; Tiphareth, light; Geburah,

[1] See *Complete Works*, vol. 5, chap. 3.

strength; Chesed, generosity; Binah, stability; Chokmah, wisdom; and Kether, omnipotence.

The extraordinary thing is that every time I have an opportunity to see some of the things human beings are producing today in the field of art I discover a tendency to move further and further away from the centre. Whether in music, dance, painting, sculpture, architecture or poetry, there is this constant pursuit of novelty and originality and no one seems to realize that it is leading artists further and further away from true beauty. This is why art is so bizarre today. There is no law against novelty; on the contrary, but why look for it always below in the regions furthest from the source? The trouble is that artists have not been enlightened by initiates. One needs considerable learning and a profound philosophy simply to recognize this estrangement from the centre. Without that philosophy and knowledge, man has to fall back on his instinct, his impulse to create. Of course, whether someone looks for inspiration in the right direction or not, he can always create. In distancing himself from the source, from the spiritual sun, he will still find an infinite variety of forms and aspects but the forms he finds will contribute to leading those who look at them still further from the centre.

Today wherever you look in music, painting or literature, you can see evidence of this estrangement; even in human relations; in the way people love. It is a wonderful thing to be a creator of music, pictures or films ... or children; but you have to be careful to examine the value of what you create, otherwise you will produce nothing but gargoyles. You have created something? Well done! But what does it do for the audience or the spectator? What effect does it have on people? Nobody thinks about that.

People will explain that they needed to get something out of their system. Well, there is nothing unusual about that: everybody needs to get certain things out of their system, but does that mean that it all has to be put on exhibition? Two or three times a day we all need to get something out of our system but we don't put it on a silver platter for other people to smell! But this is exactly what some creators in the fields of art, literature and philosophy do: they exhibit their excrement for others to smell and swallow. You will say that I am exaggerating. No; I assure you, it's no exaggeration! But in the future when artists are instructed in initiatic schools they will be shown the true path of creativity, and then they will produce works of art that reflect the beauty of heaven and inspire and delight the souls of human beings. But what inspiration can anyone possibly find in the ugliness that we are shown today?

In the past many artists were adepts of initiatic schools and were taught how to rise to the higher realms in search of forms, colours and harmonies. They meditated and contemplated in order to receive heavenly inspiration, and when their works expressed this inspiration, they inspired others to follow the same upward path. And for the same reason they continue to influence us today, centuries later.

Nowadays artists graduate from their academies armed with bundles of diplomas but no knowledge of initiatic laws. They elaborate all kinds of theories to explain that their abstract art is a vehicle for a philosophy, an idea too profound to be understood by the man in the street. But why do they have to go and get bogged down in abstractions that are so tasteless? Abstractions are for initiates, not for nitwits. But nowadays any nitwit can show you an 'abstract' painting, and even if you turn it upside down and look at from every angle you won't be able to make head or tail of it. What is there to see or understand in it? Nothing. It is idiotic; absurd! Artists themselves have no idea of the true function, the true mission of art, and yet it is very simple. It can be expressed in a few words: the mission of art is to lead human beings back to heaven, to the source.

Now I want to add a few remarks to what I have already said about simplicity. The deeper one penetrates into matter, the more one discovers the tremendous variety and complexity of forms. On the other hand one also finds a much greater similarity between the individual members of any one species. For example, an extra-ordinary variety of forms can be seen in the leaves of different kinds of trees, but the leaves of any one tree are all alike. And the same is true of fishes and insects, etc. What a fantastic variety of forms!

But can you distinguish one fly from another? And now, by contrast, compare the faces of several human beings, all of whom live an intense spiritual life: what a wealth of expression in each one and how different they all are! Whereas very crude, primitive people who have no spiritual life of any kind all look alike. On the one hand, therefore, there is simplification and on the other, complication. The nearer a person is to heaven the simpler and more unified he is, and at the same time the more expressive, vibrant, alive and subtle he becomes. And the lower one descends on the scale of life the greater the variety of forms, and at the same time the less expressiveness and light animate those forms. This fact is very important, but human beings have never even noticed it.

The higher one goes the simpler one becomes ... but this is a figure of speech. Simplicity is not the equivalent of mental deficiency, indigence, poverty or a lack of resources. No; the simpler you are the more closely you resemble the Deity, because being free of so many complications you are better able to manifest yourself truly in light, love and power. When you are immersed in complications these possibilities diminish. But they are replaced, of course, by others: you acquire a greater ability to suffer and weep and make a commotion and become wicked and destroy everything. Yes, there too you have great possibilities!

Dante, who was versed in esoteric philosophy, described hell as an inverted cone. The greater a man's guilt, the lower he was made to go and the tighter the limitations put on him. And this is quite true: the more deeply immersed you are in matter, the more you are crushed, restricted and miserable. Whereas the higher you go and the closer you come to the source, the simpler you become and the greater your possibilities of seeing, creating, moving about and expressing yourself.

Now you must understand me correctly when I talk about descending into matter. In incarnating we have all descended into matter. I am no exception. I was very well off up there, but I came down here of my own free will. When I was still very young the Master Peter Deunov told me that I had signed a contract with the twenty-four Elders, the Lords of Karma, to come and work on earth. Do you imagine that I found that descent pleasant? I too have to endure the terror of matter. Matter is all around us, hemming us in and making prisoners of us, preventing us from seeing, hearing or understanding. Yes, but the purpose of this is to oblige us to do the special work we have come to do on matter, not to encourage us to pursue all kinds of experiences which alienate us from the divine world.

You feel shackled, restricted and subjugated and you wonder, 'What on earth have I got myself into? And how am I ever going to extricate myself?' There is only one answer to this: hurry up and turn back towards a higher plane. Don't wait until you are incapable of doing anything about it. Don't be like someone who walks into some freshly-poured concrete. As long as it is still wet of course he could get out of it, but his thoughts are elsewhere and he doesn't notice where he is until it is too late: the concrete sets and he is unable to move. He is going to have to break it in order to get out and he may well injure himself in doing so. Yes, this is what happens: time hardens things. If you delay in extricating yourself from certain situations you may soon find that your feet are caught fast and you cannot move. I am here to tell you these truths. People want to explore every possibility, taste every experience for themselves because 'everybody does it'; and their explorations take them further and further from the centre. And more often than not instead of the joy, pleasure and happiness they had hoped for, they find only imprisonment and bondage.

I don't claim to have explained this question of simplicity and complication perfectly; there are always some gaps in my talks, but all the same, I can see that little by little you are beginning to see things more clearly. I can feel this. The earth is a school and we are here for several reasons: principally in order to free ourselves from the debts incurred in previous incarnations; to understand the reasons for the situation in which we find ourselves, and finally to discover, awaken and develop some of the qualities latent within us. This is the meaning of life.

Most people, having no notion of why they are on earth or what they have to do here, are content to eat and sleep, amuse themselves or quarrel with each other before going back to the other side. And when they come back again they do the same stupid things all over again. But if someone is enlightened he knows that, first and foremost, he must free himself from his karma and work to become perfect. Secondly, he will try to understand why he was born in a particular country and a particular family, what is expected of him and the reason why he is on earth. And finally he will make every effort to cultivate the seeds of qualities and virtues that the Creator has sown within him from all eternity. This is why an initiatic school is indispensable. There is nothing more important than the light that such a school can give a disciple about these three questions: where he comes from, why he is here, and where he is going.

There, that was just a few words about creation, the descent into matter. One day when God has finished his work, he will cause creation to disappear. He will absorb the universe into himself. This is the period of cosmic repose known to Hindus as *Pralaya* and which lasts for millions and millions of years. Then once again he will bring a new universe into being. God breathes: when he breathes out the universe appears and when he breathes in the universe disappears. And as we are made in his image, we too breathe in and out. But the final expiration is something quite different.

For the moment meditate on simplicity; try to get away from the state of complication in which human beings are immersed and which brings them nothing but wars and misery.

Blessed are those who have simplified their lives in the light of purity because, although they are still at work on earth, they are already living in heaven.

The Bonfin, July 19, 1967

173

iii

Nothing exists that is separate and apart from God; nothing. Angels, archangels and human beings are thoughts in the mind of God and God is at the same time actor and spectator of the drama of creation. As soon as you say that there can be something apart from God you are saying that God does not contain everything in himself, that he is neither omniscient nor omnipotent.

In reality the universe is only an illusion, a soap bubble that floats in the air for a few seconds before bursting. The only enduring reality is the Creator. You will object that the world is not going to disappear as soon as all that, that it has billions and billions of years ahead of it. True, but what is a few billion years compared to eternity? We cannot know why God created the universe and all the explanations we have been given are only fit for children. 'Mummy, how was I born?' – 'The stork brought you, darling' ... or, 'I found you under the gooseberry bush'. If you want to know the truth you had better ask an angel or an archangel – although I am not at all sure that even they know the answer. They know everything about creation, but do they know exactly what the Lord is thinking or why he does what he does? With all due apologies to the Seraphim I rather doubt that God reveals everything even to them. To put it simply, I wonder if the Lord would not put himself in great danger if he revealed everything! You will say, 'But how can the Lord be in danger?' Well, just think about it: if one archangel of light could rebel, why not others? If the Lord had revealed everything he would have given them the weapons they needed to combat him, whereas by keeping his secrets to himself he remains invulnerable.

Human beings would be devastated by the truth; that is why they have been told some harmless little lies. And this system

174

works: there is no damage done! And you too will only be told as much about reality as you can bear otherwise you would give the whole thing up. This is what happens in fact to many Hindus: they don't want to go on living once they understand the futility of so many aspects of life: earning a living or marrying and having children. They see no point in doing so many things since it is all going to end in nothingness. It is much better for human beings to keep busy and even to be obliged to sweat and strain a little, to have the impression that they are accomplishing something. They are like children building sand-castles. Parents are always happy to see the passionate interest with which their children build their sand-castles because they know that that is how they enjoy themselves. 'Ah', they say, 'They had a splendid day on the beach!' And in the same way the adults in the world above watch us and say, 'It's marvellous to see how busy they are: making all those little mud patties, playing with their dolls and building their little castles. They put their whole heart into it!' And they accept the situation; it's normal, you cannot expect children to behave like adults. And we are children!

And now you will want to say, 'But then your teaching is a lie too!' Yes, it's a lie. But it's the best lie there is: the most adequate, the most useful and the most practical. Since everything is a lie I have simply chosen the one that is best and most easily digestible. Actually it is the truth, the greatest of all truths; why should I mislead you? But there are many different degrees of truth and the ultimate degree of truth is perhaps emptiness, nothingness, the void. In any case it is not necessary to go so far and I don't advise you to try it. Stick to your normal occupations and enjoyments. We are on earth and we must fulfil our role. Although we must not forget that we are actors in a play, at the same time we must not try to avoid playing our part. Look at what happens in a play about two enemies who hate each other: one of them ends by assassinating the other. But after the play what do you see? Why, victim and murderer go off together and drink each other's health! And during a war between two countries in which there are millions of casualties on both sides, when the dead meet in the next world they laugh and congratulate each other for the part they played in the comedy on earth. They were busy slaughtering each other in this world, but in the world above they embrace and drink to each other's health. The truth is that they did not really hate each other; it was just that they had a role to play. How the French and Germans must have hugged and slapped each other on the back when they met in the next world during the war! I can just imagine them sitting round a table, drinking wine or beer and laughing about it! What a lot of things we still don't know!

But let's stop there for the moment. Some people want to know everything and that is very bad. They are like children. Only children ask endless, impossible questions; they want to know everything but they are not capable of understanding. What is the use of trying to understand why God created the universe? You should not even ask such a question for the truth is that no one will ever be able to answer you. God has kept the answer to himself. One day someone who wanted to know everything infuriated a pastor by asking him what God did all alone in heaven. And the pastor – who had no idea, of course – replied, 'He spends his time cutting some good stout sticks with which to thrash those who have the impertinence to ask such questions!'

The only thing that is useful is to live properly and do one's work without bothering one's head with such remote questions. Human beings live like animals and then they expect to learn the secrets of the universe! They lose themselves in abstractions and forget to live properly.

Sèvres, January 31, 1971

176

iv

When one examines the conditions of life on earth, one sees that because of our descent into matter which began so long ago, we now need all that exists in nature. There is nothing wrong in using all that is at our disposal therefore, as long as we use it to turn back to the source. We are so far away from that source today that if we tried to get back to it directly, without the help of any material means or instruments, the task would be even more difficult. And in this connection too I am aware that you have not always understood what I tell you. Some people think, 'Well, since we have to be simple, I'll get rid of everything that encumbers me and go directly to heaven; in that way I shall become one with the Lord'. But this is not possible. It was possible at one time when we were much closer to heaven, but now that we are so far away we are obliged to make use of all that is in us and around us. As long as we use all that we possess in order to turn back to unity, and not in order to scatter ourselves and grow even further away, it is much wiser and more reasonable to do so.

What matters is the goal, the purpose, the reason for which we do things. If everything you do is motivated by your will to return to unity, then whatever you do – eat or breathe or walk, work or make love – is always good. But if you say, 'No, no; I refuse to use any material means; neither my legs nor my lungs nor my stomach. I'm not going to walk or eat or breathe any more. I'm a spirit and I want to get back to the source ...' you will get back to be sure, but in a way that you had not intended. In a way that is not highly recommendable!

Simplicity is first and foremost a question of thought; it is to understand that we have to vibrate in unison with the divine principle. Simplicity is also a question of the heart, and simplicity

177

of heart is to be free of many different contradictory and mutually destructive desires. And finally simplicity can also be in the way we work, if we have the will to work consistently in the same direction, so that everything we do is marked by order and harmony. Knowing this it is easy to look at your own life and see whether it is a life of simplicity or of complication. As soon as you begin to sense disorder, darkness or suffering in your life, it means that you are getting further from your goal. When this happens you must immediately find out how and when you let in the element that is disrupting your harmony and proceed to get rid of it. And for this you will need the help of all the means the teaching has put at your disposal for your perfection and purification.

As a matter of fact I realize that simplicity is not really so simple. In fact it is extremely complicated! Human beings are so far out on the fringes of life that it is very difficult for them to get back to the sun, to the centre, to unity. Man needs a great deal of knowledge, adequate means and methods, and great strength in order to strip himself of all the foreign and contradictory elements that have made him the tangled mixture that he is today. Simplicity is to strip oneself, to detach oneself and be free. Isn't that complicated? One needs so much knowledge, such strength and so much will-power to achieve it. So it is not really simple after all! It is simple to talk about simplicity of course, but nothing is more complicated to achieve. And it is because it is so complicated that the teaching gives us so many different explanations, methods, exercises and activities to help us.

There is a lot of work to be done before we can hope to be cleansed of all that we have accumulated in the way of false notions, negative feelings and bad habits. And yet it is possible to become simple at a single stroke, but only on the level of thought. To introduce simplicity into our behaviour or our feelings is much more difficult. But if we make an effort every day to introduce simplicity into our thoughts, this simplicity will gradually penetrate our feelings and even our actions, and in the long run it will take over our whole being, which will become as pure, transparent, hard and precious as a diamond. To reach this state of simplicity, this degree of transparency, a disciple must free himself from all the false notions inherited from his family and society which contradict the philosophy of the initiates. He must get rid of them because they are an obstacle to his evolution.

The teaching you have here is the teaching of simplicity and light, and yet you continue to cling to the opinions and points of view of those who have never lived in this simplicity. Everything is mixed up inside you; that is why you are not making progress. It is time now to sort things out, to review and weigh up and analyse all that you have received in the past. And when you have done that, keep whatever corresponds to what you have learned here and which can help you to turn back to unity, to perfection, to the Lord, and discard all the rest.

Since we are beginning a new year this is the work that heaven is asking of you: to take a good hard look at all that you have learned, all that you have inherited, and see whether it is compatible with the fundamental ideas of the teaching of the Universal White Brotherhood. If it is, emphasize and reinforce it and try to get a deeper understanding of it. But if you find some little things that contradict the teaching and put obstacles in your way, discard them. You will be amazed at the sense of freedom and lightness this gives you, at the ease with which you begin to rise, to soar. At the moment you are burdened by so many things that keep you down; your balloon cannot rise. You must throw all that excess weight overboard. So there you are: that is the work you have to do this year. Yes, I mean this seriously, very seriously. If you don't know what work is asked of you the years will go by and you will never make any progress.

A brother said to me one day, 'Master, I feel that for years I have made no progress at all. Tell me what I should do so as not to go on wasting my time'. Here was someone who at least knew that he had wasted a lot of time. Many people think that it is enough to belong to the teaching without having any particular plan in mind; and yet it is this that is important: your plan of campaign, the target you aim for. When you fix a target for yourself, even if you are unable to achieve it, at least you are preparing the ground, marking out and beginning to dig the channels which your subconscious forces can then use to carry out your aims. If you do no digging in advance the year will go by and nothing will have been accomplished. When it rains the water runs off the ground by way of drainage ditches prepared in advance, so this is what you have to do: prepare the ground, dig some ditches. It works in the same way as in a transistor; the current flows along a printed circuit exactly as though it were wiring.

This year therefore include some sorting and sifting in your programme. Examine all the different aspects of your life – your activities, associations, friendships or business arrangements – and ask yourself this: is it leading me to unity, simplicity and perfection? Is it helping me to find God or just the opposite? There are always some warning signs: if you realize that you are not thinking very clearly about a course of action, or that you feel uneasy about it, or that your will is still hesitant, don't do it, for these are infallible signs. A lot of people are aware of warning signs of this kind, but as they are too eager to satisfy their desires they ignore them. Later of course they regret it. We are always given a warning but people don't take it seriously because the temptation before them is too strong.

Although I say all these things I know very well that human beings prefer complications. If you tell them for instance that by leading a simple, normal, natural life, it is possible to live in a world in which illness, poverty, prisons and war no longer exist, in the first place they would not believe that it was possible and, in the second place, they would do nothing to make it possible. And yet look at the alternative: every day hundreds are arrested and tried and punished by law; so many people are sick that more and more hospitals have to be built, more and more expensive equipment bought, more and more drugs and remedies developed and produced. And what about all the wars that sow death and destruction over the face of the earth? You will say, 'But it has always been like that!' No, that is not true: it has not always been like that.

The Bible, like most of the sacred scriptures of mankind, tells of a period during which men lived a simple life. Adam and Eve lived in paradise in a state of joy and light unadulterated by any foreign elements. The foreign elements were introduced when the serpent intervened; that was when things began to get complicated, and man was condemned to earning his bread by the sweat of his brow, and woman to giving birth to children in pain. Then came the first crime when Cain killed Abel, and so it went on. Moses presents this idea of man's estrangement from his source in the form of a story, but it can be presented in many different ways, and I present it in the form of a geometrical figure: the circle with its centre and its circumference.

The further human beings moved away from the centre, therefore, the more complicated everything became until today the situation has become inextricable. As soon as one country creates a network of espionage, its adversaries have to create a network of counter-espionage. Everywhere you look there are endless watchdog committees, public or secret societies, organizations and operations. You have to watch out for this, be on your guard against that, and those who know that they are being watched organize their own surveillance of the watchers! As soon as man stepped out of line, as soon as he broke a law and moved away from the light, things became more and more complicated. Let me illustrate this: it is summer, the sun is shining, it is very warm and life is very simple. But when winter comes you need supplies of coal, wood or oil. You have to lay up reserves of food. You need more clothes, more electric light. And then fog or snow adds to the complications; communications are more difficult, the danger of accidents is greater, etc., etc. In other words the less light and warmth there is, the more complicated things become.

And here again we find the symbol that I have always given you: the symbol of the sun. As you get farther away from the sun, warmth and light decline and as warmth and light decline so does life – for life is simply the warmth and light of the sun – and everything becomes more complicated: you have to find other sources of light and warmth, other ways of protecting yourself. So as human beings have drifted far from the sun in their thoughts and feelings and in every other aspect of their lives, their existence obviously has become very complicated.

As soon as human beings understand that they must turn back to the sun, to light, to the Lord, everything will become clear and simple and easy. Not all at once, of course; it will take years to get everything sorted out, but this is the only possible way: never to forget that when one is far away from light, warmth and life, everything becomes complicated. What is the fate of an animal that strays too far from its nest or its den? And what happens to a child that strays away from home? When there is a handout of some kind those who are nearest to the source of supply get the best bits and those who are farthest away get nothing. The word 'far' has a disastrous ring to it! Unless, of course, we are saying that we are far from hell, far from darkness or far from folly, for then it is the equivalent of saying that we are near to heaven, near to the light, near to wisdom.

Every day, every morning and evening, you must try to draw closer to light, warmth and life, closer to God, the spiritual sun. To be sure you have to go on living, eating and breathing, but all these things must be aimed at bringing you closer to the source. As soon as you sense that you are drifting away you must pause and readjust your course; if you are sufficiently vigilant and have the wisdom and discernment to do this you will be rewarded with renewed abundance of inner light and joy. Whereas the situation of those who ignore the warning signs and persist in wasting their energies in a disorderly, frivolous way of life continues to worsen until it ends in ruin. The thing that prevents human beings from understanding this is that it is often a long time before they feel the consequences of their acts; they see no immediate worsening or improvement of their situation so they say, 'No, I don't believe a word of it! I am perfectly fit and well; I eat well; I drink well, and my business is flourishing.' Yes, in spite of a life of disorder, folly and passion, they enjoy success. The trouble is though that this success will not last long. Human beings make the great mistake of basing their conclusions on the immediate present, on something that is only temporary; they don't know that the laws are inexorable, and that sooner or later they will have to suffer the consequences.

We have all come to earth and taken on a physical body in order to make good our past mistakes and learn something. (All, that is, with the exception of a few, very few, who have come in order to help others.) And of course it is difficult to transform or improve the physical body, for it is heavy, gross and inflexible. But we have other regions within us, the regions of the soul and spirit, which are extremely subtle, and it is in these regions that we can work to improve, embellish and enrich ourselves. This is why we have to begin on the level of our thoughts, and then our physical body will follow ... much more slowly of course, but that is not important. What is important is the fact that in our soul and spirit, in our thoughts and feelings, we are completely free to work to improve things. Our work may not reflect itself perfectly in the physical body in this incarnation – although our body will certainly show some improvement – but because of the tremendous work accomplished by our soul and spirit and our thoughts, when we come back to earth in the future it will be with a physical body that is absolutely new, supple, beautiful and expressive.

It is possible to improve the state of one's physical body to a certain extent. As you know I have always insisted on this: we can for instance slow down the ageing process and the onset of physical decay. But to prolong this effect for thousands of years ... well, that is another matter! For that we need the elixir of everlasting life, and that is not the goal of our teaching. It goes without saying that the physical body is improved by participating in our spiritual work, but this must not be our primary concern for the physical body is limited; it has a beginning and an end. Our true concern must be the rich, limitless, infinite life that exists within us; this is where our work must be concentrated.

As a result of his descent into matter man is burdened with all kinds of complications from which he is now unable to free himself. Life is complicated because man's nature is complicated, but this will not last for ever. Man will one day return to a state of simplicity. You will say, 'Oh, how boring that will be!' Perhaps.

Perhaps simplicity is boring. Complication is certainly very entertaining, very absorbing; it keeps you on your toes and gives you plenty to worry about! So it is always interesting! What on earth could you find to make a film about in the life of an honest citizen, for example? There is no plot, nothing to catch your attention., – whereas the life of a criminal, a secret agent, a spy – ah, there you will find plenty of excitement and breath-taking complications! The life of a simple, innocent young girl is very dull, but the life of a *femme fatale*, of a vicious, seductive woman, is fascinating. Yes I understand all that, but that is no reason why it should be so for eternity; if you tell me that the simple life will be very dull I must reply that you don't know what you are talking about. If you were right how could we explain the fact that the angels and archangels, and even the great masters, who live this simple, luminous, divine life, are not bored by it?

The simple life is extraordinarily abundant, varied and diversified. Light is simple but it has many colours, sounds and scents. You must not confuse simplicity and poverty. To be sure we speak of the simple life of peasants or illiterate, primitive peoples, but the simple life as it is understood by every initiate is the richest and most beautiful life possible because it disposes of all the wealth and beauty of heaven itself. A diamond is simple, it is pure carbon, and yet it is considered the most beautiful of all precious stones. Everybody admires the beauty of a diamond and many people have been ready to go to great lengths – even to commit crimes – to have diamonds on a ring or a necklace or a crown. So you see, if true simplicity is a diamond how can you say that it is poor, dull or monotonous?

So there you are, my dear brothers and sisters: is the question a little clearer now? The whole of life offers us elements that help us to understand; the whole of life, the whole of nature, the whole universe, gives us the elements, the arguments we need to see everything more clearly.

Sèvres, January 2, 1968

III

Truth, Objective and Subjective

In our everyday lives when we are talking to someone in a normal conversation, drafting a report or answering questions in the witness box, we are always asked to be objective. That is to say, to state the facts accurately, exactly as they happened, without letting our own personal impressions get in the way. There is nothing very extraordinary about that; some people are not very highly developed mentally and if they allow their feelings to get the better of them they will fumble and hesitate and get everything mixed up or go off at a tangent. So it is normal that they should be asked to be objective. But what do we understand by objectivity? And why are people so distrustful of subjectivity? In a few minutes, if you make the effort to listen and understand what I say, the question will be clear to you.

Suppose someone is giving you an account of an event that he has witnessed: if he begins to inject into his account his personal point of view, his own feelings and impressions, or even some notions drawn from his own imagination, you will not get a very clear idea of exactly what happened. This is why you will probably ask him to tell you only what he saw and heard: the words, acts, times and distances involved, as though it had all been recorded by a camera or a tape-recorder. But in asking him to confine his description to a factual account of what happened on the material, physical plane, you will learn about only one aspect of the reality and the story will still be incomplete. In fact you will know no more about the reality than in the first case, when your informant was carried away by his own subjectivity. A human being is not simply a physical form and a collection of words and gestures; he possesses an intangible inner life which emanates from him and spreads out into his surroundings, and if you can neither see nor feel that life how can you describe or explain it? And how can you truly claim to be objective?

An initiate who possesses a knowledge of the different worlds can give you the means to recognize when you have strayed into the misty, unhealthy regions of subjectivity and illusion. But he will also explain to you that the objective world is not confined to that which can be perceived by your five senses and that the information that your five senses gives you, therefore, is incomplete.

He will also give you the means to develop other faculties. He will lead you through and beyond that zone of illusory perceptions into spiritual regions in which you will perceive things as clearly, precisely and accurately as on the physical plane. In this way you will learn to see life as it really is; your vision of things will begin to embrace every aspect and dimension. In this way, when you are called on to explain or describe something, you will be in a position to do so accurately and fully, for you will not allow your own personal reactions to predominate, nor will you confine yourself merely to the husk, the external aspects. There is so much going on above and beyond all that we can see and hear, so much that is never perceptible to us, for we do not possess the more highly perfected eyes or ears or brain needed to perceive any of it. And so we go on – in a tangle of lies and inaccuracies!

And now how would you like it if I proved to you that everything was subjective? For it is you know! If you did not have that subjective life, your psychic life, the life of your thoughts and feelings, what objective reality would there be? None at all. Even the objective world would no longer exist for you. It is entirely thanks to your subjective life that the objective life you are so proud of even exists. Do away with your subjective life and you would have nothing objective any more: you would be dead, and for the dead there is neither subjective nor objective reality; it is all over. For the living, thanks to their subjective life, there is something that we call the objective world. How can a dead man know whether the sun or the stars, the trees or the mountains exist? He is dead. But what must a disciple do? Guided by his instructor he must examine his own inner life, his subjective life, and learn to rise above the murky regions of dust and fog that he finds within himself (for these regions really and truly exist) and climb to the highest peaks of the spiritual mountains, that is to say, to the causal plane. Remember: I have never said that you have to embrace everything that goes on in your inner life.

When I speak of fog, I mean all the cruder emanations of the human heart: emotionalism, sentimentality and sensuality. And when I speak of dust, I mean all the illusions and self-serving fabrications of the intellect. When someone does not work in the right way with his heart his sentimentality and sensuality become exaggerated and produce fog, and this fog obscures his vision. And when he uses his intellect wrongly and tries to probe into too many things, it stirs up a lot of dust which also prevents him from seeing clearly. This is why I say that you have to rise high above the region of fog and dust to the causal plane, the region of high spiritual peaks. On this plane one understands that although there is a lower subjective world in which human beings often lose their way, there is also a higher subjective world in which they can see things clearly, in which they can see truth.

It is the subjective not the objective world which is the origin and cause, the centre of everything. The subjective world comes first and the objective world is simply a screen, a form, a manifestation, a concretization, an emanation of the subjective world. If you don't want to be a prisoner to lies and illusions you must rise to the higher planes of the subjective world. But human beings still have many very false notions about the subjective world, because they do not know that there is a way out, a path by which they can escape from its lower reaches. They need to be enlightened, therefore, and taught to rise to a much higher plane, to the plane where all is light and clarity, to the causal plane. Don't delude yourself that the way to obtain a clear vision of reality is to focus on the objective dimension. No, because that is not where the light is. The only light in the objective world is whatever light you yourself are capable of projecting into it. If you yourself are not capable of illuminating the objective world with the light of your own subjective life, it will never become intelligible to you. The objective world has not been given any light of its own, so if no light falls on it from the subjective dimension it will always be a world of darkness and chaos. If you take refuge in it therefore – as almost everybody does – you will be alienating yourself from light, from life, from the source. Human beings must be freed from all these false notions otherwise they will never find truth.

It is not possible for a human being to be objective; one can only be subjective with a higher or a lower subjectivity. You cannot be objective because the objective world will always be something external, something foreign to you; it is not you. And this means that when somebody says to you, 'For goodness sake, be objective!' it is as though he were saying, 'For goodness sake, stop being you!' It's just not possible. What madness to think that in order to be fully truthful one has to stop being oneself! You cannot not be yourself; you can only be what you are. Is this clear now?

When an initiate describes an event, he describes what he sees – what he sees and others cannot see. Take St John for instance: was he being objective or subjective in his account of his vision in Revelations? Everybody thinks he was being subjective; in other words, he doesn't have to be taken seriously; it's better not to pay too much attention to what he says. Even the Church has been seduced by objectivity and has neglected Revelations. Tell me: what do you think? Was St John being objective or subjective? Did he really see the things he describes? Did they exist on the physical or the spiritual plane? There are some intriguing questions for you!

Why did God create the world? And what is the world? Let me try to make this a little clearer for you by taking an example. Every artist (a painter or sculptor, for instance) needs something material to work on, whether it be a block of marble or some canvas and paint. If he does not have this material he cannot exteriorize what is in him. Creation can be explained in the same way: God created matter in order to mould and fashion it, and in order to create that matter he took something of himself, of his own quintessence, and condensed it. We are told that God created the world out of nothing. The truth is that he drew it from himself and projected it outside himself. And there you have the objective world! The subjective world is God himself and the objective world is the screen on which he projected his own image. And human beings, men and women who have been created in the image of God, simply reproduce God's work on matter, and the results of their work are their children. Everything that happens here below is simply a reflection of what happens above.

God is an artist, a sculptor. He needed some matter with which to model his statuettes and each time he produced something he exclaimed, 'How beautiful it is!' In Genesis Moses says 'And God saw that it was good'. And if anything did not turn out well he destroyed it and began all over again. Don't you like my explanations? Well, if you don't think they are true, you can go and ask him. And the astonishing thing is that he will say, 'Yes, it's quite true; that explanation corresponds to the level of understanding that human beings have reached today. When they have evolved a little further they will be given other explanations.'

God is an artist and he is busy and happy and always at work. When human beings work to fashion and mould matter therefore, they are on the right path because they are doing what God does. But there is one great difference and that is that God never forgets that he is God: he is involved with matter but he never loses himself in it. He knows that he is the cause of all that is and he fashions matter, that is to say the objective world, without losing sight of the fact that everything depends on him, that the essential factor is himself and not matter. Whereas when human beings are involved with matter they get sucked into it; they forget that it is they that are the essential factor, that they possess all things within themselves, that they are divinities.

Human beings must not stop being involved with matter; they must simply understand that there are several different kinds of matter, that beyond the dense, crude matter of the physical world there is another matter that is subtler, more tenuous, crystalline, pure and luminous and that this subtle matter can take on every form and every divine shade of colour that the spirit may wish to lend it. This is the matter of man's inner world and it is on this matter that he must work in order to give it form and colour. In this way in the future all men will be artists, and the world and the whole universe will be peopled with his winged creations. Man will never reach a point where he ceases to be involved with matter, but his consciousness will expand and be enriched to such an extent that his activity, the object of his work, will change: he will continue to work on matter but on celestial, virgin matter of a higher plane.

You will say, 'But this means that you are not opposed to scientists who are wholly concerned with matter! We thought that you were always very angry with them and thought that they should be concerned only with the spirit.' Well, perhaps conditions made it difficult for me to explain my point of view clearly. If someone tried to prevent people from being concerned with matter, from being artists and creators, it would show that he had not understood the first thing about it. If I criticize scholars and scientists it is because most of them are so exclusively concerned with matter that they deny the existence of anything else. There are so many other things they could study, even in the objective world, in the world of matter. For matter exists after all in the etheric and astral worlds too. Do you think that initiates have always confined their work to the spiritual dimension? If that were so how could they have discovered alchemy, astrology and magic? How could they have left us such a vast body of knowledge about animals, crystals and plants? If all they were interested in was the spirit, how could they have explored matter? It is simply that for the initiates the word 'matter' had a much broader, much vaster meaning than for contemporary scientists, who still do not know what it is. As a matter of fact modern scientists have already had a few surprises; all their notions about the nature of matter have been turned upside down and they see it now as a form of energy. But just wait: it will not be long before they make other discoveries that will lead them closer and closer to the notions of the initiates.

The initiates knew much more about matter than today's scientists, but we must not forget that there are different kinds of matter. Don't misunderstand me: there is nothing wrong in studying matter; there is nothing wrong in working with it so as to fashion it and discover all its properties. God does this all the time and all the initiates have done it ever since the creation of the world. And what about me? What do you think I am busy with all day long? With matter. Day and night I work on a matter that is invisible to you, the matter of my own being. I do not work with a matter that is external, foreign to me, but with that which heaven has given to me as my own. Whereas scientists are busy with a matter that is not part of their own being; they will never get much out of it because it does not belong to them. They are wasting their time. Sculptors fashion wood, stone, clay and goodness knows what else, but they never fashion their own matter. Painters paint canvases or walls but never themselves. And chemists mix all kinds of elements in their test-tubes but they never attempt to enter their own inner laboratories for a work of spiritual alchemy. Of course the world will never recognize us as artists or scientists because nobody can see our paintings or statues or our laboratories. But one day everybody will be busy in this way and will understand that all the rest is nothing compared to the work one can do on oneself, on one's own matter. The only thing is that this work requires you to be omniscient: you have to be a mechanic, a chemist, a biologist, an astronomer, a painter, a musician, etc., etc. And as human beings have not got the necessary knowledge they confine their work to the objective dimension which requires very little knowledge. The work of an initiate is far more difficult, but it is a work of total fulfilment.

This work on one's own matter is the work of God. God works on his own matter; – this is why nothing is lacking to him, – he is omniscient and omnipotent. Whereas a human being who works not on himself but on something extraneous is struggling in a vacuum. When he has plenty of money, equipment and weapons he imagines that he is all-powerful. And he is right; he is all-powerful as long as he still has these things. But when he loses them he is terrified to find himself weak, impotent and vulnerable. Yes, because none of those things really belonged to him. Whereas all that an initiate possesses is truly his own. You can take away all his material possessions and he will still feel himself to be luminous, powerful and fulfilled because his wealth, his equipment and his weapons are not external. In reality those whose possessions are all external possess nothing; what they have does not really belong to them. This is the truth. And this is why I pity people like that, because they are so rich in money and arms, but all their wealth is external; they themselves are still weak and indigent. Whereas the initiates understand where true strength lies, and because they understand this they can build up an inner reserve of strength that will always be theirs; no one can take it from them. However much things may change in the world they have understood where their true strength and true wealth lie.

Do you want to convince me that it is those who rely on external achievements that are on the right path? That it is they who understand things correctly? Forgive me, but that makes me laugh: time will show how right or wrong they are. Nothing that they have ever done will belong to them if it was purely external. None of the marvellous machines they have built will remain with them. They are like an old general whose soldiers recognize and salute him when he is in uniform and wearing his medals. But if they saw the skinny, decrepit old man in his bath they would not recognize him and nobody would think of saluting him. Whereas an initiate who has spent his life working at his own inner machines carries them with him wherever he goes.

It is important to have a clear idea of what a true initiate is. Whatever you may hear to the contrary, a true initiate is always on the right path because his spirit, which is divine, is constantly at work on the matter of his own being. initiates are the true artists, the true creators and one day everybody will come and ask to learn from them, because only they possess the truth. They work in the same way as the Lord who works on the matter that he himself created and that is his.

So there you are, my dear brothers and sisters, these are

questions of eternal, vital importance. There is no getting away from that. The truths I have given you today are treasures indeed.

The Bonfin, August 11, 1965

IV

The Whole and the Parts

To be alive is to have a heart full of love; there is no need to look for anything else. Life without love is not life, it is torture. If you neglect or underestimate that state of consciousness that is love you will know nothing but disappointment. It depends entirely on yourself whether you love or not. If you want to love you can do so.

I know that you lack a great many things but I also know that there is a great deal more in your heart and in your soul. It is as though the whole earth, the whole sky, the whole universe belonged to you. You have this sensation and it is this sensation that is reality. It is useless to possess every material advantage if your consciousness is continually tormented. The important thing is to love, for if you love you will be happy whatever your circumstances. But as love counts for nothing in the minds of human beings they are always worried about satisfying all their material needs, and even when they do so they are still unhappy. Whereas look at you: you have no gas, no electricity, no cars, no money, no jewellery, no house nor wife nor husband, and you feel this lack – that is only to be expected – but then why are you all so happy here when you have been listening to some music and singing together? You will say, 'Oh yes, but it's only for a few minutes. That doesn't count!' But what is there to prevent you from stretching those few minutes out and making them last an eternity? Who is stopping you? No one; only your own ignorance, your own lack of light. So the only thing that is really lacking is light; you have everything else you need.

Now more than ever before we have everything we need. In the past it is true men lacked many things, but today even the poorest of the poor have things that the rich never had in the past. What is lacking as I say – and have often said – is light, knowledge and, to a certain extent, will-power.

Can you explain why you are happy now? I can see that from one minute to the next you have become happy. It is when you go back home that you feel unhappy because you no longer remember the power of love; you find yourself back in so-called 'reality'. Does reality always have to be ugly and sad? No; believe me, it depends to a great extent on the way in which you are in the habit of looking at things. Why are some people happy irrespective of their physical and material circumstances? True wealth and glory belong to the inner realm, but human beings are less and less in touch with their own inner realm and it is this that is the cause of all their misery. I know that you don't want to understand me; you say, 'No, no; I really need this or that!' Well, I know that you need things – we all need things – but why not attach greater importance to the power of thought, the power of love and of life? This is what you are doing today; I can see that you are really happy today as though nothing were lacking to you. Even those who were feeling unwell or tense earlier have lost that feeling. It is only later, when their present state fades, that they will remember that they were ill or worried. Until then the only things that count are life, happiness and light.

Henceforth always emphasize this aspect and you will see that whatever the circumstances you will always find a reason to be happy. If your husband abandons you, you will say, 'Oh, but he's not the only one; there are still millions of husbands in the world!' And if you are worn out you will say, 'Well, I'm exhausted today, but that doesn't mean that it has to be the same tomorrow.' It is up to you to know how to use your power of thought in order to transform the situation. Only inanimate objects are fated to submit to their destiny for all eternity. A stone is a stone, and it will never be anything else. A piece of glass will always be a piece of glass. But human beings have an extraordinary range of possibilities. The trouble is that instead of exploring their own terrain and discovering all the possibilities available to them so many people spend their time feeling sorry for themselves and complaining about what they haven't got.

I sometimes listen to people talking on television, so-called great minds, brilliant thinkers – and what nonsense they talk! Oh, to be sure they have an intellect that functions well, but their intellect can only see outward appearances. Everyone is lost in admiration; 'How original; what a profound philosophy!' Yes, it may be very original but it is not the truth. 'But it is so striking, everybody is bowled over by it!' I know, but I still say that it is not the truth. There are a lot of thinkers like that who go about poisoning everybody by propagating ideas which may seem to be true at first sight but which are really very false. And the masses are thrilled: as they have no standards by which to judge they are ready to applaud anything, however idiotic, and this is how false notions spread. Until all thinkers make up their minds to study initiatic science and begin to understand that without the knowledge of certain truths they will never be in a position to reason rightly or to evaluate things correctly, they will never perceive reality, they will never see beyond appearances.

As I was saying yesterday, when you climb to a higher level, that is to say when you get closer to the divine principle, you may no longer see the details, but you see something immense, a vast, coherent unity and this gives you an overall idea of the nature of things. When you descend to the material, physical plane on the other hand, you can see every tiny detail – and this is very interesting, to be sure – but you no longer have the same vision of the whole. Today human beings are only interested in studying matter; the trouble is that when one studies matter one has to limit oneself and concentrate on details.

So there you are: now you can see the difference between the work of scientists and the work of initiates. Initiates, because they want to achieve a view of the whole, to arrive at a synthesis, distance themselves from matter. This is why their understanding of reality is quite different from that of scientists, who have lost sight of the whole and restrict themselves to the parts. As a matter of fact the degree of specialization that exists today is a good indication of the extent to which man has had to limit himself in order to study matter. In medicine for instance there are specialists who only treat ears; others who treat the eyes or the heart, etc. There is nothing wrong with studying the parts, but it is preferable to study the whole. Actually it all depends on your goal: if you want to specialize, of course, you will know everything about one little detail, but you will lose sight of the whole. Whereas if you study the whole, your knowledge of the parts will be limited. Personally I think that, all things considered, it is better to study the whole, for it gives you greater scope: when you see things from above you have a better chance of being in control of the situation and can intervene to put things right. When you have a knowledge of the whole you are closer to truth.

Because of its almost exclusive emphasis on the study of the physical world, of matter, modern science has lost all perception of the universe and of the being who rules that universe. You surely would not think that it was enough to know about your nose or your big toe without knowing anything about the other functions of your body? And yet this is the situation human beings are in today: they are getting further and further away from what is essential, from their Creator, from the world of principles. When they specialize they become inwardly weaker and more material. I don't deny that the path of specialization is useful and even necessary, and that some people have to follow that path, but they should not do so until they have achieved a view of the whole, until they have reached a synthesis. When this is the case, they can concentrate on one little corner of the universe and study it in great detail without running the risk of losing sight of the whole. But if you start to explore in depth only one little part before having studied the whole you will always lack something essential, with the result that your judgement and your reasoning will be false and you will put things into the wrong categories.

The best of all would be to study every domain in detail, one after the other, but we have not got time for that; it would take an eternity. With his method of studying the whole first, an initiate's knowledge of the parts may not be very detailed but at least it will be exact. And if later on he decides to concentrate on a particular subject he will be in a position to study it in far greater depth than a specialist, because his knowledge of the whole will throw light on the one little part that has been isolated from the rest and allow him to see exactly where it belongs. If you are influenced by the philosophy of today you will become specialists and study only toads, or only mosquitoes or mice or butterflies, and you will never know anything of the whole, of immensity, of the life that embraces all that exists. Personally I have never specialized. Well, perhaps I should say that I have specialized a little, because after all I am on earth. I have degrees in psychology and education, but it is not because of my degrees that I know anything about psychology and education. If I know anything about them, if I am something of a psychologist, something of an educator, it is because I chose to study the most important subject of all: life, the life that flows from the source.

Let me give you an image. Suppose you have been given an apple or a pear or some other fruit. That fruit has already been detached from the tree it was growing on, and if you study it carefully you will see that it is very different from one that is still on the tree and in which the sap of life is still flowing. As long as it was attached to the tree it was nourished by the sap that flows into the tree from the whole universe, but when you pluck it, it is no longer the same: it immediately begins to lose its vitality. And the same is true of man: he should be studied while he is still attached to his tree, to the cosmic tree, of which he is the fruit, for it is only then that he is alive, rich, beautiful and radiant. When science studies man as he is today, it is studying a fruit that has already fallen from the tree and is cut off from its life forces; what science sees therefore is not really man, it is his cadaver. You will say, 'Yes, but at least when something is dead you can cut it up and see how it is made. You cannot do that if it is still alive; it would make too much fuss!' Well, that only goes to show that we should find other ways of studying man without cutting him up into little bits, without vivisection; we have to find ways of studying him while he is alive. And such ways exist. When men learn how to use them they will discover all the subtle currents that flow, not only within man's own being, but also between man and the universe. They will discover that this extraordinary current of life is exactly like that which flows between a tree and its fruit, or between a woman and the child in her womb. What a wonderful flow of life between the tree – the mother – and the fruit – the baby! Once the child is born and the umbilical cord is cut this current is interrupted, but another current continues to flow from that other tree to which the mother herself is attached: the one great tree of life, the cosmic tree.

When you are in an aeroplane you can see mountains, rivers and towns laid out below you. But when you are on earth your vision is limited; you can only see a small area with a few trees and a few houses. When you are very high up, therefore, you can see the whole planet, and not only our own planet, but the sun, the stars and the other planets as well. And this is what happens inwardly as well. So which are you going to choose?

If I had chosen to concentrate on only one area of study I would have been accepted by scientists, but as I chose to study the whole, life itself, scientists will never accept me as one of theirs. No, but I shall be counted amongst the initiates, for all initiates have followed the same path and they will recognize me as one of theirs. Actually with you I use both methods: sometimes I look at the parts so as to throw light on some little detail and help you to see it more clearly, and at other times I take you back to the whole. In other words, I use both methods, the scientific method and that of the initiates, alternately. But personally I prefer the second method, that which puts me in contact and makes me one with the whole, for it is then that the currents of energy flow through me. And this is fulfilment.

When I am alone in my room or up in the mountains or looking out at the ocean, why should I dwell on little details? I am looking at immensity and that is what I love: immensity, unity. I need to immerse my soul in the cosmic ocean and drink its waters, to spread my wings. The human soul needs immensity; only in immensity can it be happy and feel free to breathe. It suffocates and feels imprisoned when it is confined to a small space. And this is what has happened to human beings: they have restricted themselves to little things and never have a minute in which to immerse themselves in immensity and find fulfilment. They cannot spare the time apparently! Yes, and it is precisely this that makes everybody so tired: all those little things in which they lose themselves. It is true, of course, that limitation is necessary. The birth of a child is a limitation, a limitation that is accepted in order to permit manifestation. Man has to limit himself when he descends into matter, and then at the moment of death he returns to unity, to the realm of immensity. Life is made up of these two processes and your happiness depends on your learning to apply them to your life: you enter into your inner realm and put yourself in touch with the vastness of the universe, with the universal soul, and then you limit yourself again in order to carry on your work amongst human beings. But don't stay there too long otherwise you will be bored and unhappy. Turn back to the higher planes and plunge into the cosmic ocean once again. If human beings are always unhappy and have a feeling of emptiness and despair, it is because they don't know how to use this method of alternation.

We need both: the immensity of the whole and the details of the parts. Human beings neglect immensity because in their opinion it is too vague and indefinite. But I think that you will find more light in this 'vagueness' than if you confined yourself to details, for when you do this the whole slips out of focus and you lose sight of it. People think that it is in the details that they will find the light, the precision, they are looking for, but this is an illusion: you will find far more light in what is 'vague and indistinct'. This is something that you still need to prove for yourselves, but I have experienced it so often. Yes, how often I have been amazed to see that it was in this region, which is thought to be so inexact and indefinite, that one finds light and strength and joy; whereas there is no light in what is precise. Yes, this is very obvious to me; I cannot help but see it.

Sèvres, January 2, 1969

V

The Two Faces of Truth:
i
Good and evil

One must never focus exclusively on one aspect of reality, otherwise one will never grasp the whole truth – and this even applies to evil. Truth is a medal of which one face is good and the other evil. This is why the great initiates are not content to know good; they must also know evil, and for this purpose they visit the depths of hell. To be sure, before doing this they take the necessary precautions; they make sure that they are well armed, and once their protection is assured, they descend into hell to study its regions and its inhabitants. The dictum, 'Know, will, dare and hold your peace', was addressed to initiates and, as I have already told you, it is the word 'dare' that is the most mysterious. Yes, because 'to dare' means to dare to venture into hell in order to see, understand, know and conquer. And then one must hold one's peace; one must never speak of hell to those who are not capable of confronting it, otherwise it would destroy them.

Never forget, therefore, that truth always has two sides: the pure and the impure, the light and the dark, and that true knowledge must embrace both. Obviously, if you are weak and ignorant, it would be unwise to go and explore hell; I certainly don't advise you to attempt it. I am simply saying that the great initiates are those who have been capable of confronting hell, because in this way all knowledge was theirs.

The Bonfin, July 31, 1970

The Two Faces of Truth:

ii

Love and Wisdom

Truth is a medal, one side of which is love and the other wisdom. If you seek truth without love and wisdom you won't find it. On the other hand, as soon as you possess love and wisdom you will also possess truth, whether you seek it or not.

To the extent to which you possess love and wisdom you dwell in truth. No one can possess truth without the aid of the intellect and the heart. If you have neither thoughts nor feelings you are dead – and the dead cannot know truth. Except of course those of the dead who are more alive than the living; those who have departed for the other world in order to live more fully and who are now able to see all the dimensions of reality. How many people are dumbfounded when they get to the other side and look back at their family and friends! It is not worth trying to describe what they see, you can imagine it for yourselves. They even see that our teaching is truly extraordinary, and that is something that they were incapable of understanding while they were on earth.

You will be wondering how it is possible for human beings to know truth when they are dead if love and wisdom are necessary, for the dead are incapable of feeling love or of manifesting wisdom. The fact is that they have more love and wisdom than when they were on earth, for death frees man from the physical body, which maintained him in a state of ignorance and prevented him from seeing and understanding. This is why human beings suffer so terribly on the other side. When they are deprived of their protective shell they suffer far more, unless of course they have lived wisely and well on earth and have cause to rejoice on the other side. But if they have lived stupidly they will suffer, for now that they are more lucid and sensitive the least little thing makes them suffer atrociously. This is what we call hell. Hell is simply a state that we prepare for ourselves while we are on earth but which we cannot feel because our sensitivity is dulled by our physical body. You could say that hell is a soup that we have prepared but never tasted! And when we get to the other side and have to taste it, we find it horrible. The laws are the same for hell as for heaven. Here in the Brotherhood you are preparing your own heaven, but as you can neither taste nor see nor feel nor hear it, you say that you are accomplishing nothing; you are wrestling with the wind. But that is not so; it is simply that you cannot see or feel any of it yet.

So this is what truth is: love and wisdom. Never forget that you cannot find truth as something distinct and apart. Just think: how could you conceive of truth if you had neither a heart nor a mind? To the extent to which you possess love and understanding, to that extent will the world show you truth, for truth is limitless. Many books have been written about truth, but no one has ever understood it in this way before. It is always treated as though it were a world apart, whereas in reality one cannot conceive of the world of truth without reference to the heart and the intellect. To the extent to which you have a heart and an intellect, truth exists for you. And if your heart and intellect are not in order you will never know the higher levels of truth. As a matter of fact, if human beings profess so many different and contradictory truths today it is because these different truths reflect the distortion of their hearts and minds. Someone will say, 'For me, the truth is this or that ...' In fact what he sees to be 'the' truth is only 'his' truth and it speaks of his heart and mind, which may be inadequate or deformed or, on the contrary, very exalted. This explains how although there is only one truth each person can have 'his' truth.

If truth had nothing to do with the heart and the mind we would expect everybody to discover the same truth. And this as you very well know is not the case. Everybody discovers different truths; everybody, that is, with the exception of those who possess true love and true intelligence: they have all discovered the same truth, and this is why they all speak the same language. From the beginning of creation to the end, truth will always be the same, for God has placed truth in the heart and the intellect, the soul and the spirit, and if men develop these principles harmoniously they will be obliged to agree on the same truth. And this is also true for tastes. Why do some things give pleasure to some people and cause pain to others? If they were all built on the same pattern according to the same truth, shouldn't they all have the same tastes? But the tastes, ideas and beliefs of human beings are becoming more and more depraved; before long they will not have a single truth in common. Some love beauty and others ugliness; some love light and others darkness. There are even creatures who are so deformed that they end by considering that lies are truth. Yes, for the creatures of hell, lies and falsehood are truth.

It all depends, therefore, on the harmonious development of a person's heart and mind and, on a higher level, of his soul and spirit. To the extent to which they are warped or deformed he will deviate from the truth. He may write books to express his point of view, he may win many followers, and of course he will be entirely sincere, but he will not be truthful, for on the subject of light, love, purity, morality, God, justice and freedom, there are not several different points of view, several truths, but only one. It is not only here on the physical plane, but also on the spiritual plane that there is an Office of Weights and Measures that can tell you whether you conform to the norm or whether you have deviated from the model created by God in the beginning.

It is because men wanted to be free that they strayed away from the source and accepted slavery and falsehood. And now in an attempt to justify their aberration they say that there is no accounting for tastes. They even say it in Latin thinking that that makes it all the more profound and 'philosophical': '*De gustibus et coloribus non disputandum.*' Which simply means, of course, that everyone has his own form of folly and has the right to indulge every whim dictated by his folly, however depraved. No, this is false: there is a norm to which our tastes should conform: the good and the beautiful must be good and beautiful for everyone. It is only in what concerns the quantity that we are free to choose, not in what concerns the quality. We must always choose what is pure, luminous and divine. There are so many angels and archangels, for example, that no one will question your choice of one angel rather than another, and you can spend as much time with him as you please. But if you choose a demon you will be blamed for it.

And now if you have understood what I have been saying you are in a position to analyse yourselves: 'Let me see, now: how do I feel things in my heart? Is it true love? And how does my mind envisage things? Is there anything that has slipped in and that is leading me into error?' I can see that you have still not fully understood all the advantages of truthfulness. You think that you can get along perfectly well without the truth. But don't you see that if you live in truth you will be free? Truth sets us free. Jesus said this: 'The truth shall make you free'. Nothing else can set us free. Not even love; not even wisdom. You can have a great deal of love and still not be free – in fact you may well be even more tightly bound. And if you have a great deal of wisdom you may well become very proud – and that is not a liberation either. It is only with love and wisdom together that you will possess truth, and it is truth that will make you free.

And now, just in case you are wondering, let me tell you that it was not I who invented these criteria; it is cosmic intelligence that shows me how it sees and understands things. It would not be enough for me to suppose that I had found the truth for myself. Any madman can do as much; in fact he will be even more convinced than others that he is right. We always have to test the accuracy of our opinions and I know how to do this and just where to go in nature to do it. Only when nature tells me that it approves do I accept something as true. If nature says that something is not true, then I reject it; I never accept anything as true without verification.

One day I was invited to the home of someone who was an engineer and a very intelligent man. He took me into several rooms and showed me a lot of his own paintings which covered the walls. They were very interesting geometrical designs, and according to him they all had some esoteric meaning. I asked him what this or that one represented and his answers astounded me: one of them was supposed to represent such and such an event, another such and such a force of nature, the next such and such a cosmic swirling, and so on. I was astounded, as I say, because the paintings simply did not correspond to what he said. I asked him, 'But have you ever checked with nature to see if this is true?' 'What do you mean – if it's true? – Isn't it enough that I see it that way?' 'No', I told him, 'That is not enough. We can see many things that are not necessarily true. You have to check with nature and find out whether the reality of the mineral, vegetable and animal kingdoms, the reality of human nature, and even of the stars, confirms your theories. If nature endorses your view of things, then sooner or later everyone will be obliged to accept it, because what you say will be backed up by nature. But if nature does not agree with your theories, even if for the time being the whole world accepts them, sooner or later they will lose all credibility because they are not backed up by nature.' Most human beings consider that whatever enters their head is true. But a great many things enter my head too, and I am not so easily persuaded that they are true. I put them to the test, and if I find that nature has a different opinion, then out they go! If I thought that everything that entered my head was the absolute truth, I ask you: – where would I be today? And you must do as I do: learn to check all your opinions against the reality of nature.

Sèvres, February 1, 1970

Chapter Ten

FREEDOM

I

The Laws of Destiny

We have always been told that the ways of God are inscrutable. And this means that although a person's destiny may seem to all appearances to be extremely unfortunate, we can never tell where events will lead him. You can never foresee the final outcome of your marriage to a particular man or woman, of your decision to practise a particular profession or to live in a particular town, nor of the fact that you suffer from a particular illness. Even if your marriage is not a success, even if illness confines you to your bed for months on end, it may be that your destiny is taking these apparently roundabout ways to lead you to what is best for you. You cannot tell until it is all over! So many brothers and sisters have told me, 'Something terrible happened in my life several months ago and to begin with I was in despair, but it was thanks to that terrible event that I discovered the teaching'. This is how, by its own inscrutable ways, the invisible world led them to the light.

Even an initiate cannot always see the reason for the events of his life, because even an initiate does not arrive in this world in full possession of all knowledge. It may be years and years before he understands why he was born into a family that is so undistinguished or in a country that is almost unknown, for instance, or why he has so few of the talents and capacities that others seem to have, and to realize that behind all these circumstances there was a hidden wisdom. Perhaps, when it deprived him of certain favourable conditions or capacities heaven had a special destiny, a special kind of development in mind for him. Otherwise he would have followed the beaten path and lost his way in pursuit of goals that may be glorious from an earthly point of view but that are not at all glorious from heaven's point of view.

Suppose that, just when a being is about to reincarnate, he is asked if he would be willing to undertake a unique and very exalted mission on earth which could only be accomplished at the cost of terrible tribulations. He would have to be willing to be despised, defamed and disgraced, for only in that way would he eventually succeed in carrying out his mission. And suppose that, in spite of the prospect of all the suffering involved, he accepts the mission, because the only thing that matters to him is the goal; nothing else counts. Then when he reincarnates the Lords of Destiny wipe out his memory of the past, and he remembers nothing about the difficulties he will have to experience nor the reason why. He is like any other human being and he suffers until he realizes that heaven has used him to achieve a glorious task. If he had not gone through so much he would never have accomplished anything worth while – like so many others, he would have suffered in vain. Of course not everybody can say that his trials or his failings and inadequacies are due to the exalted role for which he is destined. Such cases are extremely rare and are confined to great initiates. Most human beings are simply receiving the tribulations they deserve. The important thing is to remember, when you are tempted to judge the destiny of others, that there is always a danger that some vital element will escape you.

Also, even the greatest clairvoyants can never foretell the future with absolute certainty, because human beings possess free will and the higher their degree of evolution, the greater the role of their free will. For inferior beings it is possible to foretell the future with certainty, but not for highly evolved beings, for they have the means to foil certain prophecies.

I can see that what I have just said about initiates requires a little more explanation. Once a human being has succeeded in freeing himself completely and has no more debts to pay, he is not obliged to reincarnate again; he can remain in the light and bliss of the world above; he has no more obligations on earth. Sometimes, however, amongst all those who have achieved this freedom there will be one who is moved by the suffering of human beings and, making up his mind to help them, he will go and present his case before the twenty-four Elders and ask to be allowed to return to earth. Then the twenty-four Elders deliberate and decide to take advantage of this extraordinary occurrence: a human being who wishes to sacrifice himself, and as they are the expression of the inscrutable wisdom of the Lord, they plan the most terrible and at the same time the most marvellous course of events for his life on earth. Before he actually reincarnates they will show him, as it were, a film of the life they have planned for him, with all the sufferings and difficulties he will have to endure, and will ask him if he accepts it. And of course he accepts.

It is almost as though many of those who had finished their evolution were a little tired of all that happiness and joy and light. Even some of the greatest initiates who have ever incarnated are unable to wipe out all memory of their experience or to sever the ties that bind them to the earth. They are free; they have emerged victorious; they live in eternity; and yet, from time to time, they feel the desire to be in touch once again with those poor human beings with whom they once lived and to whom, in spite of the great distance between them, they still feel bound. After hundreds, and even thousands of years, they still remember, and out of the abundance and generosity of their hearts they determine to share some of their treasures with human beings. But once they are on earth they cannot remember where they came from or why they are there. It is all wiped from their memory, because if they remembered and knew what they were going to have to live through, it might complicate things. It is only much later, if they really do have a special mission to accomplish, that it will be revealed to them. Until then they know nothing about it. Does that astonish you? Like you, I used to think that the invisible world revealed an initiate's mission to him from the start and showed him exactly what he had to do, and why, and how. No, unfortunately – or fortunately – this is not so.

As I have just said we must not be too categorical, therefore, in our predictions about the fate of individuals. It is not the same where a collectivity, a whole nation, is concerned: if heaven has ordained grave events for a country it is extremely rare that they should not occur, but individuals have a certain amount of freedom; they are more likely than a collectivity to be able to avoid certain events. You can foresee a war, for instance, but it is more difficult to foresee with absolute certainty that such or such an individual will be killed in that war. The war will happen – that you may be sure of – but you cannot tell exactly who will be killed. An individual always has a slight chance of escaping a particular destiny.

I have often spoken to you about the case of Jesus who was destined to be betrayed by one of his disciples. Although the decree was issued thousands of years before, the identity of his betrayer had never been mentioned. There was a part for a traitor and it was Judas Iscariot who acted the part. If he had not been ready to do so someone else would have come forward. You cannot eliminate the roles in a play by Shakespeare or Molière, for instance; there will always be a Falstaff and a Harpagon, but it is not known in advance which actor will play the part. He will be chosen according to his merits when the time comes.

Even Nostradamus never designated a particular person in his prophecies. You will say, 'But he does give names, or at least suggests them'. True, he gives some names, but the beings who were to bear those names are not identified. You cannot take someone, Judas for instance, and keep him bottled up for five hundred or two thousand years until it is time for him to play his part. That is not how things happen, for each individual is free to evolve. It was decreed, for example, that Henry IV of France should be assassinated. But the assassin was not identified nor, for that matter, was the entity who was to play the part of Henry IV. Only as the beings concerned gradually evolved did they become suitable for these roles.

The Lord has never forced any human being to play a particular role, for that would mean that he did not allow him freedom of choice. Human beings are free to decide which way they want to go: they can advance or they can regress; they can become monsters and murderers, or they can become sages and initiates.

The Lord has his plan of evolution. You can compare it, if you like, to a play. In order for mankind to evolve, certain events have to take place and these events involve certain individual roles for which actors have to be found. But it has never been decided who should play such and such a role. There are palaces and there are prisons, and it is up to each one of you to decide which you want to live in.

So, as I say, the Lord has written a play which is going to take billions of years to enact. The actors come and go on the stage. They make war, they make peace; they build up and they tear down. And it is true that some of the roles are determined thousands of years in advance, but human beings have not yet arrived at the finale. Sometimes the same actors come back and sometimes new ones. Yes, the life of the cosmos is a play written by God. In fact it was also God who created the actors, but he created them with the freedom to play whichever part they chose. As I have said, the role of Judas, for example, was not written for a particular actor. There had to be a Judas who would betray Jesus (in the world of traitors there were certainly several who were preparing to play the part) and he who was attracted by this part was he who had the greatest natural affinity for it. If God determined the destiny of all his creatures there would be no freedom nor would there be any responsibility. How much responsibility does a machine or a robot have? And if man were not responsible how could he be condemned? It would be neither intelligent nor just.

The amount of freedom you have depends on your degree of evolution. If you are at the bottom of the scale you can have no freedom at all. Are animals free? Are plants or stones or insects free? Even amongst human beings there are many who are not free: they are driven, influenced and ruled by others; it is not they who make the decisions. In order to be free one has to lift oneself up to the level of God, for it is only there, at the summit, that one is free; nowhere else. Only the Lord is free. None of his creatures are free, even the archangels: they are immersed in the soul of the Lord and are under his influence. You could say that they are free with the freedom of God but they are not free from God. Only the Lord himself is totally free and, to the extent that a creature is close to God, it can be free with the freedom of God, but that is all. And one of the freedoms man has is the freedom to perfect himself or, on the contrary, to degenerate; to take the path of heaven or of hell.

The ups and downs that human beings, the solar system, and even the entire cosmos, are destined to encounter are pre-determined. They are part of a plan that has already been decided and we can do nothing to alter that. You could think of the destiny of the world as an ocean voyage: you cannot change its course or the ports of call that have been decided in advance; nor can you leave the ship without finding yourself in the water. But you can decide how you are going to use your time on board: you can read, you can chat with a pretty girl, you can go to sleep in your cabin or you can go up on deck and look at the sea, etc. We are all together in the same ship whose route has been planned by the Lord himself, and no one can change any of it. Can you imagine what would happen if we could? All the Lord's plans would be devastated! We can all do whatever we like with ourselves; we can destroy ourselves or we can perfect ourselves; but we cannot change the ship's course. It is not true therefore, as the Church once taught, that some people are predestined from all eternity to be damned while others are predestined to be saved. What a stupid thing to believe! The truth is that human beings are free to choose whether they want to be damned or saved.

Sèvres, January 17, 1971

II

True Freedom is a Consecration

Those who think that freedom consists in being totally independent of everything and everyone do not realize the extreme danger of this attitude: if they have nothing to fill their minds, souls and spirits, it means that they are full of gaps, and all the spirits of darkness, all the negative, demonic entities roaming in search of shelter, find those gaps and slip into them. When they seek this kind of freedom men and women become totally submerged by other forces of which they know nothing. I have so often seen this! The devil soon finds work for those whose minds are not already occupied by a divine, sublime ideal: he urges them on to all kinds of follies and wild adventures. Yes, simply because they are 'free'! The only way to be free and safe at the same time is to be occupied, engaged, inhabited by heaven, for there is no such thing as a vacuum. This is why you must hurry to be free no longer and make yourself available to heavenly forces so that you may be filled with heavenly blessings. It is in their commitment, their submission to heaven, that the initiates find freedom, for the forces of heaven never use coercion or constraint; on the contrary, they only help to organize, harmonize and embellish your life. If you want everything to go well, therefore, it is to your advantage not to be free.

Human beings are on the dividing line between two worlds: a sublime world of harmony and light and a world of chaos and darkness. These two worlds wage war with each other in and through us, and because of our ignorance we allow the world of darkness to infiltrate our defences and set up camp within us. This is why we are always unhappy, always torn this way and that. The solution to the problem of freedom, therefore, lies in a proper understanding of two processes: advance and withdrawal.

As you see my dear brothers and sisters, everything else is easy to understand, but in order to understand and realize freedom we have to be in an initiatic school. Human beings value freedom so highly that they are willing to fight for it. They love freedom more than their lives; they are ready to sacrifice themselves, to die for freedom, and yet unfortunately they still don't really understand what it is. No one wants to be subjugated by a foreign country, that is only natural, but what if that country were heaven? Would it not be better to be invaded and ruled by a country that is so intelligent? Look at what happens in so many instances: a country struggles to free itself from the domination of a foreign power and as soon as it succeeds, its own supposedly free citizens start to dominate and subjugate each other and massacre their rivals! It is perfectly legitimate for a country to seek independence, but that is not enough.

Freedom is something that concerns the inner life. You can be outwardly free and still inwardly a slave, and vice versa. You know the story of the Stoic philosopher Epictetus who had been taken in slavery to Rome. One day when his master was torturing him by twisting his leg he calmly said, 'If you go on doing that it will break', and of course that is exactly what happened. Whereupon Epictetus remarked, 'Didn't I tell you so?' Epictetus was a slave but he was inwardly free; it was his master who was the slave.

When an initiate wants to consecrate an object by projecting forces into it, he starts by exorcizing and purifying it of any negative influences. This is because those who have handled it and the events in which it has been involved may have left fluidic layers of impure, opaque matter on it and that matter can be a barrier, an obstacle, that would prevent his magic thought from impregnating it. Only after the object has been exorcized by the use of suitable formulas and the burning of incense, therefore, will the initiate consecrate it to an entity, a principle or a virtue. In this way it is set apart and steeped in good influences and evil spirits cannot get in or use it for their own ends. It is as though it were protected by a sign: 'Private Property. Keep Out!'

Freedom

There are certain laws and interdictions in nature which even evil spirits recognize and respect. They know that if they go beyond certain limits they will be punished. But naturally, when the way is wide open to them, even God himself will not forbid them to enter in search of food, nor prevent them from ransacking and befouling everything. They are within their rights; the door was open. Some Christians wonder why God allows evil spirits to get into them. What a stupid question! If they do nothing to defend themselves why should God defend them? There are laws and rules in this respect and you must know them. If there were no fence round your orchard to keep people out, would you be surprised to find that it had been looted? Of course not! And if you appealed to a court of law you would be told that you should have put up a fence to show that it was private property. If there was no fence the law can do nothing about it.

So there it is: everybody wants to be free, free, free – but free from what? Free from whom? Free from instructors who would teach them wisdom! Free from the Lord! Free from heaven! But in that case they are at the disposal of the powers of hell, who waste no time in filling them with all kinds of insane, criminal ideas. They are surrounded by hostile forces just waiting to lead them astray and amuse themselves at their expense; and in the end their reward is illness and suffering. All these so-called 'free' people have a great emptiness inside them and, of course, evil thoughts and feelings, and the evil entities that prowl round them recognize this and enter them in search of food. Like wild animals they need to eat, and they fall upon the first victim available; anyone who cannot defend himself is immediately devoured. Every creature, everything that exists, needs nourishment, and evil entities are no exception: they will devour anything they can. Look at microbes, bacilli and viruses: the law is the same on every level.

If someone does not have the sense to defend himself he will be invaded by negative forces and then he will lament and wail and wring his hands in despair – and never understand what has happened to him or why! And yet, isn't it easy to understand? He has been too gullible; he did not realize that he should not leave

217

himself empty and exposed, his doors and windows wide open to all the ne'er-do-wells of the invisible world who feed on human beings. The thousands who fill the psychiatric clinics and hospitals of the world are ignorant men and women who failed to guard against negative forces and never realized that their very freedom would be their downfall. What do hunters do? They take their guns and their dogs and go out to shoot birds or animals which they then eat or sell or stuff in order to show off in front of others. Well, that is exactly what these mischievous entities of the invisible world do: they go hunting for some tasty human game and when they catch some they eat it! So you must be occupied, inhabited, committed, but by heaven and the angels and archangels. It is your submission to these sublime powers that makes you absolutely free, because they will never despoil you. On the contrary, as they are rich, intelligent and full of beauty and light, they bring all that wealth and splendour with them and share them with you. It is far better, therefore, to be occupied, engaged and consecrated than to be stupidly 'free'. True freedom consists in not being free!

How many boys and girls want to be free to 'live their own lives!' But what kind of lives will they live if they have neither knowledge nor learning, neither light nor will-power? They will live like animals: eating and quarrelling, laughing and crying in turns. That is what it means to 'live your own life.' You must not delude yourself that you are free just because you can do what you please and go wherever you like without a master to guide and advise you. If you do not consecrate your life to heaven, freedom is simply a form of slavery.

What I have just explained to you about exorcism and the consecration of an object is of immeasurable importance in understanding this question of freedom. If you learn to apply it to yourself you can surround and protect yourself by a magic circle of light. Heavenly spirits will be attracted by the light of your aura and will come and guard you and keep all unwelcome visitors away. But you must work, you must be occupied! Look at what happens to people when they retire: they suddenly start to age much more rapidly. I have nothing against retirement, but you must take advantage of your retirement to do another kind of work, a gigantic spiritual work. If you do that you will be sustained and revivified, and find yourself getting younger again!

If you start to look at things in this way you will free yourself from your enslavement. Every time you obey an inferior desire you are a slave; and the world is full of slaves. Human beings seem to be free but, in reality, they only act in obedience to an inner tyrant. A true initiate is free of all desire except the desire to serve, help, enlighten, support and encourage others. But there; I know you cannot really understand this: you cannot have even the dimmest notion of that state of freedom. You are forever driven, dispossessed, tossed to and fro by others, and you think that you can excuse all your faults and follies by saying, 'I couldn't help it!' When someone says that it is obvious that he is already a slave; he is at the mercy of someone or something other than himself. A free man would never say, 'I couldn't help it'. It is an admission of defeat; it is as though his visiting card bore the inscription: Mr. So-and-so, Slave! You will object, 'No; my visiting card shows that I'm Chairman of this and Director of that ...'. Yes? Well, that is possible, but what I read is something quite different. Is it my fault if I have been so conditioned by my work that I can always read between – or behind – the lines?

Every day you should say, 'Lord God, accept me as your servant, I am yours to do what you like with; guide me, work through me for the fulfilment of all your plans'. Obviously you will not notice any fantastic results in the first few days. But in the long run you will feel so powerfully guided, sustained and protected, so full of light and joy, that words will be powerless to describe it! So there you are: never be free! Don't delay: hurry to give up your own little freedom and implore heaven to come and take possession of you at once.

This is one of the greatest secrets of initiation!

Sèvres, December 31, 1975

III

Liberation Through Death
Fate and Freedom

Ah, today we can see that spring is on the way! 'What? With all that snow?' you will say. Why yes! The snow is there to announce the coming of spring. If there were no snow there would be no spring later. The snow is a promise of spring. Think about it and you will see how true this is: a present grief is a promise of a happiness to come; a failure announces a future success. How can you hope for success if you have never had any failures to teach you where your weaknesses lie? In fact I'll go even further and say that death is a promise of life, but of a different kind of life, of course. Besides if you are really too unhappy, if you have no hope of being cured or are condemned to poverty for the rest of your life, if there is really no way for you to get what you want, death is always a solution. You will say that no one has ever suggested to you that death was a solution. That is quite possible, but nature sees it as a solution. Nature tells you, 'My child, if nothing is going right any more, there is only one solution; the one that I have found. You must leave this world. There is neither hunger nor thirst nor suffering on the other side!'. Why are people so afraid of death? Nature is not afraid of death; she has been using this solution for billions of years.

Human beings do everything in their power to avoid death; in fact they consider people who accept death easily to be underdeveloped or barely civilized. Yes, western culture and education encourage people to find every possible means to combat death and they cannot understand why Orientals are so serene in the face of it. For them this tranquil acceptance of death is the mark of the primitive, uncivilized man. You will object that what I am saying will provoke an epidemic of suicides. No, not at all. I am not urging anyone to commit suicide; on the contrary, I am simply saying that if there is really no hope of curing people with medicines or surgery, why try to keep them alive, in spite of dreadful pain and suffering, instead of letting them die in peace? Why not accept the idea of death more readily? Why try to cling to life at all costs? Death is there in order to solve a great many problems. A lot of people have noticed this but, unfortunately, not always in the right way. When a man who is up to his eyes in debt and is being pursued by his creditors escapes from them by taking his own life, there is nothing they can do about it. They cannot follow him and continue to dun him in the next world. Unfortunately, however, the problem is not so easily solved. If you have not settled a certain number of questions before leaving this world, you will be pursued by them in the next. Death cannot solve every problem; it is a genuine liberation only when one has no more unfinished business on earth.

Generally speaking people cling to life on earth because they do not know that there is another, better, kind of life elsewhere; they are ready to commit every kind of crime to ensure their survival in this world. In this way they pile up countless debts, and some day they are going to have to honour those debts. But a disciple sees things quite differently. He says to himself: 'Life on earth is a drudgery. We are hemmed in and limited, trodden underfoot, tormented and abused in every way. I know, of course, that there is a good reason for all this but, one day, when I have paid all my debts, I shall live in the freedom of limitless space.' This is the truth, and it is because disciples know this that, in spite of the certainty that they would be much better off on the other side, they are not in a desperate hurry to leave. As long as they have still not settled all their problems and finished the work which heaven has assigned to them, they are not too concerned about the rest. Their minds are not obsessed with death or anything else; they are only concerned with doing the work they have been sent to do. But once it is done they have no desire to linger; they know that the earth is not worth clinging to.

When an ordinary human being comes to earth he is only interested in taking advantage of everything available: he eats and drinks and pursues pleasure, or fights tooth and nail to carve out a place for himself in the world. But a disciple of an initiatic teaching is only interested in doing the work for which heaven sent him. He does not bother about finding the means to prolong his life on earth; he knows that to do so would be to deprive himself of the freedom that will be his in the next world. We only have to look at our physical bodies to recognize that, even though they can be harmonized and purified to the point of vibrating divinely, they will never be other than matter taken from the earth and, as such, will always impose limitations on us. Repeat to yourselves, therefore, every single day: 'I must do my work. My work is the only thing that counts. It is my spiritual, divine work that is important; the only work worth doing.' In this way you will begin to feel free of all the agitation and distress around you; you will become a channel, a conductor for other currents and forces, for other lights and other entities, and you will begin to understand the meaning of life. The important thing is to raise your level of consciousness, and then all at once all kinds of dark, noxious elements will leave you, because they will no longer find in you the food and shelter they need. Even the fear of death will leave you.

Death has been portrayed in fearsome forms and colours, and in reality none of that is true. Death is a liberation. Yes, but not for all and sundry, of course; only for an initiate. For an initiate it is a change of address, a change of circumstances. When an initiate dies he is going to a royal welcome, to his crowning. Death is linked to life just as life is linked to death. At the very instant that a baby is born on earth, death dwells in him and begins its work of disintegration. The best understanding of this mystery of life and death is given to us in that phrase from the Gospel: 'Except you die you shall not live.' This can be applied to the physical plane, of course, but it applies most particularly to the spiritual plane. If you do not die to all that is dark, unjust and ignoble, you cannot live to all that is meaningful, ordered and luminous. These words show us how strongly death is bound to life. To obtain life we have to touch death; in one way or another life and death always walk hand in hand. And the snow speaks to us of spring! What a deeply philosophical, initiatic question the snow has led to. But this is always the way for me: the smallest things contain the greatest initiatic, philosophical and scientific truths.

From now on, therefore, you must get this question of life and death in proper perspective: you must not be afraid of dying. The only thing you need be afraid of is being prevented from finishing your work. That attitude changes everything and gives you the right to ask heaven for the right conditions and the time and skill you need to bring your work to a fitting conclusion. But you must never pray for your life to be prolonged simply in order to go on enjoying money and pleasure.

As I said, as soon as a child comes into the world death gets a foothold in him and begins watching and waiting, determined never to let him out of its sight, and sooner or later it will take possession of him. And it is when he dies that life triumphs. Yes, life and freedom. 'I chose freedom!' Only the dead can say that; not the living. The freedom of the living is too often a bondage. Outwardly they are free but inwardly they are enslaved, because the thoughts and feelings that pursue them deprive them of all freedom. True freedom can only be understood in an initiatic school in which we learn that it must not be sought only on the physical plane. A great many people are free on the physical plane; they can go anywhere and do whatever they want, but they are not inwardly free; their bonds are too many and too strong. How can you talk of freedom in these conditions? It is out of the question! Freedom must be seen as an inner state created by one's thoughts and feelings. It is highly desirable to be physically free also, but physical freedom must never take priority over inner freedom, for physical freedom can shackle you and trip you up. You cannot be free if you are not inwardly enlightened, and external freedom alone gives you plenty of opportunities to make mistakes. How often we see this! People learn, for instance, that they are going to have an accident so they try to avoid it by going a different way; and it is precisely there that the accident is waiting for them! As long as you do not enjoy inner light and freedom you are always in danger of falling into a trap.

Let me tell you a story that I heard in India. There was once a very rich man who had the gift of understanding the language of animals. One evening he heard his dog talking to another dog who had come to invite him to go for a walk. 'No', said his dog, 'I have to stay with my master; his house is going to burn down tonight and I can't leave him alone'. The dog's master was very astonished to hear this and told himself that, of course, he should not take it seriously. But he still decided to take everything of value out of his house and to get some fire-fighting equipment ready, just to be on the safe side! And, sure enough, a fire broke out in the night and, thanks to the precautions he had taken, it did not do much damage. Not long after this the man overheard another conversation between the two dogs. His dog was saying, 'No, I can't go with you. I have learned that there are some jackals and hyenas coming to attack the sheep-fold tonight. I must stay and protect the animals.' Once again the dog's master took the necessary precautions and put all but one sick ewe away in a safe place so that when the hyenas and jackals invaded the sheep-fold they found only the one sick ewe. As you can imagine the man was very glad to have such a clairvoyant dog. Some weeks went by, and once again he overheard a conversation between the two dogs. 'No', his dog was saying, 'I can't come with you tonight; my master is going to die. I must stay and watch over him.' The other dog asked in surprise, 'But why does he have to die? Can't you do anything to prevent it?' 'No; there's no way out', replied the man's dog. 'He has got to die because he has never sacrificed anything. He has used his knowledge to avoid the losses he was supposed to incur. If he had been ready to accept certain inconveniences in the past, his life would not be in danger today; but he has always refused and now he has got to die.' These oriental notions will certainly seem very bizarre to you but there is a very profound lesson in this story, and it is that we must be ready to accept certain sufferings or the loss of certain things in order to gain other things. Those who are incapable of sacrificing anything can never gain anything in exchange.

The question of destiny – the problem of whether man is free or bound to a predetermined fate – has been hotly debated for hundreds and hundreds of years but I have never heard anyone who had the right ideas on the subject. The great mistake is to believe that all human beings without exception are subject to the same laws. Obviously, if human beings are like animals and obey only their sensations and passions and their purely instinctive impulses, they come under the rule of fate and their lives will adhere strictly to the pattern written in the stars. But those who are much more highly evolved escape the clutches of fate and enter the realm of providence and grace, in which reign light and liberty. The great spiritual masters of mankind belong to this second category, but most men drift about in an intermediate zone, somewhere between animals and divinities; in some areas they are bound, in others they are free. It would be equally mistaken to think that everyone was totally free or that everyone was subject to an implacable fate. No, the truth is that freedom depends on a person's degree of evolution. It is man's way of thinking, feeling and behaving that determines his position in relation to fate on one end of the scale, and providence on the other. Until he attains total freedom, therefore, he will continue to be subject to the law of karma in some areas of his life, whilst he will be free in others. There – quite simply and clearly – that is the truth of the matter.

All sorts of different philosophies of freedom circulate today, and men are really persuaded that they are free. They know nothing about the pattern on which the universe is built or about the cosmic forces which surround and influence them. They imagine that when they decide on a course of action they are free to choose and make up their own minds; it never occurs to them that they are pawns in the hands of forces they know nothing about and to which they owe obedience. Even astrologers are constantly perplexed by the question of human liberty. In ancient times astrologers used to say that the stars influence but do not determine man; that the wise man is above the influence of the stars. Some modern astrologers insist that it is not the stars that influence people but that the events and accidents of a person's life are all determined in advance and the stars simply indicate when they will occur; they don't actually have any influence. But this is untrue. The stars do affect human beings and influence their decisions. When someone is very highly evolved, to be sure, the stars will influence him but they cannot force him to do anything. But for those who are still very weak it is a different matter: it is as though the stars drove them irresistibly. The stars are like pretty girls. When a pretty girl wants to attract a boy she does not say, 'Come here; come and kiss me'. She does not throw herself at his head. She smiles coyly and makes eyes at him and eggs him on until he besieges her with his attentions. She does not say or do anything, and yet she manages to attract him and he, being weak, lets himself be influenced. And this is what the stars do: they arouse something in you – anger, for instance – knowing very well that you will follow through with it and do something violent. And then they say, 'But we didn't force you; you acted freely!' Yes, but by then you have gone too far and broken somebody's head!

We still do not really know what the stars are. The ancients knew them far better than we do. I read some of the books that are being published today and I see that they do not correspond to the truth that I was taught in this initiatic school. I could give you many examples to show you how events happen exactly as planned for some people, whilst for those who are more highly evolved they happen too, but on another level. Let's say that someone has a debt to pay: instead of paying it on the physical plane he may be allowed to pay it on the astral or mental plane. In one way or another he is going to have to pay, but he can choose on what level he wants to do so. Those who have not reached the same degree of evolution however must pay as planned, on the level that was planned. This is something that you must always bear in mind. Above all, bear in mind that no one can avoid paying his debts; his freedom only allows him to choose on which level he will pay them. No one is free to elude his karmic debt, therefore; only to choose how to pay it.

This means that if an astrologer tells you that on such and such a day you are liable to have an accident but that you can avoid it by doing this or that, he is telling you to do something dishonest. He does not realize this, of course, but if all you had to do to avoid future events was to know about them in advance it would be too easy. You could avoid everything. And let me tell you that I have never seen an astrologer avoid any unpleasantness in this way! It may happen in an unexpected way; it may happen a few days earlier or later than expected but it always happens, whatever precautions may be taken to prevent it. Astrologers are now saying that events always happen a few days later than foreseen. That is true. More often than not there is a discrepancy in the timing, but if they were versed in true astrology they would be able to determine the exact moment. Nothing occurs haphazardly in the heavens; on the contrary, everything is regulated with mathematical precision. It is just that the elements and notions of modern astrologers are not very good or very adequate, because so much knowledge has been lost. The ancient astrologers could foresee exactly the time and place of a future event and even the part of a person's body, for instance, that would be affected; in fact it was this accuracy that made their predictions so valuable. But nowadays that knowledge has been lost.

You probably remember a story I once told you of the king whose astrologer predicted that the prince, his only son, would be assassinated on a certain date. The king, naturally, was dreadfully upset and tried to think of some way of saving his son, so he sent his servants to prepare an underground palace on a desert island where his son could live in safety. This was done as the king had ordered, but what no one knew was that, in the meantime, a ship had been wrecked not far from the island and one young man had escaped and managed to swim to the island where he now lived all alone, surviving as best he could on wild fruit.

One day this boy was up a tree picking fruit when he saw a ship anchoring off the shores of the island. An imposing procession of people in rich garments came ashore, and amongst them was a very handsome youth. Not long after the boy saw everybody except the beautiful young man board the ship and sail away again. Once the ship was out of sight the boy went straight to where he had seen the people go when they first arrived, and there he found a large flat stone with a ring set in it. Seizing the ring he pulled up the stone, and finding a staircase he went down until he found himself in a large room, most beautifully furnished and decorated. The young man he had seen with the sailors earlier was there all alone and very alarmed at this unexpected intrusion. However, the boy told him of his own plight, of how his ship had gone down, how he had managed to swim to this island, and above all of how intrigued he had been by the arrival of all those people so splendidly arrayed. The prince's fears were calmed so completely that he asked the boy to stay with him and keep him company during his stay underground.

The two got along very well together and time passed agreeably enough. The king had spared no expense and furnished the palace with a magnificent library full of books, and they spent a lot of time together reading. One day the prince wanted a book which was on a shelf over his head and the boy climbed up to get it and was sitting on the step-ladder cutting the pages of the book with a little gold-handled knife. Suddenly the knife slipped from his hand and struck the prince on the temple and he fell to the floor in a pool of blood. In a panic the boy rushed out of the underground chamber and, at that very moment, the king's ship came in sight: he was coming to fetch his son, trusting in the prediction that if nothing terrible had happened to him by then (and, of course, he firmly believed that this was the case), he would no longer be in danger. And behold, he found his son lying dead! Now of course it is probable that none of this really happened, but the tale is interesting because it illustrates the conception that the ancients had of destiny.

And I have my own ideas on the subject, too. You cannot escape events: what is written is bound to come to pass. I have already told you: the only freedom that a reasonable man enjoys is that of being allowed a choice in the way he pays. Suppose, for instance, that you know that a serious illness is going to force you to interrupt your work. That illness is a debt you have to pay. Well, you can pay off your debt differently by doing a great deal of spiritual work with prayer and meditation and then, when the illness comes, it will not be so serious and will keep you in bed for only a few days. You will have paid off your debt with light and love. If you live reasonably, spiritually, your whole system will be stronger and, when some mishap occurs because of the aspect or the passage of the planets, you will be in a position to pay your debt with some of the 'money' accumulated in your cells. That is to say that you can use your reserves of strength and energy to divert the danger. A sensible, pure, intelligent way of life enables you to save up a lot of 'money' in your system with which to pay your debts.

You may find this a bit surprising, but a spiritual teaching teaches you to save money – symbolically speaking! Every day through meditation, prayer and contemplation, you can put a handful of gold dust into your bank account in the world above and then, when you find yourself in difficulty, instead of trying to cheat and avoid honouring your debts, you can say, 'Wait: I have the money. Here is the gold I have been saving up!' You will be like the old woman who put aside some money in case a burglar came to rob her. One day, of course, the burglar did come – that was inevitable – and what was his surprise when the old woman exclaimed, 'Ah, there you are. I was expecting you. I have got something for you.' And the burglar went away happy! That old woman did not know that by putting money aside for a burglar it was she who attracted his attentions. I have always told people not to save up for 'a rainy day' because that is the surest way of making the 'rainy days' happen. It is magic; an unconscious form of black magic. You should save up for the good days; save up so that when the princess appears you will be in a position to marry her. The princess is symbolic of course: a symbol of all that is good in life.

You must not plan for bad days ahead – whatever precautions you take there are bound to be some; we cannot expect perfection as long as we are on this earth – but you must have something saved up for when they do come; that is to say, you must have lived sensibly. When you grumble and say, 'What's the use of being a vegetarian and having to attend the sunrise and do all those exercises? They don't bring us wealth or fame!' it just shows how ignorant you are. You don't realize that all that is like money; you can become rich by saving it up.

I am telling you this because I see that so many of you are always complaining about not having the things you want. I was saying only yesterday to someone who was complaining in this way: 'As far as I can see, dear lady, you are highly privileged. Your health is good, you have plenty of money and a good education; you have no worries and, above all, you are free to devote all your time to the things you enjoy. And yet instead of being happy, you are constantly depressed and miserable.' 'That's true'. she replied, 'But I don't know what the future has in store for me and it worries me dreadfully!' You see? People are always thinking about the future and, as they do not know what it will be like, their imagination runs riot and invents all kinds of disasters. People make themselves unhappy; they never see how rich they really are nor how many possibilities are open to them, how much freedom they have. Freedom does not mean anything to them; they are bored by it and they spend all their free time worrying about the future!

The trouble is that human beings are not sufficiently conscious of the fact that they are creating their future by the way they are living in the present. It is 'now' that counts. The future is an extension of the present and the present is simply a consequence of the past. Everything is linked together: past, present and future don't belong in separate compartments. Your future will be built on the foundations you are laying today. If the foundations are not sound, of course, you cannot expect the future to be very bright, but if they are solidly built there is no need to worry about the future. The trunk, the branches and the fruit of your tree will be what its roots are. The past is past, but it gave birth to the present, and the present is the roots of the future. It is up to you now to build your own future by improving the present.

Try to appreciate everything that God has given you, the slightest capacity or talent in every dimension: physical, moral, social and intellectual, and try to use all these talents to do a nobler work. It is so stupid to ignore all the gifts and capacities you possess and spend your time weeping and complaining. We have to work with what is positive and real and it is what you have today that is real for you. The future does not belong to you; you must work with what you have in the present.

Sèvres, January 13, 1968

IV

Attachment and Detachment

i

The Emerald Tablet says, 'You shall separate the subtle from the gross gently and with great diligence'. But where shall we find the subtle and the gross that need to be separated? Are they in the alchemist's crucible? Are they in our own thoughts and sentiments? Is this what we witness in death when it separates the subtle – the soul – from the gross – the physical body? Of the four great archangels, the one who separates things is the Archangel Mikhaël, and this is why his feast is at the end of September, for he rules the autumn, the season of separations: the season in which the fruit is separated from the tree and the husk from the seed. Separation is a very important element in the alchemical process but it is not confined to the alchemist's laboratory; it exists in every area of life, although you may often think of it rather as a cleansing or sifting, a distillation, purification or liberation.

There are always things that have to be separated in life. If a child is to have a life of its own it has to be separated from its mother. If a man is drowning he has to be separated from the water. If two enemies are fighting they have to be separated, otherwise they would kill each other. And then, too, people try to separate a girl and boy who are in love, and by doing so they only succeed in uniting them even more strongly. At other times it is when one tries to bring people together that one separates them even further. There is a great deal that could be said about these two words, separation and union – as much as about the words give and take, which I have already talked to you about[1].

[1] See *Complete Works*, vol. 11, chap. 3.

Freedom

If you were clairvoyant you would see the innumerable threads that link all human beings to other creatures, other regions, other entities or occupations. Wherever one looks there are these threads, these subtle, etheric threads, which you cannot see but which tie you down, and the important thing is to be able to cut some of them, otherwise they bind you so tightly that you can no longer move; you are no longer free. The only problem is that one cannot detach oneself from something or someone without attaching oneself to someone else. One cannot be totally detached: absolute detachment does not exist. Whatever you do you will always be attached. Suppose you are tormented by a passion or another person: if you try to detach yourself without knowing how to set about it you will not succeed, because you will probably rely exclusively on your own strength, and that is just what you must not do. Try instead to detach yourself from one thing by attaching yourself to an activity or a person that is the exact opposite. Bring the two of them face to face. You know how to do this in your everyday life: you combat fire with water, dirt with soap, and so on. In other words, you must always look for an ally, another force that can help you to overcome whatever is tormenting you.

This is the law to go by therefore: always look for the opposite of that from which you are trying to disengage yourself. But there is no such thing as total, absolute disengagement or freedom, for the law of attraction is always in effect. As soon as you escape the influence of one thing you necessarily come under the influence of something else. If people imagine that they can be completely free it is because they are ignorant. Freedom as it is understood by most people simply does not exist. If you want to free yourself from darkness you must attach yourself to light, for only light has the chemical – or, if you prefer, the physical – properties that enable it to drive out darkness. And once you succeed in attaching yourself to light it will never leave you again. But to be the slave of light is the best possible thing that could happen to you. When Jesus said, 'Come to me ... for my yoke is easy', this is what he was saying, for it is far better to be bound and totally dependent on all that is luminous and divine. Therefore, as you cannot free yourself from

233

the devil by relying only on your own strength, you have to depend on the Lord, for only he has the power to set you free. Yes, but then you are not free! And so much the better, for this lack of freedom is true freedom, the only real freedom: to be the servant of God and to depend completely on him and on his wisdom, his beauty, his love, and his eternity. You must learn to become more and more detached in order to be more attached. Yes, we have to detach ourselves in order to be attached. Or to attach ourselves in order to be detached!

I often hear the comments of people who know nothing about human nature or how human beings are constructed and who say that they need neither God nor a master nor the light; that people should detach themselves from all that. What they don't realize is that by detaching themselves from 'all that' they are necessarily going to attach themselves to something else, something that will lead to disaster. Some people have wanted to detach themselves from the teaching because they felt that it tied them down. They had to pray and meditate, listen to lectures, eat in silence and keep trying to become better, and they got bored with it all, so they left the teaching. And then, before long, they found not only that they were attached but that they had become a prey to other things which were tormenting and devouring them. And their life was no easier; on the contrary. It was not long before they wanted to come back and attach themselves to the teaching again in order to be free.

We continually have to detach, disengage, free ourselves; free ourselves even from certain activities or habits which are good in themselves but which are not the best, for we must constantly adjust our sights and aim for what is best. There is nothing wrong in spending our leisure time travelling, visiting museums, going to concerts or the theatre, but even the best of these things is often a waste of time, for there is always so much that is mediocre and really not worthwhile. But this whole question, the necessity of choosing nothing but the best, is very vast. We would have to talk about it much more in order to make it quite clear.

Sèvres, January 19, 1969

Yes, as I have said, nothing and nobody in the whole universe is completely and absolutely free and independent. If an object escapes from the gravitational field of the earth, for instance, it is instantly drawn into that of the sun. There is no corner of the universe where you can be totally free. You will always be subject to different influences: you may escape from some but you cannot avoid becoming subject to others. If you refuse to expose yourself to positive, beneficial influences, you will receive negative, harmful ones. And vice versa. But one thing is certain: you cannot withdraw from all influence. This is why I so often tell you that it is far better to be subject to the Lord's influence, otherwise you will be subject to that of the devil.

Look at the angels: they have no self-will; they are instruments in the hands of the Lord, they never do anything against his will and carry out all his commands instantaneously. When I referred to the words of Jesus, 'My yoke is easy and my burden light', I did not explain something important, and that is that goodness, wisdom, light, kindness, all weigh something. Yes, but that weight is so light and so desirable! Even the sun's rays weigh something. Every form of matter, however subtle, weighs something. Even primeval matter, that which is closest to God himself, has a certain weight and exerts a certain amount of pressure. And from this we can conclude that there is no place in the universe in which man could be totally independent, because everywhere in the universe are forces, influences and entities. Every part of the universe is populated, and when you leave one zone you necessarily enter another and become subject to its laws. Similarly, you might leave one country in the world because you don't like it or its laws and customs, but you necessarily have to go to another country with other laws – which may be worse – and you have to get used to them and learn to conform.

Reasonable beings who understand this important truth accept the yoke of Christ, the yoke of light, in order to find the freedom they desire. If we want to be free we have to submit to the divine will. The freedom that human beings dream of and which consists in never having to submit to any authority other than themselves, simply does not exist. The desire for that kind of liberty, that kind of independence, is the result of ignorance, and in this sense freedom does not exist any more than equality. For there is no equality in nature either.

You will object that when people speak of equality they mean equality before the law. Yes, but even there, there is no equality, for the law treats those who are rich, influential and well-informed very differently from those who are poor, ignorant and without influence. If a desire for equality leads you to apply the same laws to those who are very highly evolved as to those who are not, that 'equality' is not founded on truth. Divine justice, which is superior to human justice, proceeds very differently; it evaluates and judges beings according to their degree of evolution and not just according to their actions. Earthly justice looks only at what you do; it knows nothing about who you may be, your degree of evolution, the reason why you did this or that; it takes into account only the fact, the action, the event. Whereas in every region of the universe, throughout rational nature, you are judged according to your intentions, your emanations, for the same act can mean two quite opposite things. The kiss of a criminal, for instance, will contaminate a woman for years, whereas that of an initiate will heal her.

There is no such thing as freedom, liberty. The liberty that most people wish for is not liberty but licence. They want to be independent and free of anything that will prevent them from indulging their whims and fancies; they are blind to the fact that it is precisely these whims and fancies that deprive them of true freedom. You must understand that in order to be free you must become the servant of the only being who is absolutely free, God himself. No other being in the whole universe is totally free, not even the Seraphim. Only God is absolutely free and dependent on none. He alone is Master and Lord, and yet he knowingly imposed limitations on himself in the act of creation. In creating the world part of him had to submit to certain limitations and abide by the laws which he himself decreed. If you aspire to be free, therefore, you must become servants of God, become one with him, because then the freedom which is his will pass into you. You can be free only through God's own freedom. There is no other! This is something that philosophers have never understood. They imagine that they can be free apart from God. No, never! As we have already seen, when you escape from the influence of one kind of force you necessarily fall under the influence of another kind. If you are not within the sphere of light you will be the prey of darkness. If you are not within the sphere of health, you will be plagued by illness, and so on. And those who adhere to that pernicious philosophy which drives people to get rid of all sense of religion and to cut themselves off from the Creator are very ignorant; sooner or later they will have to suffer the consequences of their ignorance.

Imagine for a moment that you wanted to cut yourself off completely from the world around you and never go out of your house. You have stored up quantities of food in your attic, but your reserves are not unlimited and you will only be able to eat and drink and stay alive as long as your supplies last. And when they have run out? Well, you will simply die! Those who have cut their ties with heaven are living on their reserves, and their reserves are not unlimited. They say, 'We're perfectly fit and well; we can work like anybody else, and business is flourishing!' Perhaps, but one day their supplies will run out and death will be imminent: spiritual death. Human beings are so ignorant that they get rid of all that is best for them and then boast that they feel perfectly well! But they do not know how the laws operate. They do not know that even if their affairs go well for a long time, the slightest deviation on the philosophical level leads to inextricable difficulties in the long run.

What you have to understand is that you cannot detach yourself from anything or anyone in the broad sense of the term without, by that very fact, attaching yourself to something or someone else. We are always subject to an influence of some kind: the influence of the weather, the temperature, the times in which we live, the stars. We are obliged to eat and drink, to breathe and sleep, to wear clothes, to meet other people and to listen and talk to them, and in all these activities we are influenced by certain forces. A woman leaves her husband in order to be free and soon finds herself committed to someone else, and her situation becomes even worse. When ignorant, unsuspecting human beings try to free themselves, there are always other forces waiting to intercept them and pull them into their zone of influence. Would you throw petrol on a fire to put it out? No, you would use water. And if you are in the dark, would you try to use money or water to lighten your darkness? Of course not. The only thing that can release you from darkness is light. Everything that exists, both in the external world and in our inner world, has its own particular properties, and it is important to know them. You want to put out a fire (a burning desire, a passion that is consuming you) but if, through ignorance, you pour oil on it, symbolically speaking, the blaze will be fiercer than ever. And generally speaking this is what human beings so often do.

If you want to rid yourself of misunderstandings and suffering you have to find the element, region, entity or virtue which can help you to do so. The same is true if you want to be free and, for my part, I have always found that nothing is more effective than to attach myself to something better. If you work in a government office, for example, you are at the beck and call of your superior and have to do what he tells you, and this may be very galling. The only way out of the situation is to be promoted; so you study and pass all kinds of exams and, in the long run, you end up as head of the department and your one-time boss cannot badger you any longer. Of course you will still have to put up with others in higher echelons, so perhaps you will set out to climb even higher, above them too. And as there will always be someone above you, you will keep climbing until you reach the Lord himself!

I have known a number of people who, in order to be free, abandoned their families, their work and their friends. Selling all their belongings, they left everything behind them and went to seek happiness in some other country. They did not know that one cannot find freedom that way. They may have freed themselves from external ties but they forget to work on their inner reality, they forget to free themselves from certain thoughts and desires, with the result that, wherever they go, they continually find themselves faced with the same difficulties. I have seen so many people in my life who have tried to free themselves, but they all go about it so clumsily, in ways that are dangerous for themselves and for others! I tell them, 'Now look, suppose your house is old and tumbling down, it is very uncomfortable and you don't want to live in it any more. I quite understand; that's normal. But don't pull it down until you have built another one in its place, otherwise you'll be out on the street, at the mercy of the wind and rain – symbolically speaking.' This is exactly what I mean when I tell you that before you can detach yourselves you have to attach yourselves to something new. This new attachment is the new house you have to build, and once it is built you will be free to pull down the old one. But don't do it the other way round and detach yourself before you are safely attached to something else, otherwise your detachment will be useless; you will simply find yourself attached to all kinds of contradictory elements and you will be worse off than before. So remember – never detach yourselves before attaching yourselves; never destroy before you have built anew.

And now, just to show you that when I tell you something you can always find confirmation of it in all the manifestations of nature, let me give you one more example. When you cut yourself a scab forms over the wound and the new skin begins to grow under the scab. But if you pull the scab off before the new skin is fully formed you will reopen the wound and then you will have to wait for the whole process to take place all over again. Before pulling off the scab you must 'build your new house', that is to say, you must give the new skin time to form. If you are observant you will see that the human organism, nature, trees and the whole universe respect this order of things. Human beings are the only exception. They want to be free, but as they do not know how dangerous it is to break away from old attachments before creating new ones, they are always getting tied up in unexpected difficulties. Yes, because if you do not invite higher realities to fill the places you have cleared out in your heart and mind, all kinds of other entities will slip in, and you will be in a terrible situation. Your heart and mind must be occupied by a magnificent ideal, by all that is best, most noble and most luminous. That is why initiates teach their disciples always to give first place to the Lord. Even if this strikes you as ridiculous, even if it is in complete contradiction to all modern ideas – do it; put the Lord firmly in first place.

Most educators know nothing about this law of creating new bonds before releasing oneself from the old ones. Suppose, for instance, that the parents of a young girl want to detach her from a boy who has seduced her. If they do not know how to go about it they will criticize him and point out all his faults and failings, with the result that the girl will be even more attached to him. Without saying anything they should simply make sure that their daughter meets other young men who are better-looking, more intelligent, more honest and altogether more suitable. The girl will see for herself how blind and stupid she has been and will detach herself from her seducer. You have to show people alternatives, let them taste other realities. That is what I do: I know very well that I could never detach you from certain habits or mental attitudes if I did not begin by attaching you to something else. That is why I put before you all the glories of heaven and the beauty of the soul and the spirit: I want you to see for yourselves how beautiful these things are and to feel the need to attach yourselves to all that beauty. Later, when you look at all the rest, you will want to flee from it in horror. One must always let people find out for themselves what is best.

I expect you remember the example which I have often given you. Suppose I go to visit some friends in winter: all the doors and windows of the house are tightly shut and the stench is overpowering because the cat and the dog, and even the horses and pigs, have all been brought in to keep warm. It is more economical this way they explain; there is no waste of warmth. Yes, but they are all quite groggy because of the fumes and are incapable of thinking or feeling anything clearly. So what do I do? If I tried to explain to them how unhealthy, offensive and unsightly their living habits were it would only trigger interminable discussions. They would find all kinds of arguments to prove that they were in the right and I was in the wrong and I would simply be wasting my time. So I use guile! I invite them to go out for a walk with me, or to go with me to pick up something I have forgotten, and we all go out into the fresh air for a few minutes. When we go back into the house it is they who exclaim in horror at the foul smell and wonder how they ever managed to live in such an atmosphere, that is to say – for all this is symbolic – with such a philosophy, with such notions. This is the point at which they begin to understand me. And it is they who understand for themselves; they make the comparison instinctively. It is quite possible that as they left the house they did not realize at once how marvellous it was to breathe the pure, fresh air, but when they get back and are greeted with that suffocating stench they understand. Then I can talk to them to some purpose and get results, but not before. Before detaching them from that poisonous atmosphere they have to be attached to the fresh air out of doors.

Anyone who does not know this law and tries to improve human beings without first giving them a taste of something better, something that dazzles and attracts them, will necessarily fail. It does absolutely no good to rant and rave against evil if you don't help people to see what is good, and to attach themselves to it so as to advance.

Sèvres, April 9, 1969

V

Free for a Divine Work

The goal of most oriental spiritual teachings is liberation. The initiates of India, Tibet and Japan have worked for thousands of years to find methods which would enable them to free themselves. But for my part I do not like that selfish liberation. Why try to free oneself? I have no desire to be free; on the contrary, I want consciously to limit and commit myself. When someone is intent on freeing himself there is one simple solution: to walk out on everything and everyone. Nothing else matters. It is wonderful to be free, to float in light, bliss and ecstasy, to know the beatitude of nirvana but, personally, that is not what I want. What I want is to limit myself and commit myself totally. And that is what I have done. I came down to earth because I thought it was selfish to stay up there, in such freedom and happiness. I saw that it would be better to come into the world to be harried and criticized and defiled. But perhaps you are complaining that you do not understand what I am talking about. Be patient for a little while and you will soon understand. You are in too much of a hurry: you always want to understand everything at once!

We have to free ourselves, that is true, but only in order to limit ourselves. We have to free ourselves inwardly from all our lower instincts and tendencies in order to bind ourselves, that is to say in order to work for the collectivity. This to my mind is the meaning of life and liberty. Happiness and joy consist in freeing oneself. Not in shirking one's obligations, but in freeing oneself inwardly from all one's weaknesses in order to commit oneself even more whole-heartedly to helping others. Yes, if you want to be inwardly free, you have to begin by limiting yourself and sacrificing certain things in order to commit yourself more fully.

How can anyone who is not free commit himself to working for a divine goal? This is quite obvious to me: those who are not free cannot be very useful; they are busy serving other gods (and, believe me, there are quantities of other gods). They are not free because ever since they were young they have cherished all sorts of personal plans and ambitions and their first priority has always been to achieve these goals. The result is that they are now so deeply involved elsewhere that they have no time to give to the collectivity. What can you do if you are not free? Even if you do come and listen to one of my lectures you will not understand it if your mind is not free, if you are besieged by all kinds of incongruous thoughts and feelings and memories.

In fact if I were to ask you, 'What is the difference between a spiritual master and a university professor of any discipline you like?' I am certain you would not know what to answer. Perhaps you would say, 'Well, it's the type of knowledge, the syllabus and the goal they pursue'. Yes, that is certainly true. But there is a much more important difference that you have not mentioned, because you have never thought about it. I'll tell you: once a university professor has completed his course of lectures he can forget about his students. He has enough concerns of his own to occupy him: his personal problems, his private thoughts, feelings and suffering. Once he has given his lecture his job is finished. Whereas a master's work is never finished; he never puts aside his concern for his disciples. Night and day, eating, working or sleeping, he never relaxes his care for the souls and spirits of his disciples; ceaselessly, every moment of every day, he is at their side, helping them.

Some of the more intuitive and sensitive brothers and sisters tell me that, even during our meals together, they sense that I am thinking of them and taking care of them, that I am speaking to their soul and spirit. How is that possible? It is possible simply because a master, an initiate, is free, and when someone is free and has solved all his own personal problems, he can help his friends, disciples and pupils. Whereas if one is engaged and preoccupied and constantly entangled in one's personal problems, as is the case with most human beings, what can one do for others? There, now you see the difference between an authentic spiritual master and an ordinary instructor: a master is free!

Everyone thinks that the spiritual teachings of the East are marvellous – and you are no exception! But do you realize that if I followed them it would mean that I would abandon you and devote myself to my own spiritual work? And tell me: is that what you want? Would you be pleased if I abandoned you? No, it is by committing myself more and more deeply that I am attaining greater freedom. That is quite a new light on the question, isn't it? Those who are interested only in achieving personal liberation are on the wrong track; there is no love in that attitude; it is sheer selfishness! The time has come now to put the emphasis on collective work, for it is through work that one attains freedom. For my part this is how I have resolved the problem: I don't want to be free, I want to do the work that needs to be done, and it is in that work that I find my joy.

The history of mankind is an endless series of wars waged by men struggling to free themselves, by men who are ready to shed their blood for liberty. But all those men have never known the true nature of freedom. For them it is simply a question of not being conquered by their enemies: that is the only freedom they are looking for. But that is not enough. What about all those enemies inside them? They have never even realized that they are there. They fight to free themselves from the yoke of a foreign power but they never take up arms to free themselves from their own inner enemies. They shed their blood but they are no freer for that. Bulgaria is no longer under Turkish rule, but are Bulgarians any freer?

Human beings are ready to sacrifice everything for external freedom. I have known a great many women who were so eager to have money and be free to travel and amuse themselves and do what they like that they were ready to marry rich men whom they did not love, never realizing that they were tying themselves down and would end by being enslaved. Outwardly, perhaps, they were free; but what about their inner freedom? Outer freedom is often deceptive. The initiates prefer to be outwardly bound so as to be inwardly free. Look at the example of Socrates: he deliberately married the most shrewish woman in Greece because he knew that, because of her, he would be obliged to master his own reactions and in this way attain a very high degree of inner freedom. When you want to conquer yourself it is useful to have someone who keeps you on your toes and forces you to make an effort. And Xanthippe was well qualified to do just that! In fact it is partly thanks to her that Socrates was what he was!

If you want to be strong in life you have to accept certain self-imposed restrictions. If you scatter a handful of gunpowder on the ground and throw a lighted match on it, it will just go 'pfft' and fizzle out because it has too much free space. But if you pack it tightly into a container before igniting it, it will explode with a roar and demolish everything around it. Human beings are like gunpowder: they have to be compressed before they feel the urge to burst out and conquer the world. If they have too much free space they will never do anything. Freedom often chloroforms people and puts them to sleep. They achieve nothing useful; they are too free! This is why cosmic intelligence packs some people into terribly tight situations, so as to get them to set the whole world ablaze! It would be a good idea to think about these things a little. I am not saying that you should always be hemmed in, exploited and trampled underfoot. No; I am simply saying that this question of freedom is not quite so simple as you might think. When you have had no instruction in initiatic science you can have a very false view of things; it is not easy to understand why you have to put up with certain circumstances nor to distinguish the good from the bad in a given situation. Someone who is very well off on the material level, for instance, may think that he is very privileged: he does not realize the dangers of his situation. What counts for him is the external aspect. But the fact is that there is always a good and a bad side to everything: this is something that you must think about. Even if you cannot immediately find the significance of a situation in which you are struggling, the simple fact that you use your mind to think about it is already something; in fact it is a great deal!

As far as I am concerned, the difficult conditions I have experienced in life have been enormously helpful in stimulating my reflection. If, very early on in life, I had not encountered conditions which seemed on the surface to be utterly deplorable and miserable, I would never have discovered or achieved anything. That is why I thank heaven for all the privations, difficulties and misfortunes I have had to endure. Yes, really! I thank heaven for them! Once one understands one can see the good side of these things. And I am saying this for you, too, so that when you find yourselves obliged to live through something very difficult, instead of being discouraged, you may recognize the positive aspects and learn, as I have, to thank heaven every day for the trials and tribulations you have to live through. Before rebelling against your lot you must try to understand it. Before deciding to hold everyone else, even the Lord himself, responsible for your tribulations, you must think, reflect and meditate and, just as I am doing, you will certainly discover the positive aspect of them. There are a great many qualities that one would never develop if one did not have to experience certain trials. In fact I would go so far as to say that our enemies are often friends in disguise, because they oblige us to make an effort and, thereby, to liberate ourselves. This is why we must love them.

Jesus said, 'Love your enemies'. Yes, because that is really meritorious. It is too easy to love your friends; anyone can do that. But it is very difficult to love one's enemies. In fact one can only love them if one realizes that they are friends in disguise, thanks to whom we can make great strides on the path towards self-mastery and liberation.

So, there you are, my dear brothers and sisters: isn't life wonderful? Once you know that you can love even your enemies and that the greatest possible blessings are hidden in all the most distressing circumstances, how can you avoid being glad? Once one has understood that, one is free. Yes, free! But free to chain oneself all the more securely to the divine work.

Sèvres, May 20, 1974

By the same author :

'Complete Works' Collection

VOLUME 1 — THE SECOND BIRTH

1. The Second Birth — 2. 'Ask, and it shall be Given to You. Seek, and You shall Find. Knock, and it shall be Opened to You.' — 3. Truth is Hidden in the Eyes — 4. Wisdom is Hidden in the Ears — 5. Love is Hidden in the Mouth — 6. Love, Wisdom and Truth — 7. The Master of the Universal White Brotherhood - Peter Deunov — 8. The Living Chain of the Universal White Brotherhood.

VOLUME 2 — SPIRITUAL ALCHEMY

1. Gentleness and Humility — 2. 'Except Ye Die Ye Shall Not Live' — 3. Living in Conscious Reciprocity with Nature — 4. The Unjust Steward — 5. Lay Up for Yourselves Treasures — 6. The Miracle of the Loaves and Fishes — 7. The Feet and the Solar Plexus — 8. The Parable of the Tares — 9. Spiritual Alchemy — 10. Spiritual Galvanoplasty — 11. The Mother's Role During Gestation.

VOLUME 5 — LIFE FORCE

1. Life — 2. Character and Temperament — 3. Good and Evil — 4. Pitting Oneself Against the Dragon — 5. Presence and Absence — 6. Thoughts are Living Entities — 7. Unwanted Guests — 8. The Strength of the Spirit — 9. Sacrifice — 10. A High Ideal — 11. Peace.

VOLUME 6 — HARMONY

1. Harmony — 2. Medical Science Must be Based on Initiatic Science — 3. The Future of Medicine — 4. A Disciple Must Develop His Spiritual Senses — 5. What Can We Learn From a House ? — 6. How Thought is Materialized on the Physical Plane — 7. Meditation — 8. The Human Intellect and Cosmic Intelligence — 9. The Solar Plexus and the Brain — 10. The Hara Centre — 11. The Initiatic Heart — 12. The Aura.

VOLUME 7 — THE MYSTERIES OF YESOD

Yesod reflects the Virtues of All the Sephiroth — *Part I. Purity :* Purity is a Question of Nourishment — Sorting and Selecting — Purity and the Spiritual Life — Purity in the Three Worlds — The River of Life — Purity and Peace — The Magic of Trusting — Purity and Speech — To Find Purity — Blessed are the Pure in Heart — The Gates of the New Jerusalem — *Part II. Love and Sex* — *Part III. Realization* — The Spring — Fasting — Washing — The Real Baptism — The Angels of the Four Elements.

VOLUME 10 — THE SPLENDOUR OF TIPHARETH

1. Surya-yoga - The Sun, Centre of our Universe - All that Exists on Earth Exists Etherically in the Sun — 2. Obtaining Etheric Elements from the Sun - When We Gaze at the Sun Our Soul Begins to Resemble it — 3. Our Higher Self Dwells in the Sun — 4. The Creator Sows Seeds in Us and the Sun Makes Them Grow - The Sun Reflects the Blessed Trinity — 5. Every Creature Has a Home - The Seven Beads of the Rosary — 6. The Master and the Seven-bead Rosary - Every Creature Needs to Own and Protect its Dwelling

Place - The Aura - 7. The Heliocentric Point of View - 8. Love as the Sun Loves - 9. A Master Must be Like the Sun and Remain at the Centre - Some Prayers to Say at Sunrise - 10. Rise Above the Clouds - The Sephirah Tiphareth - 11. The Spirits of the Seven Lights - 12. The Prism, Symbol of Man - 13. A New Heaven and a New Earth - Spiritual Grafting - 14. The Sun Has the Solution to the Problem of Love - 15. The Sun is in the Image and Likeness of God - 'In Spirit and in Truth' - 16. Christ and the Solar Religion - 17. Day and Night - Consciousness and the Subconscious - 18. The Sun, Originator of Civilization - A Disciple's Clairvoyance Must Begin on the Highest Levels - 19. The Sun Teaches Unity - The Power of Penetration - 20. The Sun Teaches by Example - The Sun, Heart of our Universe - 21. Three Kinds of Fire - 22. Making Everything Converge Towards One Goal.

VOLUME 11 - THE KEY
to the Problems of Existence

1. The Personality - 2. Jnani-yoga - 3. Giving and Taking - 4. Evil is Limited, Good is Limitless - 5. Eternal Happiness - 6. Fermentation - 7. Which Life ? - 8. The Image of the Tree - The Individuality Must Consume The Personality - 9. Working on the Personality - 10. The Personality Keeps You from Reflecting the Sun - 11. Identify with the Individuality - 12. The True Meaning of Sacrifice - 13. The Balance Restored - 14. Render Therefore Unto Caesar - 15. The New Philosophy - 16. The Personality Devoured by The Individuality - 17. Call On Your Allies - 18. The Further Down, The Less Space - 19. Your Inner Animals - 20. But Which Nature ? - 21. Sexual Sublimation - 22. Toward Universal Brotherhood.

VOLUME 12 - COSMIC MORAL LAW

1. The Law of Cause and Effect ; 'As Ye Sow, so Shall Ye Reap' - 2. The Importance of Choice - Seek Work, not Pleasure - 3. Creative Action as a Means of Evolution - 4. Justice - 5. The Law of Affinity : Peace - 6. The Law of Affinity : The True Religion - 7. The Moral World is an Extension of the Physical World - The Measure - 8. Reincarnation - 9. Do not Stop Half-way ! - 10. Knowing How to Use Energy - 11. How to Obtain the Quintessence - 12. The Morals at the Source - 13. Look to Heaven for Models - 14. Through His Thoughts and Feelings, Man is a Creator in the Invisible - 15. 'All That is Below is Like That Which is Above' - 16. 'If You Are Light, You Will Go Towards The Light' - 17. Everything has its Double - Making a New Recording - 18. Moral Law Becomes Entirely Significant in the Hereafter - 19. Example : the Best Method of Pedagogy - 20. 'Whosoever Shall Smite Thee on the One Cheek...' - 21. The New Year.

VOLUME 13 - A NEW EARTH
Methods, Exercices, Formulas and Prayers

1. Prayers - 2. A Daily Programme - 3. Nutrition - 4. Actions - 5. Overcoming the Evil in Us - 6. Methods of Purification - 7. Human Relations - 8. Man's Relations with Nature - 9. The Sun and the Stars - 10. Mental Work - 11. Spiritual Galvanoplasty - 12. The Solar Plexus - 13. The Hara Centre - 14. Methods for Working with Light - 15. The Aura - 16. The Body of Glory - 17. Formulas and Prayers.

VOLUME 14 - LOVE AND SEXUALITY - PART I

1. The Masculine and Feminine Principles - The Love of God, the Love of Others, Self

Love – 2. Taking the Bull by the Horns - The Caduceus of Mercury – 3. The Serpent - Isis Unveiled – 4. The Power of the Dragon – 5. Spirit and Matter – The Sexual Organs – 6. Manifestations of the Masculine and Feminine Principles – 7. Jealousy – 8. The Twelve Doors of Man – 9. From Yesod to Kether : The Path of Sexual Sublimation – 10. The Spiritual Screen – 11. Nourishment and Love – 12. Woman's Role in the New Culture – 13. The Initiatic Meaning of Nudity – 14. Exchanges and Relationships – 15. Wealth and Poverty – 16. To Love is the Work of the Disciple – 17. Love in the Universe – 18. A Wider Concept of Marriage I – 19. The Twin-Soul – 20. Everything Depends on Your Point of View – 21. A Wider Concept of Marriage II and III – 22. Analysis and Synthesis – 23. Like the Sun, Love Brings Order to Life – 24. Mother Love – 25. The Meaning of Renunciation – 26. The Bonds of Love – 27. Youth and the Problem of Love - The New Currents - Marriage - Why Self-Control - The Need for a Guide - Give Your Love to God First.

VOLUME 15 – LOVE AND SEXUALITY – PART II

1. A Question of Attitude – 2. True Marriage – 3. The Sun is the Source of Love – 4. The Goal of Love is Light – 5. The Manifestations of the Masculine and Feminine Principles – 6. Master or Mistress ? – 7. Vestal Virgins ; the New Eve – 8. Materialism, Idealism and Sexuality - 'On Earth as in Heaven' – 9. Heart and Mind ; the Universal White Brotherhood – 10. Seek the Soul and the Spirit – 11. Restoring Love to its Pristine Purity – 12. Love Transforms Matter – 13. Love and Identification – 14. The Task of a Disciple – 15. Open Yourself to Others and They Will Love You – 16. Tantra-Yoga – 17. Emptiness and Fullness : the Holy Grail – 18. Love is Everywhere – 19. Look for Love at its Source – 20. Know How to Use Your Powers of Love – 21. A Broader Concept of Marriage, Part IV – 22. It Rises from Earth and Descends from Heaven – 23. The Secret of Happiness is in an Expanded Consciousness – 24. 'Whatever you Bind on Earth' – 25. Love God so as to Love Your Neighbour Better – 26. Live Lovingly – 27. Our Only Weapons : Love and Light – 28. Never Stop Loving – 29. Towards a Broader Concept of the Family.

VOLUME – 17 'KNOW THYSELF' JNANA YOGA

1. 'Know Thyself' – 2. The Synoptic Table – 3. Spirit and Matter – 4. The Soul – 5. Sacrifice – 6. Food for the Soul and the Spirit – 7. Consciousness – 8. The Higher Self – 9. Truth – 10. Freedom.

VOLUME – 25 A NEW DAWN:
Society and Politics in the Light of Initiatic Science – Part I

1. The Age of Aquarius – 2. The Dawn of Universal Brotherhood – 3. Youth and Revolution – 4. Communism and Capitalism – 5. True Economics – 6. Wealth – 7. Aristocracy and Democracy – 8. Politics in the Light of Initiatic Science.

VOLUME 26 – AQUARIUS, HERALD OF THE GOLDEN AGE – Part II

1. Forms and Principles – 2. The Religion of Christ – 3. The Idea of a Pan-World – 4. The Cosmic Body – 5. The Kingdom of God and His Righteousness – 6. The New Jerusalem.

VOLUME 29 – ON THE ART OF TEACHING
from the Initiatic Point of View

1. On the Spiritual Work – 2. On Responsibility – 3. On Building the New Life – 4. On the Living Knowledge – 5. On Perfection – 6. On the Reality of the Invisible

World – 7. On Participating in the Work of the Universal White Brotherhood.

VOLUME 32 – THE FRUITS OF THE TREE OF LIFE

1. How to Approach the Study of the Cabbalah – 2. The Number Ten and the Ten Sephiroth – 3. Structure and Symbols of the Tree of Life – 4. The Tetragrammaton and the Seventy-Two Planetary Spirits – 5. The Creation of the World and the Theory of Emanation – 6. The Fall and Redemption of Man – 7. The Four Elements – 8. Evening Vigils Round the Fire : I. The Power of Fire – II. Fire and the Sun – III. The Fire of Sacrifice – 9. Water and Fire – 10. A Bowl of Water – 11. The Living Logos : I. The Alphabet and the Twenty-Two Elements of the Word – II. The Universal Language of the Word – III. The Power of the Word – 12. The Esoteric Church of Saint John – 13 Binah, the Realm of Stability – 14. The Human Spirit is Above Fate – 15. Death and the Life Beyond – 16. Human and Cosmic Respiration – 17. The Cardinal Feasts – 18. The Moon and its Influence on Man – 19. The Glorified Souls – 20. The Land of the Living – 21. A Magic Wand – 22. Nature Spirits – 23. Objects are Receptacles of Life – 24. The Holy Grail – 25. Building the Inner Sanctuary.

By the same author

Izvor Collection

TABLE OF CONTENTS

201 — TOWARD A SOLAR CIVILIZATION

1. The Sun, Initiator of Civilization — 2. Surya Yoga — 3. Seeking the Centre — 4. The Sun our Provider — 5. The Solar Plexus — 6. Man is Made in the Image of the Sun — 7. The Spirits of the Seven Lights — 8. The Sun as our Model — 9. The True Solar Religion.

202 — MAN, MASTER OF HIS DESTINY

1. The Law of Cause and Effect — 2. You will Separate the Subtle from the Gross — 3. Evolution and Creation — 4. Two Justices: Human and Divine — 5. The Law of Correspondences — 6. Natural and Moral Law — 7. Nature's Records — 8. Reincarnation.

203 — EDUCATION BEGINS BEFORE BIRTH

1. The First Priority : Educating Parents — 2. Education Begins before Birth — 3. A Blueprint for the Future of Mankind — 4. Don't Neglect Your Children — 5. A New Understanding of a Mother's Love — 6. The Magic Word — 7. Never Let Your Children be Idle — 8. Prepare Your Children for Adult Life — 9. Protect Your Children's Sense of Wonder — 10. Love without Weakness — 11. Education versus Instruction.

204 — THE YOGA OF NUTRITION

1.Eating : An Act which Concerns the Whole Man — 2. Hrani-Yoga — 3. Food : A Love-Letter from God — 4. Choosing Your Food — 5. Vegetarianism — 6. The Ethics of Eating — 7. Fasting : I — Means of Purification. II — Another Form of Nutrition — 8. Communion — 9. The Meaning of the Blessing — 10. The Spirit Transforms Matter — 11. The Law of Symbiosis.

205 — SEXUAL FORCE OR THE WINGED DRAGON

1. The Winged Dragon — 2. Love and Sexuality — 3. The Sexual Force is Essential for Life on Earth — 4. Pleasure : I — Do not Seek Pleasure for it Will Impoverish You — II — Replace Pleasure with Work — 5. The Dangers of Tantric Yoga — 6. Love without Waiting to be Loved — 7. Love is Everywhere in the Universe — 8. Spiritual Love is a Higher Way of Feeding Ourselves — 9. A High Ideal Transforms Sexual Energy — 10. Open Your Love to a Higher Path.

206 — A PHILOSOPHY OF UNIVERSALITY

1. What is a Sect ? — 2. No Church is Eternal — 3. The Spirit Behind the Form — 4. The Advent of the Church of St. John — 5. The Foundations of a Universal Religion — 6. The Great Universal White Brotherhood — 7. For a Universal Notion of the Family — 8. Brotherhood, a Higher State of Consciousness — 9. The Annual Conventions at the Bonfin — 10. The Universal Dimension of All Our Activities.

207 – WHAT IS A SPIRITUAL MASTER ?

1. How to Recognize a True Spiritual Master – 2. The Necessity for a Spiritual Master – 3. The Sorcerer's Apprentice – 4. The Exotic Should not be Confused with Spirituality – 5. Learn How to Balance the Material and Spiritual Worlds – 6. A Master is a Mirror Reflecting the Truth – 7. A Master is There Only to Give Light – 8. The Disciple and His Master – 9. The Universal Dimension of a Master – 10. The Magical Presence of a Master – 11. Identification – 12. 'Except Ye Become as Little Children...'

208 – THE EGREGOR OF THE DOVE OR THE REIGN OF PEACE

1. Towards a Better Understanding of Peace – 2. The Advantages of Unity amongst Nations – 3. Aristocracy and Democracy – 4. About Money – 5. The Distribution of Wealth – 6. Communism and Capitalism – 7. Towards a New Understanding of Economics – 8. What Every Politician Should Know – 9. The Kingdom of God.

209 – CHRISTMAS AND EASTER IN THE INITIATIC TRADITION

1. The Feast of the Nativity – 2. The Second Birth – 3. Birth on the Different Planes of Being – 4. 'Except Ye Die Ye Shall not Live' – 5. The Resurrection and the Last Judgment – 6. The Body of Glory.

210 – THE TREE OF THE KNOWLEDGE OF GOOD AND EVIL

1. The Serpent of Genesis – 2. What Good is Evil ? – 3. Beyond Good and Evil – 4. Until the Harvest – 5. The Philosophy of Unity – 6. Into the Wilderness to Be Tempted – 7. The Undesirables – 8. Suicide is not the Answer – 9. The Real Weapons – 10. The Science of the Initiates, or the Inner Lamps.

211 – FREEDOM, THE SPIRIT TRIUMPHANT

1. Man's Psychic Structure – 2. Mind over Matter – 3. Fate and Freedom – 4. Freedom through Death – 5. Sharing in the Freedom of God – 6. True Freedom : a Consecration of Self – 7. Freedom through Self-Limitation – 8. Anarchy and Freedom – 9. The Notion of Hierarchy – 10. The Synarchy Within.

212 – LIGHT IS A LIVING SPIRIT

1. Light : Essence of Creation – 2. The Sun's Rays, their Nature and Activity – 3. Gold is Condensed Sunlight – 4. Light Enables us to See and be Seen – 5. Working with Light – 6. The Prism : a Symbol of Man – 7. Purity Clears the Way for Light – 8. Living with the Intensity of Light – 9. The Spiritual Laser.

213 – MAN'S TWO NATURES, HUMAN AND DIVINE

1. Human Nature or Animal Nature ? – 2. The Lower Self is a Reflection – 3. Man's True Identity – 4. Methods of Escape – 5. The Sun Symbolizes the Divine Nature – 6. Put the Personality to Work – 7. Perfection Comes with the Higher Self – 8. The Silent Voice of the Higher Self – 9. Only by Serving the Divine Nature – 10. Address the Higher Self in Others – 11. Man's Return to God, the Victory.

214 – HOPE FOR THE WORLD : SPIRITUAL GALVANOPLASTY

1. What is Spiritual Galvanoplasty ? – 2. Reflections of the Two Principles – 3. Marriages Made in Heaven – 4. Love Freely Given – 5. Love on the Lower Plane – 6. Love on

the Higher Plane – 7. Love's Goal is Light – 8. The Solar Nature of Sexual Energy – 9. Mankind Transformed – 10. The Original Experiment and the New One – 11. Replenish the Earth ! – 12. Woman's place – 13. The Cosmic Child.

215 – THE TRUE MEANING OF CHRIST'S TEACHING

1. 'Our Father Which Art in Heaven' – 2. 'My Father and I Are One' – 3. 'Be Ye Perfect, Even as Your Father Who is in Heaven is Perfect' – 4. 'Seek Ye First the Kingdom of God and His Justice' – 5. 'On Earth as it is in Heaven' – 6. 'He That Eateth My Flesh and Drinketh My Blood Hath Eternal Life' – 7. 'Father, Forgive Them, For They Know Not What They Do' – 8. 'Unto Him that Smiteth Thee on the One Cheek...' – 9. 'Watch and Pray'.

216 – THE LIVING BOOK OF NATURE

1. The Living Book of Nature – 2. Day and Night – 3. Spring Water or Stagnant Water – 4. Marriage, a Universal Symbol – 5. Distilling the Quintessence – 6. The Power of Fire – 7. The Naked Truth – 8. Building a House – 9. Red and White – 10. The River of Life – 11. The New Jerusalem – Perfect Man. I – The Gates. II – The Foundations – 12. Learning to Read and Write.

217 – NEW LIGHT ON THE GOSPELS

1. 'Men do not Put New Wine into Old Bottles' – 2. 'Except Ye Become as Little Children' – 3. The Unjust Stewart – 4. 'Lay up for Yourselves Treasures in Heaven' – 5. The Strait Gate – 6. 'Let Him Which is on the Housetop not Come Down...' – 7. The Calming of the Storm – 8. The First Shall Be Last – 9. The Parable of the Five Wise and the Five Foolish Virgins – 10. 'This is Life Eternal, that they Might Know Thee the Only True God'.

218 – THE SYMBOLIC LANGUAGE OF GEOMETRICAL FIGURES

1. Geometrical Symbolism – 2. The Circle – 3. The Triangle – 4. The Pentagram – 5. The Pyramid – 6. The Cross – 7. The Quadrature of the Circle.

219 – MAN'S SUBTLE BODIES AND CENTRES
the Aura, the Solar Plexus, the Chakras...

1. Human Evolution and the Development of the Spiritual Organs – 2. The Aura – 3. The Solar Plexus – 4. The Hara Centre – 5. Kundalini Force – 6. The Chakras: The Chakra System I. – The Chakra System II. Ajna and Sahasrara.

220 – THE ZODIAC, KEY TO MAN AND TO THE UNIVERSE

1. The Enclosure of the Zodiac – 2. The Zodiac and the Forming of Man – 3. The Planetary Cycle of Hours and Days – 4. The Cross of Destiny – 5. The Axes of Aries-Libra and Taurus-Scorpio – 6. The Virgo-Pisces Axis – 7. The Leo-Aquarius Axis – 8. The Fire and Water Triangles – 9. The Philosophers' Stone : the Sun, the Moon and Mercury – 10. The Twelve Tribes of Israel and the Twelve Labours of Hercules in Relation to the Zodiac.

221 – TRUE ALCHEMY OR THE QUEST FOR PERFECTION

1. Spiritual Alchemy – 2. The Human Tree – 3. Character and Temperament – 4. Our

Heritage from the Animal Kingdom — 5. Fear — 6. Stereotypes — 7. Grafting — 8. The Use of Energy — 9. Sacrifice, the Transmutation of Matter — 10. Vainglory and Divine Glory — 11. Pride and Humility — 12. The Sublimation of Sexual Energy.

222 — MAN'S PSYCHIC LIFE : ELEMENTS AND STRUCTURES

1. Know Thyself — 2. The Synoptic Table — 3. Several Souls and Several Bodies — 4. Heart, Mind, Soul and Spirit — 5. The Apprenticeship of the Will — 6. Body, Soul and Spirit — 7. Outer Knowledge and Inner Knowledge — 8. From Intellect to Intelligence — 9. True Illumination — 10. The Causal Body — 11. Consciousness — 12. The Subconscious — 13. The Higher Self.

223 — CREATION : ARTISTIC AND SPIRITUAL

1. Art, Science and Religion — 2. The Divine Sources of Inspiration — 3. The Work of the Imagination — 4. Prose and Poetry — 5. The Human Voice — 6. Choral Singing — 7. How to Listen to Music — 8. The Magic Power of a Gesture — 9. Beauty — 10. Idealization as a Means of Creation — 11. A Living Masterpiece — 12. Building the Temple — Postface.

224 — THE POWERS OF THOUGHT

1. The Reality of Spiritual Work — 2. Thinking the Future — 3. Psychic Pollution — 4. Thoughts are Living Beings — 5. How Thought Produces Material Results — 6. Striking a Balance between Matter and Spirit — 7. The Strength of the Spirit — 8. Rules for Spiritual Work — 9. Thoughts as Weapons — 10. The Power of Concentration — 11. Meditation — 12. Creative Prayer — 13. Reaching for the Unattainable.

225 — HARMONY AND HEALTH

1. Life Comes First — 2. The World of Harmony — 3. Harmony and Health — 4. The Spiritual Foundations of Medicine — 5. Respiration and Nutrition — 6. Respiration: I. The Effects of Respiration on Health — II. How to Melt into the Harmony of the Cosmos — 7. Nutrition on the Different Planes — 8. How to Become Tireless — 9. Cultivate an Attitude of Contentment.

226 — THE BOOK OF DIVINE MAGIC

1. The Danger of the Current Revival of Magic — 2. The Magic Circle of the Aura — 3. The Magic Wand — 4. The Magic Word — 5. Talismans — 6. Is Thirteen an Unlucky Number — 7. The Moon — 8. Working with Nature Spirits — 9. Flowers and Perfumes — 10. We All Work Magic — 11. The Three Great Laws of Magic — 12. The Hand — 13. The Power of a Glance — 14. The Magical Power of Trust — 15. Love, the Only True Magic — 16. Never Look for Revenge — 17. The Exorcism and Consecration of Objects — 18. Protect Your Dwelling Place.

227 — GOLDEN RULES FOR EVERYDAY LIFE

1. Life: our most precious possession — 2. Let your material life be consistent with your spiritual life — 3. Dedicate your life to a sublime goal — 4. Our daily life: a matter that must be transformed by the spirit — 5. Nutrition as Yoga — 6. Respiration — 7. How to recuperate energy — 8. Love makes us tireless — 9. Technical progress frees man for spiritual work — 10. Furnishing your inner dwelling — 11. The outer world is a reflection

of your inner world – 12. Make sure of a good future by the way you live today – 13. Live in the fullness of the present – 14. The importance of beginnings... etc.

228 – LOOKING INTO THE INVISIBLE
Intuition, Clairvoyance, Dreams

1. The Visible and the Invisible – 2. The Limited Vision of the Intellect, The Infinite Vision of Intuition – 3. The Entrance to the Invisible World : From Yesod to Tiphareth – 4. Clairvoyance : Activity and Receptivity – 5. Should We Consult Clairvoyants ? – 6. Love and Your Eyes Will be Opened – 7. Messages From Heaven – 8. Visible and Invisible Light : Svetlina and Videlina – 9. The Higher Degrees of Clairvoyance – 10. The Spiritual Eye – 11. To See God – 12. The True Magic Mirror : The Universal Soul – 13. Dream and Reality – 14. Sleep, an Image of Death – 15. Protect Yourself While You Are Asleep – 16. Astral Projection While Asleep – 17. Physical and Psychic Havens – 18. The Sources of Inspiration – 19. Sensation is Preferable to Vision.

229 – THE PATH OF SILENCE

1. Noise and Silence – 2. Achieving Inner Silence – 3. Leave Your Cares at the Door – 4. Make Your Meals an Exercise in Silence – 5. Silence, a Reservoir of Energies – 6. The Inhabitants of Silence – 7. Harmony, the Essential Condition for Inner Silence – 8. Silence, the Essential Condition for Thought – 9. The Quest for Silence is the Quest for the Centre – 10. Speech and the Logos – 11. A Master Speaks in Silence – 12. The Voice of Silence is the Voice of God – 13. The Revelations of a Starry Sky – 14. A Silent Room.

230 – THE BOOK OF REVELATIONS: A COMMENTARY

1. The Island of Patmos – 2. Introduction to the Book of Revelations – 3. Melchizedek and Initiation into the Mystery of the Two Principles – 4. Letters to the Church in Ephesus and Smyrna – 5. Letter to the Church in Pergamos – 6. Letter to the Church in Laodicea – 7. The Twenty-Four Elders and the Four Holy Living Creatures – 8. The Scroll and the Lamb – 9. The Hundred and Forty-Four Thousand Servants of God – 10. The Woman and the Dragon – 11. The Archangel Mikhaël Casts Out the Dragon – 12. The Dragon Spews Water at the Woman – 13. The Beast from the Sea and the Beast from the Land – 14. The Wedding Feast of the Lamb – 15. The Dragon is Bound for a Thousand Years – 16. The New Heaven and the New Earth – 17. The Heavenly City.

231 – THE SEEDS OF HAPPINESS

1. Happiness : A Gift to be Cultivated – 2. Happiness is not Pleasure – 3. Happiness is Found in Work – 4. A Philosophy of Effort – 5. Light Makes for Happiness – 6. The Meaning of Life – 7. Peace and Happiness – 8. If You want to be Happy, Be Alive – 9. Rise Above your Circumstances. – 10. Develop a Sensitivity to the Divine – 11. The Land of Canaan – 12. The Spirit is Above the Laws of Fate – 13. Look for Happiness on a Higher Level – 14. The Quest for Happiness is a Quest for God – 15. No Happiness for Egoists – 16. Give Without Expecting Anything in Return – 17. Love Without Asking to be Loved in Return – 18. Our Enemies are Good for Us – 19. The Garden of Souls and Spirits – 20. Fusion on the Higher Planes – 21. We are the Artisans of Our Own Future.

By the same author
(translated from the French)

Brochures :
New Presentation

301 – The New Year
302 – Meditation
303 – Respiration
304 – Death and the Life Beyond

Life Lectures on Tape
(available in French only)

K 2001 F – La science de l'unité
K 2002 F – Le bonheur
K 2003 F – La vraie beauté
K 2004 F – L'éternel printemps
K 2005 F – La loi de l'enregistrement
K 2006 F – La science de l'éducation
K 2007 F – La prière
K 2008 F – L'esprit et la matière
K 2009 F – Le monde des archétypes
K 2010 F – L'importance de l'ambiance
K 2011 F – Le yoga de la nutrition
K 2012 F – L'aura
K 2013 F – Déterminisme et indéterminisme
K 2014 F – Les deux natures de l'être humain
K 2015 F – Prendre et donner

Editor-Distributor
Editions PROSVETA S.A. – B.P. 12 – 83601 Fréjus Cedex (France)

Distributors

AUSTRIA
MANDALA
Verlagsauslieferung für Esoterik
A-6094 Axams, Innsbruckstraße 7

BELGIUM
PROSVETA BENELUX
Van Putlei 105 B-2548 Lint
N.V. MAKLU Somersstraat 13-15
B-2000 Antwerpen
VANDER S.A.
Av. des Volontaires 321
B-1150 Bruxelles

BRAZIL
NOBEL SA
Rua da Balsa, 559
CEP 02910 - São Paulo, SP

BRITISH ISLES
PROSVETA
The Doves Nest
Duddleswell, Uckfield,
East Sussex TN22 3JJ

CANADA
PROSVETA Inc.
1565 Montée Masson
Duvernay est, Laval, Que. H7E 4P2

CYPRUS
THE SOLAR CIVILISATION BOOKSHOP
PO Box 4947
Nicosie

GERMANY
EDIS GmbH
Daimlerstr.5
D - 8029 Sauerlach

GREECE
PROFIM MARKETING Ltd
Ifitou 13
17563 P. Faliro
Athens

HOLLAND
STICHTING
PROSVETA NEDERLAND
Zeestraat 50
2042 LC Zandvoort

HONG KONG
SWINDON BOOK CO LTD.
246 Deck 2, Ocean Terminal
Harbour City, Tsimshatsui, Kowloon

IRELAND
PROSVETA IRL.
84 Irishtown – Clonmel

ITALY
PROSVETA Coop. a r.l.
Cas. post. 13046 – 20130 Milano

LUXEMBOURG
PROSVETA BENELUX
Van Putlei 105 B-2548 Lint

MEXICO
COLOFON S.A.
Pitagora 1143
Colonia del Valle
03 100 Mexico, D.F.

NEW ZEALAND
PSYCHIC BOOKS
P.O. Box 87-151
Meadowbank Auckland 5

NORWAY
PROSVETA NORDEN
Postboks 5101
1501 Moss

PORTUGAL
PUBLICAÇÕES
EUROPA-AMERICA Ltd
Est Lisboa-Sintra KM 14
2726 Mem Martins Codex

SPAIN
ASOCIACIÓN PROSVETA ESPAÑOLA
C/ Ausias March n° 23 Ático
SP-08010 Barcelona

SWITZERLAND
PROSVETA
Société Coopérative
CH - 1808 Les Monts-de-Corsier

UNITED STATES
PROSVETA U.S.A.
P.O. Box 49614
Los Angeles, California 90049

VENEZUELA
J.P. Leroy
Apartado 51 745
Sabana Grande
1050 A – Caracas

PRINTED IN FRANCE IN JULY 1992
EDITIONS PROSVETA, Z.I. DU CAPITOU
B.P.12 – 83601 FRÉJUS
FRANCE

– N° d'impression : 1988 –
Dépôt légal : Juillet 1992
Printed in France